FARM
HOUSING

A VOLUME IN THE CENSUS MONOGRAPH SERIES

FARM

HOUSING

by

GLENN H. BEYER

Cornell University

and

J. HUGH ROSE

Bureau of the Census

for the
Social Science Research Council
in cooperation with the
U. S. Department of Commerce
Bureau of the Census

JOHN WILEY & SONS, INC., NEW YORK
CHAPMAN & HALL, LIMITED, LONDON

Copyright © 1957

BY

The Social Science Research Council

———

Library of Congress Catalog Card Number: 57-10802

PRINTED IN THE UNITED STATES OF AMERICA

FOREWORD

The statistical results compiled by the Bureau of the Census constitute a tremendous mass of detailed information about the population of the United States and its characteristics and economic activities. To meet the requirements of government agencies, business concerns, and investigators of social problems and to satisfy the needs of individual citizens, facts must be gathered and published, showing the distribution of the population in each large and small political unit with respect to age, sex, color, marital status, occupation, income, education, national origin, and other characteristics. This information provides the basis for apportionment of representatives in Congress, for answering many questions by direct reference, and for formulating many plans, at least in preliminary form.

It is the first business of the Bureau of the Census to put into print the census results that directly answer as many such questions as possible. Along with these results, similar data from one or two previous censuses are usually included. Limitations of time, space, and money prevent any extensive statement of the relations between particular results, the long-term trends of significant totals and subtotals, the shifting proportions of the people belonging to different categories, various interesting and important relations such as those between income, occupation, and age. It is not that the Bureau of the Census fails in any sense to appreciate the value and need for such analyses, but rather that it must concentrate on its basic concern with the summary statistics that constitute its unique contribution to knowledge.

When plans for the 1950 Census were made, the need for more extensive analysis was recognized and a series of census monographs similar to those issued after the 1920 Census was proposed. Because of the pressures caused by the depression in the early 1930's and by defense and war in the early 1940's, plans for monographs based on those censuses could not be carried out. Late in the 1940's interested persons from business, research, and government agencies expressed the need for a series that would provide analyses of the most significant results of the 1950 Census. The Social Science Research Council, with the assistance of Russell Sage Foundation, took the lead in stimulating the formulation of suitable plans and in June 1950 appointed a Committee on Census Monographs to cooperate with the Bureau in organizing this project. The members of the Committee are:

Ralph G. Hurlin, Russell Sage Foundation (Chairman)

Robert W. Burgess, formerly Western Electric Company, since February 1953 Director of the Bureau of the Census

John D. Durand, United Nations

Ernest M. Fisher, Columbia University

F. F. Hill, Cornell University

Frederick F. Stephan, Princeton University

Conrad Taeuber, Bureau of the Census

Ralph J. Watkins, Dun & Bradstreet, Inc.

Paul Webbink, Social Science Research Council

J. Frederic Dewhurst, Twentieth Century Fund, and William F. Ogburn, University of Chicago, were members of the Committee during the first year and a half.

It is essential in any sound census monograph program to obtain the cooperation of authors with a broad understanding not only of the statistical information provided by the regular tabulations of the current census but also of the results of earlier censuses and other relevant knowledge and points of view from other sources and even from other countries. The preparation of a monograph should include broad exploration of new questions suggested by the new information, as well as narrowing the elements of doubt and controversy on old questions. The Social Science Research Council Committee early undertook, in consultation with leading figures in various professional fields, to develop a suggested list of monograph titles and authors and persuaded experts in the subject areas selected to undertake the preparation of memoranda outlining and discussing the topics proposed. Then, in 1951, arrangements were made for continuing cooperation between the Committee and the Bureau concerning the selection of topics, proposals of authors and consultants, and editorial supervision.

Throughout the conduct of the project there has been close collaboration with a number of interested Federal agencies and with universities and research organizations, which provided staff and facilities to help bring the project to completion. They and the Council, which also obtained necessary funds from the Rockefeller and Russell Sage Foundations, provided assistance without which the monographs could not have been prepared.

The task of preparing monographs is an essential part of the broad function of making the information secured by censuses fully available to satisfy the needs and interests of the community and to constitute a broad base for further studies in the social sciences. As Director of the Census and President of the Social Science Research Council, respectively, we wish to record our full approval of the monograph project. It is not implied, of course, that the views expressed in these reports are necessarily those of the Bureau of the Census, the Department of Commerce, or the

Social Science Research Council.   The views are those of the individual
authors, each of whom has been given the freedom to interpret available
materials in the light of his technical knowledge and competence.   This
freedom of the individual authors is an essential element in making the
most useful analyses and interpretations generally available to the
community.

ROBERT W. BURGESS, DIRECTOR
BUREAU OF THE CENSUS

PENDLETON HERRING, PRESIDENT
SOCIAL SCIENCE RESEARCH COUNCIL

PREFACE

Farm life has been exposed to the many influences of our modern civilization: distances have been effectively reduced by improvements in transportation; mechanization has changed the way of life on a farm; new methods of communication have increased the social contact possible for the farm family; and the spread of urban areas into the surrounding countryside has increased the number of contacts between the farm and the nonfarm family.

What effect have these and other aspects of life in America today had upon the farmhouse itself? In this monograph we have described the farmhouse and household in the United States in 1950 and have analyzed the changes which occurred during the preceding decade. Our major sources of data were the 1950 and 1940 Censuses of Population and Housing and the 1950, 1945, and 1940 Censuses of Agriculture. As supplementary materials we used special tabulations of census data, as well as information obtained from the Housing Research Center at Cornell University.

We have described the farmhouses of 1950 in terms of geographic location, economic class of farm, condition, age, size, equipment, and facilities. We have also studied the occupants of different kinds of farm homes according to their family characteristics and sizes, tenure status, race, income, and sources of income.

A principal purpose of our study has been to determine the extent to which the farm home is a unique phenomenon in the United States housing picture. We were interested in finding out whether the trends over a decade have intensified or modified differences between farm and other housing. With this purpose in mind we have focused attention on the comparison of farm and other rural housing and households, on studies of the relationships of distance from urban centers to farm housing, and on the analysis of changes within the farm housing inventory itself.

We gratefully acknowledge the assistance we have received from many persons, both in the Bureau of the Census and outside. Without this assistance our monograph could not have been completed. We are indebted to Conrad Taeuber, who has given many helpful suggestions during all stages of the monograph preparation; to Mrs. A. M. Dodds for editing the manuscript; to Howard Brunsman for his critical review of the manuscript; to Mildred M. Russell, Meriam B. Perrie, Edna L. Brogdon, and Zetta Whitson for help in preparation of both the tables and manuscript; and to many others who have supplied material and checked the tabulated data.

GLENN H. BEYER

J. HUGH ROSE

October 1, 1957

CONTENTS

CHAPTER 1

BACKGROUND

Ninety-five percent of the foods that supply America's well-stocked larder are produced on the farm lands of this country. Production of foods and fibers has more than kept pace with a population which, between 1910 and 1950, grew by two-thirds. At the same time, there have been great shifts of emphasis in both rural and urban living habits. Some of these shifts have resulted from increasing commercialization and the accompanying mechanization of farm practices.

Today the market is largely specialized; and because fewer persons are needed to achieve greater production, there has been a steadily growing trend toward larger and more specialized farms. In 1920 the average-sized farm was 148 acres; by 1950 it had increased to 210 acres. Census figures indicate as part of this trend that the predominating medium-sized farms have become fewer (although the number of small farms of under 20 acres have shown a small increase). At the same time, between 1920 and 1950, larger farms of 500 to 999 acres increased by 40 percent; farms occupying 1,000 acres or more increased nearly 200 percent.

To a very great extent, farm mechanization and commercialization account also for the relative decline in rural population that has been a marked trend of the first half of the century. Whereas, in 1910, rural areas housed 54 percent of the population, in 1950 they accounted for only 41 percent, of which only one-third lived on farms.

Although increased farm efficiency has encouraged the transfer of large numbers of farm workers to other occupations, this is not the only factor involved in the shift of population. Today, more capital than ever is needed to begin a farming operation and to maintain it. The spread of city suburbs into the countryside, relative ease of transportation and communication, a growing interdependence of city and rural peoples—each of these trends facilitates the transition from rural to urban occupations.

But the changeover does not always imply abandonment of residence. Many families continue to live on their farms while working in nearby cities and operate their farms on a part-time basis. When abandoned, some farms, formerly operated on a commercial scale, are taken over by people whose incomes derive from the city. There was a noticeable increase from 1920 to 1950 in the number of "part-time" and "residential" farms, so designated by the Bureau of the Census.

1

The changing pattern of the farming industry reflected by these trends may be expected to have some influence on the quality of the houses on the farms. Construction has been noticeably greater in some parts of the Nation in recent years, although much of it has served to replace old, inferior dwellings with new, scarcely superior ones. Facilities known as "modern conveniences" have increased, but the quality of farm housing, in general, is low. It could scarcely be otherwise, since about 60 percent of the Nation's farms are low-production farms.

Standards of farm housing

In contrast to the usual urban house, which can be appraised as an independent unit, the value of a farmhouse, as separate from that of the total farm plant, is less easily judged. The one is generally in no small way dependent on the other. And, since the efficient production of farm commodities is basic to the welfare of his family, the farmer must apportion his money outlay as well as the effort he expends in the upkeep of house, barns, and equipment.

A variety of factors have influenced rural housing standards across the country. The generally low income of farm families from 1920 to World War II undoubtedly prevented any extensive rebuilding or remodeling. Among tenant farmers—a group which in 1950 comprised nearly a third of all farm operators—a factor in poor-quality housing is their landlords' tendency to delay necessary repairs. This tendency is reflected in the average standards of all farm housing.

But rural housing standards are not wholly governed by income. Tradition is a contributing factor. Despite the fact that modern communications and transportation have in recent years widened the horizons of farming families and brought rural people into a closer relationship with city dwellers, farm families have for generations become accustomed to a way of life that yields only slowly to change.

Farm and nonfarm housing

Shifts in the economic status of American families, in general, or in the relationships between population groups must obviously be reflected in family housing. For this reason the greater efficiency of farming operations and the accompanying interdependence of rural and urban people are clearly demonstrated by statistics of the Nation's housing situation.

In the Nation as a whole, approximately 8,658,000 more dwelling units of all types existed in 1950 than in 1940, an increase of approximately 23 percent. Of the total increase, some 7,953,000 dwelling units were in urban areas. The increase in urban units during the 10-year period was approximately 37 percent. During this same decade, rural-nonfarm units increased by about 2,000,000—an increase of approximately 25 percent.

The trend in farm housing provides a strong contrast. In 1940 the Nation contained approximately 7,642,000 farm housing units. By 1950 this number had *declined* to approximately 6,358,000,[1] representing a decrease of approximately 17 percent.

This decline in farm housing follows closely the decline in rural population as a whole, and explanations for both downward trends are largely similar.

First, at some time during the 10-year period some of the householders changed their occupation from farming to other activities but did not actually move out of the family house.

Second, there was a considerable change in occupancy. Because of the general expansion of farm size throughout the Nation, many houses occupied by farm families in 1940 were later sold to families who do not work the farm lands.

In addition, some farmhouses—because of fire or decay, or because they are no longer used for housing purposes—have been taken out of the farm inventory. The precise number of farm housing units this involves is difficult to judge, but it has been estimated that from the total of all housing units—urban, rural farm, and rural nonfarm—the inventory lost at least 900,000 in this way between 1940 and 1950.[2]

Finally, to a limited extent, part of the decline may be attributed to changes in the procedure by which the census is taken. After 1940, the Bureau of the Census instituted changes in the definition of a farm and in the rural-urban classification. (See glossary, p. 186.) Estimates vary as to the effect of these revisions. However, since the new rural-urban classification resulted in a decrease of only 28,000 in the rural-farm population, its influence on farm housing can be of slight significance. The effect of changes in the farm definition cannot be measured accurately.

A summary of relative increases in the number of urban, rural-nonfarm, and farm dwelling units in the Nation between 1940 and 1950 is given in table 1. As will be seen from table 2, these increases have varied considerably in the four geographic regions of the United States. The most significant change has taken place in the South. Here, between 1940 and 1950, urban dwelling units increased by 61 percent and rural-nonfarm units, by 36 percent. Meanwhile, rural-farm units declined by 21 percent, although the South still maintained the largest percentage of rural-farm housing.

The greatest increase in urban units during this decade was in the West, where they increased by 68 percent. Rural-nonfarm units increased by 19 percent, and the number of rural-farm units decreased by 11 percent.

The North Central and Northeast geographic regions were more stable, but here, too, some important changes were taking place. In the North

---

[1] This estimate is liberal. Many of the families are part-time farmers—a term which includes those who live on farm land but are not farm operators in the generally accepted sense of the term. Many of them probably are commuters.

[2] Another factor that influences the farm housing inventory is that of migration. It is discussed later in this chapter.

Central Region urban units increased by 28 percent, and rural-nonfarm units, by 25 percent; while rural-farm units declined by 12 percent. In the Northeast the increase in urban units was 20 percent; in rural-nonfarm units, 13 percent. The decline in rural-farm units amounted to 14 percent.

TABLE 1.—RELATIVE GROWTH IN URBAN, RURAL-NONFARM, AND RURAL-FARM DWELLING UNITS: 1950 AND 1940

[Because of revisions in the definitions of urban and farm residences between the two censuses, the figures for 1940 and 1950 are not strictly comparable; see glossary, p. 190. Minus sign (−) denotes decrease]

Area	1950		1940		Increase, 1940 to 1950	
	Number	Percent	Number	Percent	Number	Percent
United States.............	45,983,398	100.0	37,325,470	100.0	8,657,928	23.2
Urban......................	29,569,073	64.3	21,616,352	57.9	7,952,721	36.8
Rural nonfarm..................	10,056,382	21.9	8,066,837	21.6	1,989,545	24.7
Rural farm....................	6,357,943	13.8	7,642,281	20.5	-1,284,338	-16.8

Source: *1950 Census of Housing*, Vol. I, *General Characteristics*, Part 1, U. S. Summary, table 2; *1940 Census of Housing*, Vol. II, *General Characteristics*, Part 1, U. S. Summary, table 4.

In each geographic region except the West the percentages of rural-nonfarm housing were remarkably similar in 1940 and in 1950. And in the Northeast the proportions of total housing in urban, rural-nonfarm, and farm categories remained almost the same.

Today, the growing tendency of many city workers to make their homes in rural areas confuses the rural housing situation. A recent study of rural housing in New York State[3] identifies seven modern types of rural residents:

Full-time farmer: A family in which the head of the household derives the major proportion of his income from the farm; that is, he has minor or no other employment.

Part-time farmer: A family in which the head of the household is working 40 hours or more per week in other employment, in addition to farming. (Included here also are the subsistence farm families who have no other apparent source of income.)

Farmer—other: A family in which the head of the household is employed on the farm but neither owns nor rents it; that is, he is a hired hand or a manager.

Rural resident—commuting: A family that lives in the open country but whose head is employed in an urban area of 2,500 population or over.

Rural resident—noncommuting: A family that lives in the open country and whose head is engaged neither in a farming operation nor in employment in an urban area. The head may be retired, unemployed, working in a nearby village, or in some such open-country occupation as a job with the highway department.

Village resident—commuting: A family that lives in a village and whose head is employed in an urban area.

Village resident—noncommuting: A family that lives in a village and whose head is employed in the same village, is retired, or unemployed.

The study points out a number of interesting relationships between farm families of the first three types listed above and also with other rural fam-

---

[3] Glenn H. Beyer, *Rural Housing in New York State*, Bulletin 893, Cornell University Agricultural Experiment Station, October 1952.

ilies. For example, though farmers generally have a higher income than rural nonfarm families, proportionately fewer of them live in homes with such facilities as central heat, complete bathrooms, and septic tanks. Apparently, families living in villages and "commuting rural residents" more frequently enjoy these facilities than families who live in the open country and who do not commute to urban areas. The study also indicates, on the other hand, that in recent years full-time and part-time farmers as a group have undertaken more repair work than any of the other groups. Two explanations for this situation are possible. First, since a majority of rural nonfarmhouses are relatively new, they are in less need of repair. And second, since the farmer himself often undertakes the job of repairing his house, labor costs are minimized and repairs can be made more frequently.

TABLE 2.—RELATIVE GROWTH IN URBAN, RURAL-NONFARM, AND RURAL-FARM DWELLING UNITS, FOR GEOGRAPHIC REGIONS: 1950 AND 1940

[See headnote, table 1]

Area	1950		1940		Increase, 1940 to 1950	
	Number	Percent	Number	Percent	Number	Percent
Northeast..................	12,051,182	100.0	10,312,732	100.0	1,738,450	16.9
Urban.....................	9,351,830	77.6	7,768,225	75.3	1,583,605	20.4
Rural nonfarm..................	2,175,301	18.1	1,933,658	18.8	241,643	12.5
Rural farm.....................	524,051	4.3	610,849	5.9	-86,798	-14.2
North Central...............	13,745,646	100.0	11,597,471	100.0	2,148,175	18.5
Urban.....................	8,673,933	63.1	6,803,785	58.7	1,870,148	27.5
Rural nonfarm..................	2,919,902	21.2	2,335,997	20.1	583,905	25.0
Rural farm.....................	2,151,811	15.7	2,457,689	21.2	-305,878	-12.4
South......................	13,653,785	100.0	10,876,056	100.0	2,777,729	25.5
Urban.....................	6,963,307	51.0	4,324,822	39.8	2,638,485	61.0
Rural nonfarm..................	3,618,051	26.5	2,664,771	24.5	953,280	35.8
Rural farm.....................	3,072,427	22.5	3,886,463	35.7	-814,036	-20.9
West......................	6,532,785	100.0	4,539,211	100.0	1,993,574	43.9
Urban.....................	4,580,003	70.1	2,719,520	59.9	1,860,483	68.4
Rural nonfarm..................	1,343,128	20.6	1,132,411	25.0	210,717	18.6
Rural farm.....................	609,654	9.3	687,280	15.1	-77,626	-11.3

Source: *1950 Census of Housing*, Vol. I, *General Characteristics*, Part 1, U. S. Summary, table F; *1940 Census of Housing*, Vol. II, *General Characteristics*, Part 1, U. S. Summary, table 4.

When a farmhouse is taken over by a nonfarm family, it ceases to be classed as a farmhouse. And as more urban families follow the trend toward rural living, the houses they occupy will gradually take on the characteristics of urban rather than rural houses.[4]

Classifications Basic to This Study

Three classifications were used in analyzing the data on which this study is based: the economic subregion (used by the 1950 Census of Housing), type-of-farming region (combining economic subregions into larger regions),

---

[4] The influence of these homes on the housing of farmers in the same area is dealt with in Chapter 5, p. 89.

FIGURE 1.—ECONOMIC REGIONS AND SUBREGIONS: 1950

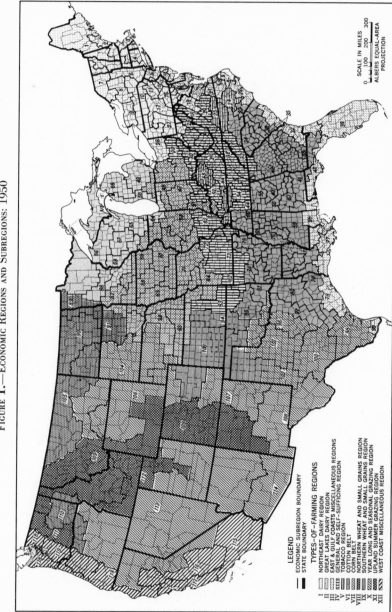

Source: U. S. Bureau of the Census.

and the economic class of farm (used by the 1950 Census of Agriculture). In addition, total incomes reported by farm families for the 1950 Census of Population provided a further means of examining the data and verifying conclusions. Some explanation of the nature of these classifications is relevant to an appraisal of the conclusions.

Economic subregions and type-of-farming regions

Farm housing varies widely from one section of the country to another. Not only is it affected by the physical conditions of its region—weather, type of soil, and topography—but it is also influenced by such economic factors as type of farming, size of farm, nearness to markets, and the price structure of the farm products involved. In addition, as will be evident throughout this study, traditions, attitudes, and values may well be reflected in the housing of a particular group. Thus, in order to compare the characteristics of the farm houses of the United States effectively, some sort of geographical classification into approximately homogeneous cultural regions is essential.[5]

Statistical comparisons can be made for a large number of small areas identified in the 1950 Census of Housing volume on farm housing[6] as "economic subregions." But these, used alone, are too detailed to be useful in a comprehensive survey of farm housing characteristics. On the other hand, figures for the United States as a whole can obscure important regional differences. For the purposes of the present study, an intermediate level was found to be needed, and some compromise between the broad type-of-farming regions set up in 1950 by the Bureau of Agricultural Economics and economic subregions seemed most logical.[7] Since the data for the study were drawn primarily from tabulations of housing characteristics by economic subregions, it was necessary that the larger regions be made up of combinations of economic subregions. And because type of farming can be expected to have a definite influence upon the housing of farm families, the combination of economic subregions into approximations of type-of-farming regions appeared to be justified.

The map (figure 1) on page 6 shows how these subregions were combined into 12 regions. Neither the number nor the boundaries of these regions are the same as the type-of-farming regions developed by the Bureau of Agricultural Economics.[8]

---

[5] T. J. Woofter, Jr., defines a cultural region as "an area within which the combination of environmental and demographic factors have created a homogeneity of economic and social structure." See Carl C. Taylor, *et al.*, *Rural Life in the United States*, Alfred A. Knopf, New York, 1949, p. 336.

[6] *1950 Census of Housing*, Vol. III, *Farm Housing Characteristics.*

[7] Bureau of Agricultural Economics, "Generalized Types of Farming in the United States," *U. S. Dept. of Agr. Inf. Bul. 3*, 1950.

[8] A brief survey of the problems of rural classification and details of the relationships between the type-of-farming regions established by the Bureau of Agricultural Economics and those worked out for this study will be found in Appendix B, p. 131. Further reference to the differences in regional classifications is also to be found in Chapter 3, which deals with characteristics of farm housing, region by region.

The economic class of farm

Of the numerous factors that influence standards of farm housing, the farm family's economic level might be expected to exert the most direct influence. To the extent that each of the economic subregions is a homogeneous unit, where similar crops are raised and similar factors affect farm income, the housing in each region is of a certain general standard, though wide individual variations owing to differences in cultural backgrounds, topography, initiative, and the like exist within this standard. In general, however, as will be shown later in this study, the higher the economic class of the farms in an area, the larger will be the proportion of farmhouses that are in good condition and equipped with modern facilities.

The 1950 Census of Agriculture divides farms into economic classes in order to provide a statistical basis for analyzing the agricultural industry in meaningful groups.[9] The classification is based on three factors: total value of farm products sold, number of days the farm operator worked off the farm, and the relationship of income received from nonfarm sources by the operator and members of his family to the value of all farm products sold. Certain types of farms, such as experimental farms or those associated with institutions or community projects, are always classed as "abnormal" regardless of income or other factors.

In making this classification, farms are divided into two major groups, "commercial farms" and "other farms." Farms whose farm products were sold for $1,200 or more are placed in the commercial classification. Commercial farms also include those whose products in 1949 were sold for $250 to $1,199, provided that the farm operator had worked off the farm less than 100 days during the year, and provided also that the income of the operator and members of his family, from nonfarm sources, was less than the total value of all products sold. Farms whose total sale of farm products in 1949 was less than $250, as well as county, State, private institutional, and experimental farms, are classified as "others."

Commercial farms are divided into six groups, according to total value of farm products sold:

Class	Value of farm products sold in 1949
I	$25,000 or more
II	10,000 to $24,999
III	5,000 to 9,999
IV	2,500 to 4,999
V	1,200 to 2,499
VI	[1] 250 to 1,199

[1] See qualification noted in preceding paragraph.

---

[9] For discussions of uses of farm classification, see M. R. Benedict, F. F. Elliott, H. R. Tolley, and C. Taeuber, "Need for a New Classification of Farms," *Journal of Farm Economics*, November 1944; and K. L. Bachman, J. C. Ellickson, W. D. Goodsell, and Ray Hurley, "Appraisal of the Economic Classification of Farms," *Journal of Farm Economics*, November 1948.

Noncommercial or "other" farms are grouped into three classes:

Part-time farms. Farms whose sales of farm products in 1949 were
$250 to $1,999 are classified as "part time," if the farm operator reported
(*a*) that he had worked 100 or more days off the farm in 1949, or (*b*) that
the year's nonfarm income received by him and members of his family
had been greater than income from the sale of farm products.

Residential farms. These include all farms except abnormal farms,
whose total sales of farm products in 1949 amounted to less than $250.
Some of these represent farms on which the operator worked off the
farm more than 100 days in 1949. Some represent farms on which the
year's income from nonfarm sources had been greater than income from
sales of agricultural products. Others represent subsistence and marginal
farms of various kinds. Some farms included here might, under different
conditions, have qualified as commercial farms.

Abnormal farms. Insofar as identification is possible, abnormal farms
include public and private institutional farms, community enterprises, and
experiment station farms. In most of the tables in this study, data for
abnormal farms are included with those for part-time farms.

Distribution of farms by economic class shows that in 1950 over two-
thirds of the farms in the United States were commercial farms (figure 2).
The largest group consisted of farms in class V, that is, farms whose sales
of farm products ranged from $1,200 to $2,499 in 1949. There were
almost as many class IV farms, where sales ran from $2,500 to $4,999.
Only 2 percent of all farms sold their farm products for $25,000 or more.

FIGURE 2.—NUMBER AND PERCENT OF FARMS, BY ECONOMIC CLASS: 1950

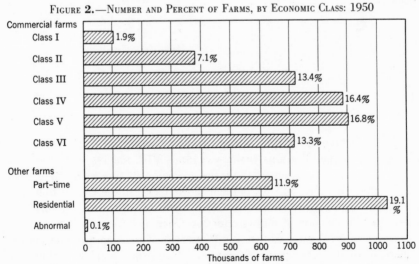

Source: *1950 Census of Agriculture*, Vol. II, *General Report, Statistics by Subjects*, Chapter XII.

The largest subgroup in the total economic classification is the residential
group. Despite their low agricultural rating the more than 1 million
farms in this group do not necessarily have the poorest housing, since the

group includes farms whose owners are dependent upon nonfarm sources of income.

Each of the 12 type-of-farming regions includes at least a few class I farms (although in 2 there are less than half of one percent), and each includes some class VI and noncommercial farms. The West Coast Region (XII) contains the greatest proportion of class I farms, and the Cotton Belt (region VI), the greatest proportion of class VI farms. The sharecropper farms in that area undoubtedly account for most of these low-production farms.

If the first four economic classes are combined, and if classes V and VI are combined with part-time and residential farms, the separation of high- and low-production farms that results is convenient for evaluating the relative economic positions of the region as compared with the position of the United States as a whole. On this basis, almost 40 percent of the farms are in the high-production group.

TABLE 3.—PERCENT DISTRIBUTION OF FARMS BY ECONOMIC CLASS, FOR TYPE-OF-FARMING REGIONS: 1950

Region	Number of farms	Percent of all farms by economic class								
		Total	I	II	III	IV	V	VI	Part time[1]	Residential
Northeast Dairy	485,000	100.0	2.1	9.0	15.7	15.6	11.9	6.8	14.7	24.2
Great Lakes Dairy	412,700	100.0	0.8	5.8	20.2	26.0	17.7	7.7	10.7	11.1
East and Gulf Coast Misc	263,100	100.0	2.9	5.6	8.2	14.4	16.5	12.3	13.2	26.9
General and Self-Sufficing	825,200	100.0	0.4	1.9	5.0	10.9	15.7	17.6	15.4	33.1
Tobacco	234,800	100.0	0.4	2.0	8.9	26.0	27.6	14.6	7.2	13.3
Cotton Belt	1,384,500	100.0	0.5	1.8	4.1	10.9	21.3	23.7	14.3	23.4
Corn Belt	906,500	100.0	2.4	15.2	27.7	22.1	13.0	6.5	6.6	6.5
Northern Wheat and Small Grains	136,400	100.0	3.7	14.7	27.0	26.5	14.2	5.4	4.3	4.2
Southern Wheat and Small Grains	112,000	100.0	5.9	17.0	25.3	23.0	13.4	4.9	5.1	5.4
Year-Long and Seasonal Grazing	275,300	100.0	6.0	14.5	18.2	18.2	14.4	7.6	9.4	11.7
Upland Summer Grazing	105,700	100.0	4.5	11.3	17.9	18.8	13.9	6.5	12.4	14.7
West Coast Miscellaneous	214,900	100.0	7.0	10.7	13.5	13.7	12.9	5.3	15.0	21.9

[1] Includes abnormal farms.

Source: Derived from *1950 Census of Agriculture*, Vol. I, *Counties and State Economic Areas*, economic area table 2. Data from State economic area tables were combined into regions.

The most favorable ratios of high- to low-production farms are in the two wheat and small grains regions, regions VIII and IX. In these two regions, 72 and 71 percent of the farms, respectively, are high production. At the other extreme, only 17 percent of the farms in the Cotton Belt (VI) are in the high-production group. (See table 3.) The two regions with the largest proportion of high-production farms include only 4 percent of the farms in the United States, but 9 percent of the high-production and 3 percent of the low-production farms. The crops in these regions are mostly wheat and other small grains for which high prices and high yields have been sustained in recent years. Consequently, more of the farms have been in the high-production group than during some other periods such as the dust storm years of the early part of the 1930 decade.

In the General and Self-Sufficing Region (IV), which stretches from the Piedmont Plateau in Virginia and North Carolina to the Ozark Mountains in Arkansas and Missouri, only 18 percent of the farms are in the high-production group. This region and the Cotton Belt together include nearly 40 percent of all farms in the United States and more than 55 percent of the low-production farms. On the average, the farms in these regions are somewhat smaller than those in other regions, particularly in the West; but low production here is due not so much to the size of farm as to the high proportion of nonproductive land in the mountainous country and to worn-out single-crop land.

Farm Family Income

A farm's economic class is largely determined by farm income,[10] i.e., the gross income from farm sources. This is true of substantial numbers of noncommercial as well as commercial farms. In considering the effect of income on farm housing, however, it is necessary to take into account other income factors, namely, net income from farm operations and income from other sources.

The 1950 Census of Population was the first decennial census to collect information on total family income. The complex nature of a farm's activities and the variety of sources which may contribute to a farm family's total income may, in many cases, lead to errors in reporting of money income.[11]

Distribution of occupied farmhouses by family income

Table 4 shows that more than half the families occupying houses on farms in 1950 reported their total farm and nonfarm money income during 1949 to be less than $2,000. The median income was $1,607. Families in owner-occupied units reported slightly higher incomes than those in renter-occupied units. There was a difference of only $450 in the median incomes of owners and renters. However, within the classes whose money incomes were over $5,000, there were proportionally more than twice as many owners as renters.

The relatively low median income results largely from the inclusion of low-production farms—commercial classes V and VI and part-time and residential farms. If these low-production groups are separated from the group that includes the better commercial farms, the income curve changes quite drastically (table 5). Nearly half the farm operators in classes V and VI combined had family incomes of less than $1,000 in 1949. Almost one-third of the part-time and residential farm operators were also in that group, but only 13 percent of the operators in the upper economic classes had such low incomes.

---

[10] For distribution of farm family income by type-of-farming region, see Chapter 3, table 35, p. 69.

[11] An explanation of the methods used in collecting census information on total family income appears in Appendix C, p. 137.

TABLE 4.—FAMILIES BY TOTAL FAMILY INCOME IN 1949 AND TENURE: 1950

Family income	Total		Owner		Renter and rent free	
	Number	Percent	Number	Percent	Number	Percent
Total......................	5,659,570	100.0	3,701,875	100.0	1,957,695	100.0
Income reported................	5,393,290	95.3	3,522,180	95.1	1,871,110	95.6
Income not reported............	266,280	4.7	179,695	4.9	86,585	4.4
Total reporting income......	5,393,290	100.0	3,522,180	100.0	1,871,110	100.0
Under $1,000....................	1,861,495	34.5	1,110,505	31.4	750,990	40.1
$1,000 to $1,999................	1,270,815	23.6	785,050	22.3	485,765	26.0
$2,000 to $2,999................	915,955	17.0	611,550	17.4	304,405	16.3
$3,000 to $3,999................	562,415	10.4	404,760	11.5	157,655	8.4
$4,000 to $4,999................	296,495	5.5	223,805	6.4	72,690	3.9
$5,000 to $5,999................	172,655	3.2	133,860	3.8	38,795	2.1
$6,000 to $6,999................	98,175	1.8	77,625	2.2	20,550	1.1
$7,000 to $9,999................	122,310	2.3	97,675	2.8	24,635	1.3
$10,000 and over................	92,975	1.7	77,350	2.2	15,625	0.8
Median income.........dollars..	1,657	...	1,829	...	1,380	...

Source: Derived from *1950 Census of Housing*, Vol. III, *Farm Housing Characteristics*, table 2.

TABLE 5.—PERCENT DISTRIBUTION OF FARM OPERATORS BY TOTAL FAMILY INCOME IN 1949, BY ECONOMIC CLASS OF FARM: 1950

Family income	Total farms	Commercial farms						Other farms		
		Total	Classes I and II	Class III	Class IV	Class V	Class VI	Total	Part time[1]	Residential
Total reporting income..............	100	100	100	100	100	100	100	100	100	100
Under $1,000..............	28	27	5	8	20	31	67	30	22	36
$1,000 to $1,999.........	25	25	11	20	29	33	24	24	29	21
$2,000 to $2,999.........	18	17	16	24	21	18	6	19	21	18
$3,000 to $3,999.........	12	12	16	18	15	9	2	12	13	12
$4,000 to $4,999.........	7	7	14	10	8	4	1	7	7	6
$5,000 and over..........	10	12	38	20	7	5	(2)	8	8	7
Median income...dollars..	1,880	1,920	4,143	2,917	2,048	1,576	746	1,833	1,966	1,667

[1] Includes abnormal farms.
[2] Less than 0.5 percent.

Source: U. S. Bureau of the Census, *Farms and Farm People—Population, Income, and Housing Characteristics by Economic Class of Farm*, 1953, Chapter 3, table 6.

Comparison of farm and nonfarm family incomes

Income differences arising from income "in kind" (farm products consumed on the farm) and other problems inherent in the nature of farm income do not account for all of the spread between farm and nonfarm incomes. The fact is that on the average the farm family has to do with less of the goods and services that contribute to the usual concept of an American standard of living than has the average nonfarm family. Table 6 shows that only about 15 percent of the farm families, as compared with more than 30 percent of the nonfarm families, reported incomes of $4,000 or more. However, the income levels of nonfarm families living in the same general areas as most of the farmers (i.e., rural-nonfarm families outside metropolitan areas) are more nearly like those of farm families. Sixteen percent reported incomes of $4,000 or more. The median income of this group was roughly 30 percent higher than that of farm families,[12] but the median income of nonfarm families in general was nearly 90 percent higher.

TABLE 6.—Percent Distribution of All Nonfarm Families, Nonfarm Families Outside Metropolitan Districts, and Farm Families, by Money Income in 1949: 1950

Family income	All nonfarm families	Nonfarm families outside metropolitan areas	Farm families
Total..........................	100.0	100.0	100.0
Under $1,000.......................	16.1	22.4	34.5
$1,000 to $1,999....................	13.5	18.0	23.6
$2,000 to $2,999....................	18.8	20.5	17.0
$3,000 to $3,999....................	19.4	17.1	10.4
$4,000 to $4,999....................	12.1	9.5	5.5
$5,000 to $5,999....................	7.8	5.3	3.2
$6,000 to $6,999....................	4.3	2.7	1.8
$7,000 to $9,999....................	4.8	2.6	2.3
$10,000 and over...................	3.2	1.9	1.7
Median income.............dollars..	3,082	2,468	1,657

Source: *1950 Census of Housing*, Vol. II, *Nonfarm Housing Characteristics*, Part 1, Chapter 1, United States; and Vol. III, *Farm Housing Characteristics*, table 2.

Sources of farm family income

Over 60 percent of the farm operators in the United States reported that their gross income from farm operations amounted to less than $2,500 in 1949, a year when farmers generally were receiving favorable prices for farm products. Even with the advantage of some income "in kind," many farm families depended on other sources to supplement farm income. These other sources were, principally, wages and salaries received by either the operator or by members of his family. According to an analysis in *Farms and Farm People*,[13] nearly 30 percent of the income received by the average farm family came from wages and salaries (approximately 20 percent earned by the operator and 9 percent by other family members). The operation of the average farm provided 60 percent of the family income, and the balance came from miscellaneous sources. (See figure 3.)

---

[12] It should be noted that "farm-operator families" had slightly higher incomes than "all farm families." This is because the groups "farm-operator families" and "all farm families" represent slightly different universes. Statistics for farm-operator families were taken from small matched samples of the Censuses of Agriculture, Population, and Housing, whereas figures on all farm families were taken solely from the Censuses of Population and Housing. The same definition of a farm was not used in the two censuses. The Census of Agriculture defined a farm according to the amount of produce it sold or according to an inventory of equipment and livestock if nothing was produced for sale. The Censuses of Population and Housing, however, defined a farm according to the respondent's answer to the question, "Is this house on a farm or ranch?" If the answer to the question was "Yes," the dwelling unit was considered as being on a farm unless cash rent was paid for the house and yard only. (A detailed discussion of differing census classifications and definitions appears in Appendix A, p. 120.) Data drawn from both farm definitions are used in this section in order to make it possible to relate income to economic class of farm (Census of Agriculture) as well as to both income of nonfarm families and housing characteristics (Censuses of Population and Housing). Differences in the income distributions of these groups can be seen by comparing tables 5 and 6.

[13] U. S. Bureau of the Census, *Farms and Farm People—Population, Income, and Housing Characteristics by Economic Class of Farm*, 1953, Chapter 3, table 6.

The proportion of family income derived from farm operations differed widely with economic class. It ranged from 87 percent on class I commercial farms to only 16 percent on residential farms. Part-time and residential farm families combined received, on an average, almost 70 percent of their incomes from wages and salaries and only 17 percent from farm operations.[14]

Figure 3 shows that wages and salaries were relatively more important for class V farm families than for families on commercial farms of any other class; a little more than one-third of their incomes was derived from this source. This accounts in large part for the fact that the median income of these families was more than twice that of class VI farm families. By definition, class V farm families were those whose gross income from farm operations ranged from $1,200 to $2,499, and class VI families were those whose incomes ranged from $250 to $1,199. The median net farm income for class V farms was, however, only a little over $300 more than that of class VI farms.[15] In addition, class V farm families received relatively less of their incomes from sources other than the farm or from wages and salaries than did class VI families.

Class V farms tend to be concentrated in areas like the Piedmont Plateau and the Mississippi Valley (figure 4), where there are opportunities for work in the Piedmont mill towns, or on the larger farms located in both areas. Class VI farms, while generally in the same broad region, are concentrated more in the mountainous areas. The availability of more part-time work is apparently the reason that the average class V farm operator was able to earn 22 percent of his total family income in wages or salaries, while the average class VI farmer earned only 17 percent in that manner.

The average family on part-time and residential farms depended on the operator's wages and salaries for half or more of the family income in 1949. Another 16 percent was contributed by the wages and salaries of other family members. Chiefly as a result of these off-farm earnings, the median wage and salary income was $1,600 for part-time and $1,700[16] for residential farm families; medians for classes V and VI were $790 and $350, respectively. In other words, income from wages and salaries resulted in higher incomes, generally, for part-time and residential farm families than for families on other low-production farms.

Another method of evaluating the relationship of income to economic class of farm is to compare the distribution of total income of farm families by economic class with similar distributions for each source of income.

---

[14] In the analysis of sources of farm family income, income from other self-employment, if any, was included with farm income, since the 1950 Census schedule did not provide for separate entries for incomes from farm and nonfarm self-employment.

[15] *Op. cit.*, table 7.

[16] *Ibid.*

FIGURE **3.**—DISTRIBUTION OF AVERAGE FARM-OPERATOR FAMILY INCOME IN 1949 BY SOURCE OF INCOME, BY ECONOMIC CLASS OF FARM, FOR THE UNITED STATES

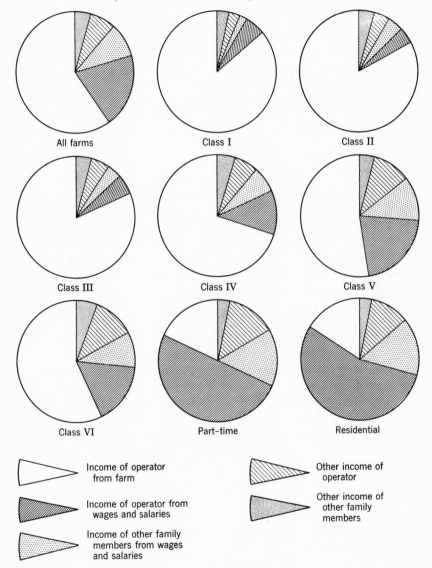

Source: U. S. Bureau of the Census, *Farms and Farm People—Population, Income, and Housing Characteristics by Economic Class of Farm*, 1953, Chapter 3, table 5.

FIGURE 4.—DISTRIBUTION OF FARMS BY ECONOMIC CLASS: 1950

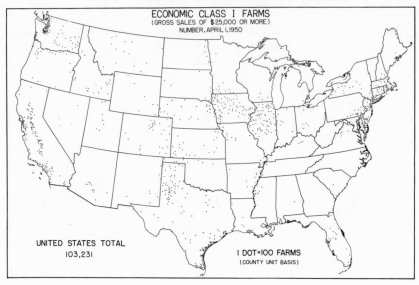

ECONOMIC CLASS I FARMS
(GROSS SALES OF $25,000 OR MORE)
NUMBER, APRIL I, 1950

UNITED STATES TOTAL
103,231

I DOT=100 FARMS
(COUNTY UNIT BASIS)

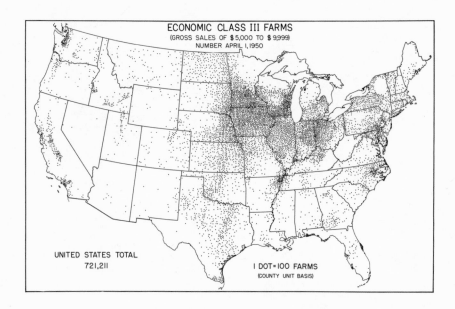

ECONOMIC CLASS III FARMS
(GROSS SALES OF $5,000 TO $9,999)
NUMBER APRIL I, 1950

UNITED STATES TOTAL
721,211

I DOT=100 FARMS
(COUNTY UNIT BASIS)

The percentage of the total money income in 1949 that went to each economic class of farm was almost precisely the same as the percentage of the total number of farms in each of the classes (see figure 2 and table 7). There were greater variations in the way that incomes from the various sources were distributed. The operators of commercial farms of every

FIGURE **4.**—DISTRIBUTION OF FARMS BY ECONOMIC CLASS: 1950—Cont.

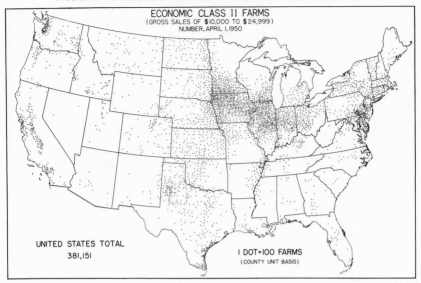

ECONOMIC CLASS II FARMS
(GROSS SALES OF $10,000 TO $24,999)
NUMBER, APRIL 1, 1950

UNITED STATES TOTAL
381,151

I DOT=100 FARMS
(COUNTY UNIT BASIS)

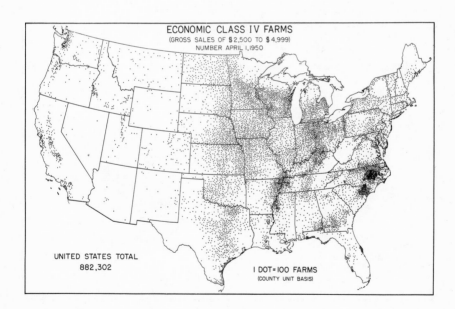

ECONOMIC CLASS IV FARMS
(GROSS SALES OF $2,500 TO $4,999)
NUMBER APRIL 1, 1950

UNITED STATES TOTAL
882,302

I DOT=100 FARMS
(COUNTY UNIT BASIS)

class had a more than proportionate share of the income from farm or other self-employment. Noncommercial farm operators, even though their farm income included most of the nonfarm business and professional income (see footnote 1, table 7), had a less than proportionate share of the income from farm and other self-employment.

FIGURE 4.—DISTRIBUTION OF FARMS BY ECONOMIC CLASS: 1950—Cont.

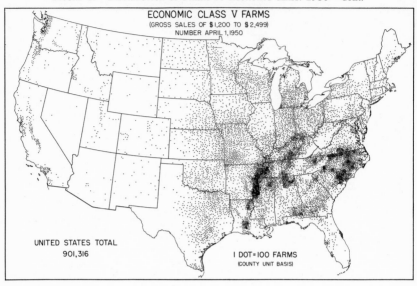

ECONOMIC CLASS V FARMS
(GROSS SALES OF $1,200 TO $2,499)
NUMBER APRIL 1, 1950

UNITED STATES TOTAL
901,316

1 DOT = 100 FARMS
(COUNTY UNIT BASIS)

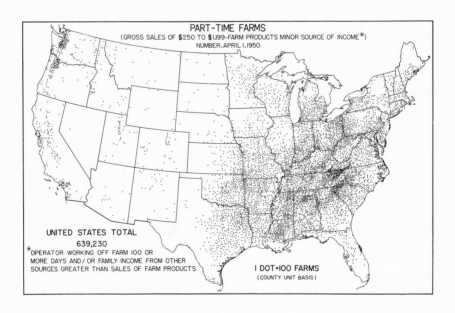

PART-TIME FARMS
(GROSS SALES OF $250 TO $1,199—FARM PRODUCTS MINOR SOURCE OF INCOME*)
NUMBER, APRIL 1, 1950

UNITED STATES TOTAL
639,230
*OPERATOR WORKING OFF FARM 100 OR
MORE DAYS AND/OR FAMILY INCOME FROM OTHER
SOURCES GREATER THAN SALES OF FARM PRODUCTS

1 DOT = 100 FARMS
(COUNTY UNIT BASIS)

Over half of the income received by all farm operators from wages and salaries went to the operators of part-time and residential farms. Similarly, more than half of the income earned from other sources went to these operators. Residential farm operators received a third or more of the total income from wages and salaries and from other sources.

FIGURE 4.—DISTRIBUTION OF FARMS BY ECONOMIC CLASS: 1950—Cont.

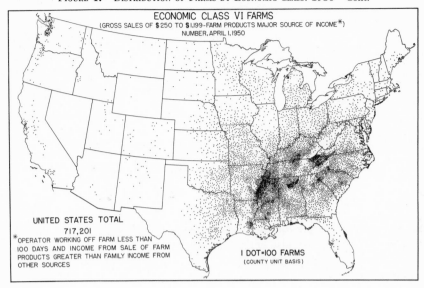

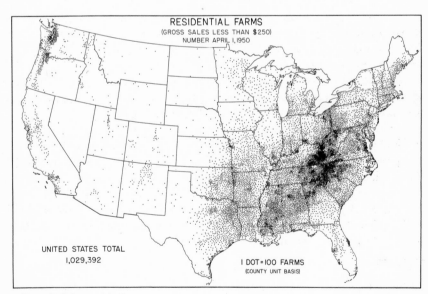

Source: U. S. Bureau of the Census.

Members of the operators' families also received income from farm operations and other self-employment. The farm income was not necessarily from the same farm as that of the operator. Income from this source was more evenly distributed among all classes than any other type of income.

TABLE 7.—PERCENT DISTRIBUTION OF TOTAL FAMILY MONEY INCOME IN 1949, BY ECONOMIC CLASS OF FARM AND SOURCE: 1950

Economic class of farm	Total money income from all sources	Income of operators			Income of other family members		
		Income from farm[1]	Wages and salaries	All other	Income from farm[1]	Wages and salaries	All other
Total....................	100	100	100	100	100	100	100
Classes I and II.............	9	11	4	5	12	7	10
Class III....................	14	17	6	7	16	12	9
Class IV.....................	17	20	11	9	19	15	13
Class V......................	17	19	15	12	17	17	15
Class VI.....................	13	15	9	11	12	10	11
Part time[2].................	12	9	23	17	11	18	20
Residential.................	18	8	32	38	13	21	23

[1] Includes other business or profession, if any; applies mainly to noncommercial farms.
[2] Includes a few abnormal farms.
Source: Same as table 5.

Wage and salary income and all other income earned by the operators' family members were distributed among the economic classes in approximate proportion to the size of the classes. As might be expected, however, families on part-time and residential farms received a little more than their proportionate share.

Migration as a Factor in the Farm Housing Supply

It has already been indicated how great has been the decline in the farm housing supply during the decade 1940 to 1950. Changes in use from farm to nonfarm represent only one aspect of this decline.[17] Another important factor is migration.

Recent migration statistics yield some interesting data on which to base tentative conclusions as to the nature and location of the farmhouses that are likely to be taken out of the inventory within the next decade or two. According to the 1950 Census, 9 percent of the families living on a farm in 1950 reported having lived in a different house in the same county during the previous year; 5 percent had lived in a different county or abroad. Although many families had moved from farm to farm, others had moved away from farms. It would seem that the trend away from the farm, so evident in the period 1940 to 1950, will continue into the foreseeable future.

The history of migration in this country up through the 1940's is amply dealt with in other volumes.[18] Discussion here will be limited to pointing

---

[17] See p. 3.

[18] Basic data on migration are reported in the *1940 Census of Population, Internal Migration in the United States, Social Characteristics of Migrants, Economic Characteristics of Migrants,* and *Age of Migrants.* For studies that focus on the movement of the rural population, see especially John H. Kolb, and Edmund deS. Brunner, *A Study of Rural Society,* Houghton Mifflin Co., Boston, 1952, pp. 25–33; and T. Lynn Smith, *The Sociology of Rural Life,* Harper & Brothers, New York, 1953, pp. 160–195.

In addition, there are a number of *Current Population Reports* of the Bureau of the Census covering the period since 1940. See Series P–20, No. 14, April 1940 to April 1947; No. 22, April 1947 to April 1948; No. 28, April 1948 to April 1949; No. 36, March 1949 to March 1950; No. 47, April 1952; and No. 49, April 1952 to April 1953.

up some of the newer details that have a direct bearing on the farm housing situation. These details are derived chiefly from data taken from special tabulations of the census migration data covering the period 1949 to 1950. More men than women qualify as "heads of households"; therefore, in order to make the analysis relate as closely as possible to migration trends of the farm households, the data selected apply solely to male migrants; but, except in the case of data relative to income, it should be noted that they do not separate the total number of male heads of households from the total number of male migrants. Some idea of the relative difference in numbers may be gained from the fact that only about half (46 percent) of the males who moved during the year were heads of households.[19]

While the data analyzed here cover only a single year's migration, there seems to be considerable validity for assuming that they are representative, in general, of migration for longer periods. This assumption has been confirmed by comparisons with several earlier and later migration surveys.

A study of the 1949–50 movement shows that, for the rural-farm population as a whole, about the same proportion of movement took place from one farm to another (11.3 percent of the 1950 farm population) as from a farm to a nonfarm area (10.6 percent). However, offsetting some of the loss is the movement back to farms from nonfarm areas—6.6 percent of the 1950 farm population.

During this one-year period, therefore, approximately 4 percent of the males living on farms moved to a nonfarm location.[20] This movement is analyzed by regions, and by other factors, in the following paragraphs.

Regional patterns

Considerable variation is shown in the amount and kind of migration taking place among farmers in the different regions. Table 8 shows that the highest proportion of movement took place in three regions—the Tobacco Region, the Southern Wheat and Small Grains Region, and the Upland Grazing Region. In the Tobacco Region the percentage moving from a farm to a nonfarm area during this one-year period represented one-fifth of the region's 1950 farm population, and the percentage moving from one farm to another farm represented a smaller proportion. For the other two regions, the percentage was about one-third of the 1950 male population for farm-to-nonfarm migrants and about one-fifth for the farm-to-farm

---

[19] Apparently this percentage figure is fairly representative since Bogue and Hagood reported 47.6 percent as heads of households in the Corn Belt and 44.2 percent in the Cotton Belt in 1940, ten years earlier. See Donald Bogue and Margaret J. Hagood, *Differential Migration in the Corn and Cotton Belts*, Vol. II, *Subregional Migration in the United States, 1935–1940*, No. 6 in a series, Scripps Foundation, Miami University, 1953.

[20] What is normally termed "migratory farm labor" is not discussed in this volume, largely because their housing problems, while serious, frequently represent requirements for temporary rather than pemanent shelter. For the person interested in this particular problem, reference may be made to a report of the President's Commission on Migratory Labor, *Migratory Labor in Agriculture*, U. S. Government Printing Office, Washington, D. C., 1951.

migrants. The farm-to-nonfarm movement did not represent a net loss in the Tobacco Region, since there was a migration from nonfarm areas to farms of about the same proportions of the 1950 total farm population.

The East and Gulf Coast Region had the next most significant farm-to-nonfarm movement (16 percent of the 1950 population). In this case there also was no net loss to farms since the "reverse" migration amounted to 17 percent.

TABLE **8.**—MOVEMENT OF THE MALE POPULATION TO AND FROM FARMS, BY TYPE-OF-FARMING REGIONS: 1949 TO 1950

Region	Total male farm population, 1950	Type of mover					
		Farm to nonfarm		Nonfarm to farm		Farm to farm	
		Number	Per-cent	Number	Per-cent	Number	Per-cent
Total......................	12,078,599	901,720	7.5	967,330	8.0	560,045	4.6
Northeast Dairy....................	1,165,810	99,255	8.5	38.610	3.3	57,615	4.9
Great Lakes Dairy.................	961,919	65,650	6.8	35,985	3.7	38,380	4.0
East and Gulf Coast Miscellaneous..	619,714	100,780	16.3	107,360	17.3	74,035	11.9
General and Self-Sufficing.........	1,881,566	60,835	3.2	41,935	2.2	27,175	1.4
Tobacco...........................	546,496	116,375	21.3	121,615	22.2	86,780	15.9
Cotton Belt.......................	3,192,341	30,490	1.0	71,035	2.2	19,915	0.6
Corn Belt.........................	1,888,254	224,870	11.9	423,370	22.4	131,420	7.0
Northern Wheat and Small Grains....	286,113	15,960	5.6	10,565	3.7	9,425	3.3
Southern Wheat and Small Grains....	204,831	67,130	32.8	56,805	27.7	45,745	22.3
Year-Long and Seasonal Grazing.....	622,380	22,180	3.6	16,455	2.6	17,375	2.8
Upland Summer Grazing..............	245,248	81,685	33.3	31,520	12.9	42,940	17.5
West Coast Miscellaneous...........	463,927	16,510	3.6	12,075	2.6	9,240	2.0

Source: Unpublished data from the 1950 Census of Population.

The net loss of male migrants from farms in the regions that lost male population during 1949 and 1950 ranged from 1 to 5 percent for most regions. The loss in the Upland Summer Grazing Region exceeded this range.

The greatest relative net loss of any region during this one-year period was in the Upland Grazing Region, where one-third of the male population moved away from farms and only 13 percent moved from nonfarm areas to farms. The greatest relative gain in male farm population occurred in the Corn Belt where 12 percent moved away from, and 22 percent moved to, farms.

Proportions of migrants were low in the Cotton Belt—an interesting fact when it is considered that the Cotton Belt and the Tobacco Region (with one of the highest rates of migration) are the two regions showing the lowest family incomes.[21] The different migratory habits apparently stem from the different attitudes the farmers in the two regions have toward their lands, even though tenancy patterns are similar. The short growing season for tobacco enables the farmer to cast around for another farm or even for a job in the city. The sharecropper and other small farmers of the Cotton Belt, on the other hand, are tied to a much later harvest. Even so, nearly

---

[21] See Chapter 3, table 35, p. 69.

780,000 of the 3 million male farmers in the Cotton Belt made moves of some sort during the 1949–50 year (see table 8).

Farmers in the General and Self-Sufficing Region also tend to remain on their land.   Here, some three-fourths of the farmers own their farms,[22] and many of them subsist on their own production.   These factors result in a low rate of migration.

The rate of migration is low in such regions as the West Coast Miscellaneous Region, the Year-Long and Seasonal Grazing Region, the Northern Wheat and Small Grains Region, and the two dairy regions.   In these regions, unlike the Cotton Belt, higher income appears to be a factor in the farmers' attachment to their lands.

Factors in migration trends

Income.   It has been seen that income is not always a determinant with respect to farm migration, but it is clear that in a great many cases it is a major factor.[23]   When income distribution of the heads of migrant families is compared with that of all farm family heads, the percentage of farm-to-farm movers in 1949–1950 in the "less than $1,000" group is considerably higher (42 percent) than the proportion of the total farm population in this group (33 percent).   A similar pattern can be seen in the "$1,000 to $1,999" group (see table 9).

TABLE 9.—MOVEMENT TO AND FROM FARMS, BY INCOME OF FAMILY HEADS: 1949 TO 1950

| Income of family head | Total farm family heads | | Type of mover | | | | | |
| | | | Farm to nonfarm | | Nonfarm to farm | | Farm to farm | |
	Number	Per-cent	Number	Per-cent	Number	Per-cent	Number	Per-cent
Total..............	5,659,570	100.0	376,780	100.0	212,951	100.0	390,865	100.0
Under $1,000.............	1,861,495	32.9	99,760	26.5	43,391	20.4	166,735	42.4
$1,000 to $1,999.........	1,270,815	22.5	96,620	25.6	55,730	26.3	108,700	27.9
$2,000 to $2,999.........	915,955	16.2	72,620	19.3	48,065	22.6	53,695	13.8
$3,000 to $3,999.........	562,415	9.9	44,980	11.9	29,605	13.9	24,045	6.3
$4,000 to $4,999.........	296,495	5.2	21,575	5.7	13,160	6.2	10,465	2.7
$5,000 to $5,999.........	172,655	3.1	12,180	3.2	6,930	3.3	5,255	1.4
$6,000 to $6,999.........	98,175	1.7	5,645	1.5	3,035	1.4	2,875	0.7
$7,000 and over..........	215,285	3.8	9,640	2.6	5,965	2.8	5,790	1.5
Income not reported......	266,280	4.7	13,760	3.7	7,070	3.3	13,305	3.3

Source: Unpublished data from the 1950 Census of Population.

For the lowest income group (i.e., below $1,000) the percentages of migrants from a farm to a nonfarm area, and of "reverse" migrants, are lower than in the total farm group.   But this picture is changed in each of the categories from $1,000 to $5,999.   It may, therefore, be concluded that, with specific exceptions such as families in the Cotton Belt, lower income families are more likely to move than families with higher incomes. And since there is a general correlation between income and quality of

---

[22] See appendix table E–7, p. 181.
[23] For a general analysis of farm family income and its relation to tenure, see p. 11.

housing, it may also be concluded that families in poor-quality housing tend to move more commonly than families occupying houses of better quality.

Tenure. That farmers who rent are more mobile than farmers who own their houses is borne out by a tabulation of census migration data covering the patterns of migration between 1949 and 1950 by families residing in (a) the open country, in both farm and nonfarm houses, and (b) rural communities, also in farm and nonfarm houses.[24] The results, shown in table 10, indicate that 7 to 13 percent of the owners and 31 to 42 percent of the renters moved during that one-year period. Variations of movement between open-country areas and rural communities were not great.

TABLE 10.—MOBILITY STATUS AND RESIDENCE OF THE RURAL POPULATION, BY TENURE: 1949 TO 1950

	Residence in 1950							
	Owner				Renter			
Mobility status	Open country		Rural community		Open country		Rural community	
	Farm	Non-farm	Farm	Non-farm	Farm	Non-farm	Farm	Non-farm
Total......................	100	100	100	100	100	100	100	100
Same house........................	90	87	93	85	65	69	58	65
Different house on a farm..........	3	2	2	2	12	15	4	5
Different house not on a farm......	2	9	1	12	8	16	21	26
Previous residence not reported....	...	2	...	1	1	...	13	3
Previous tenure not reported.......	5	...	4	...	14	...	4	1

Source: Special tabulation from the 1950 Censuses of Population and Housing.

Nonwhite migrants. Another factor in migration flow is the color of the migrants.[25] In 1950, 11.7 percent of the farmhouses in the Nation were occupied by nonwhite families. It may be seen from table 11 that the proportion of nonwhite male migrants moving from nonfarm to farm areas during the 1949–50 period (as a percentage of all movers) was somewhat less than the proportion of dwelling units occupied by nonwhite farm households (as a percentage of all occupied units). Undoubtedly, the ratio is influenced by the low rate of migration away from farms in the Cotton Belt during this period.

On the other hand, there were a disproportionately large number of nonwhite farm-to-farm movers when compared with the proportion of units occupied by nonwhite households. In the farm-to-nonfarm group, the proportion of nonwhite movers to total movers is approximately the same as the proportion of units occupied by nonwhite is to total occupied farm units.

These data would indicate that during recent years there has been a greater movement of nonwhite males from farm to nonfarm areas than the reverse. This could be accounted for by a continuation of the wartime flow of nonwhite farmers from the land to urban jobs.

---

[24] This tabulation covered 6,723 migrants, of which, 4,343 were owners and 2,380 were renters.
[25] The housing of nonwhite farm operators is fully discussed in Chapter 6, p. 101.

Table **11.**—Movement of the Male Population to and from Farms by Color, and Number of Dwelling Units by Color of Occupants: 1949 to 1950

Color	Percent by type of mover			Color of occupants	Occupied dwelling units, 1950	
	Farm to nonfarm	Nonfarm to farm	Farm to farm		Number	Percent
Total............	100.0	100.0	100.0	Total..................	5,659,570	100.0
White...............	87.4	91.5	77.1	White......................	4,995,770	88.3
Nonwhite............	12.6	8.5	22.9	Nonwhite..................	663,800	11.7

Source: *1950 Census of Housing*, Vol. III, *Farm Housing Characteristics*, tables 1 and 3, and unpublished data from the 1950 Census of Population.

C H A P T E R 2

CHARACTERISTICS OF FARM HOUSING
IN 1950

The Census of Housing uses several criteria to describe the Nation's farm housing. These are tenure, year built, condition and plumbing facilities, heating fuel and equipment, cooking fuel, number of rooms, number of persons, persons per room, sex and age of head, electric lighting, type of household, and income in 1949.

In the following pages these criteria are used, first as an indication of the trends in farm housing across the Nation during the 1940–50 decade and later as they are related to 1949 farm family income and to farm economic levels in 1950. Finally, they are used as a means of estimating the influence of low-production farms on national housing standards and of measuring the contributions of new construction to these standards.

National Trends, 1940 to 1950

Between 1940 and 1950 the number of farmhouses declined by approximately 17 percent, but the proportion of owner-occupied farmhouses in relation to tenant-occupied houses actually increased.[1] Table 12 gives comparative figures on this and other occupancy data. In 1950 almost two of every three occupied farmhouses were lived in by the family that owned and operated the farm; in 1940 the proportion was slightly over half.

During the same period the size of farm households declined slightly. In 1950, 3.6 persons was the median for a farm household, compared with 3.8 in 1940.

If, as is commonly accepted, an average of 1.01 or more persons to a room means "overcrowding," only one of every five farmhouses was overcrowded in 1950. In 1940 almost one of every three farmhouses fell into this category. Obviously, overcrowding is a more serious problem in houses occupied by tenants than in those occupied by owners. In 1950 one of every three tenant-occupied houses was overcrowded—a decline of about 40 percent from the 1940 percentage.

---

[1] It has been pointed out in the section on migration, p. 24 that renters tend to move away from farms more readily than owners. The number of owner-occupied farmhouses actually remained practically unchanged between 1940 and 1950, but the number of renter-occupied farmhouses declined by 41 percent. Thus, the fact that there was an increased rate of owner occupancy in 1950 does not necessarily reflect a proportionate shift from tenancy to ownership.

TABLE **12.**—OCCUPANCY CHARACTERISTICS OF DWELLING UNITS: 1950 AND 1940

Characteristic	1950	1940	Characteristic	1950	1940
ALL OCCUPIED UNITS			ALL OCCUPIED UNITS-- Cont.		
Total....................	5,721,022	7,106,559			
			Percent by color of		
Percent by tenure......	100.0	100.0	occupants............	100.0	100.0
Owner.......................	65.7	53.2	White.......................	88.5	85.9
Renter......................	34.3	46.8	Nonwhite....................	11.5	14.1
Percent by number of persons in household..	100.0	100.0	RENTER-OCCUPIED UNITS		
1 person....................	5.0	5.1	Total....................	1,962,702	3,323,832
2 persons...................	23.4	19.5			
3 persons...................	20.4	19.9	Percent by persons per		
4 persons...................	18.1	17.8	room..................	100.0	100.0
5 persons...................	12.8	13.3	1.00 or less..............	64.0	58.8
6 persons or more..........	20.3	24.4	1.01 or more..............	33.8	39.9
Median number of persons in household..................	3.6	3.8	Not reported.............	2.2	1.3
Percent by persons per room..................	100.0	100.0			
1.00 or less................	76.1	68.7			
1.01 or more................	21.9	30.0			
Not reported................	2.0	1.3			

Source: *1950 Census of Housing,* Vol. I, *General Characteristics,* Part 1, U. S. Summary, tables 3, 10, and 11; and *1940 Census of Housing,* Vol. II, *General Characteristics,* Part 1, U. S. Summary, tables 9 and 10.

Nonwhite farmers occupied a slightly smaller proportion of farmhouses in 1950 than in 1940—a ratio of 12 to 14 percent.[2]

Data on the condition of farmhouses occupied in 1940 and in 1950 (see table 13) are not strictly comparable, since the basis for the 1940 Census term for houses "needing major repairs" underwent some revision before the 1950 Census, and the term itself was changed to "dilapidated."[3] However, it is generally assumed that on the basis of the definitions used for each of the terms, a house classified as "dilapidated" in 1950 would be in poorer condition than one "needing major repairs" in 1940. Thus, it would be natural to expect a lower proportion of farmhouses considered to be dilapidated in 1950 than of farmhouses needing major repairs in 1940. But difference in the comparative percentages shown is sufficiently marked to warrant the conclusion that the condition of farm housing during the decade did, in fact, improve—a result, no doubt, of the period of national prosperity.

The size of farmhouses, as measured by number of rooms, appears to have increased during the 10-year period from 1940 to 1950. In 1950 the median number of rooms for farmhouses in the United States was 5.1, compared with 4.7 in 1940. The greatest relative increase is shown in farmhouses of 6 rooms or more, although some increase is evident in

[2] The figures cited are relative. The number of nonwhite occupants declined 34 percent between 1940 and 1950, while white occupants declined 17 percent. See Chapter 6, p. 102, for a detailed analysis of the trends in nonwhite farm housing.

[3] A dwelling unit was reported as dilapidated when it had serious deficiencies, was run down or neglected, or was of inadequate original construction. The 1940 and 1950 terms are defined in the glossary, p. 187.

houses of only 5 rooms. The greatest decrease is in houses of the "3 rooms or less" group. It is likely that many of the units taken out of the farm housing inventory during this period were small in size. This may account in large part for this change.

TABLE **13.**—PHYSICAL CHARACTERISTICS OF DWELLING UNITS: 1950 AND 1940

Characteristic	1950	1940
CONDITION OF HOUSING[1]		
Number of dwelling units reporting........	6,134,576	7,303,434
Percent................................	100.0	100.0
Not dilapidated............................	80.5	66.1
Dilapidated................................	19.5	33.9
ROOMS		
Number of dwelling units...................	6,357,943	7,642,281
Percent................................	100.0	100.0
1, 2, or 3 rooms..........................	17.5	26.7
4 rooms...................................	20.3	19.7
5 rooms...................................	17.8	15.0
6 rooms or more...........................	41.4	37.3
Not reported..............................	3.0	1.3
Median number of rooms....................	5.1	4.7
YEAR BUILT		
Number of dwelling units reporting........	6,148,150	7,333,850
Percent................................	100.0	100.0
1920 or later.............................	46.6	34.8
1919 or earlier...........................	53.4	65.2

[1] The 1950 and 1940 data on condition are not entirely comparable; see glossary for explanation of differences.

Source: *1950 Census of Housing*, Vol. I, *General Characteristics*, Part 1, U. S. Summary, tables 6, 7, and 9; and *1940 Census of Housing*, Vol. II, *General Characteristics*, Part 1, U. S. Summary, tables 5, 6, and 8b.

Table 13 also shows that approximately 53 percent of the farmhouses in the 1950 United States Inventory were built before 1920. A total of 560,000 farmhouses were built between the beginning of 1945 and 1950—approximately 10 percent of the 1950 total.

A substantial increase, some 140 percent, in the proportion of farmhouses piped for indoor running water is further evidence of farmhouse improvement during the decade. Table 14 shows approximately 43 percent of all farmhouses with running water in 1950, as against only 18 percent in 1940. The proportion of farmhouses with private flush toilet or with bathtubs or showers showed a slightly greater relative increase, but the improvement is less meaningful when it is considered that by 1950 only 28 percent of all farm households had installed private flush toilets; and only 30 percent, bathtubs or showers. It is possible, too, that the increased proportions of units with any of the above plumbing facilities may, in part, reflect the loss between 1940 and 1950 of dwelling units not so equipped.

In 1950, four of every five farmhouses were still heated with a heating stove, or with the more modern space heater. Only 18 percent had central heat; nevertheless, this percentage nearly doubles the proportion of farm-houses so heated in 1940.

While, in 1950, wood retained its importance as a cooking fuel, the preceding decade had seen a great decline in the number of farm households using it. This decline in relative use, from 68 to 38 percent, was offset by a marked increase in the number of households using gas and electricity. Only an insignificant proportion of families used this type of cooking fuel in 1940; but by 1950 more than one of every five households used gas and almost one of every seven used electricity for cooking. In 1950 more than three of every four households were equipped with electric lights; this compares with less than one out of every three so equipped in 1940.

TABLE 14.—FACILITIES AND EQUIPMENT OF DWELLING UNITS: 1950 AND 1940

Facilities and equipment	1950	1940	Facilities and equipment	1950	1940
WATER SUPPLY[1]			ELECTRIC LIGHTING		
Number of dwelling units reporting..................	6,248,867	7,547,321	Number of dwelling units reporting..................	6,202,235	7,512,796
Percent.................	100.0	100.0	Percent.................	100.0	100.0
Piped running water in structure..................	42.7	17.8	With electric lights........	77.7	31.3
No piped running water in structure..................	57.3	82.2	Without electric lights......	22.3	68.7
TOILET FACILITIES			HEATING EQUIPMENT		
Number of dwelling units reporting.................	6,253,901	7,525,221	Number of occupied units reporting.................	5,588,245	6,954,587
Percent.................	100.0	100.0	Percent.................	100.0	100.0
With private flush toilet....	27.7	11.2	Steam or hot water...........	3.3	2.0
Without private flush toilet......................	72.3	88.8	Warm air (piped or pipeless).	14.9	8.0
			Heating stove, other, or none.......................	81.8	90.0
BATHING FACILITIES			COOKING FUEL		
Number of dwelling units reporting.................	6,187,000	7,452,533	Number of occupied units reporting.................	5,636,520	7,001,145
Percent.................	100.0	100.0	Percent.................	100.0	100.0
With private tub or shower...	29.8	11.8	Coal or coke.................	12.3	14.1
Without private tub or shower......................	70.2	88.2	Wood........................	38.6	69.5
			Gas (utility and bottled)....	22.7	3.8
			Liquid fuel.................	8.9	9.0
			Electricity, other, none.....	17.5	3.6

[1] In 1950 a dwelling unit was enumerated as having piped running water when that facility was anywhere within the structure whereas in 1940 the dwelling unit had to have the piped running water within the dwelling unit itself.

Source: *1950 Census of Housing*, Vol. I, *General Characteristics*, Part 1, U. S. Summary, tables 8, 12, and 13; and *1940 Census of Housing*, Vol. II, *General Characteristics*, Part 1, U. S. Summary, tables 7, 7a, 7b, 8, 10a, and 11a.

Family Income and Housing Quality

The 1950 Census of Housing provides the basis for examining the distribution of occupied dwelling units by condition and plumbing facilities for families in each of several income classes. The direct relationship between family income and farm housing characteristics is obvious. Table 15 shows that the percentage of dwelling units in good structural condition and with all specified plumbing facilities increases with each rise in income class. Further evidence of this trend is apparent in the next section where housing characteristics are analyzed by economic class of farm. No time-series information is available to show directly what happens to farm housing as farm family income increases. That farm housing did markedly improve between 1940 and 1950 is evident from the preceding pages, and other data do show that this improvement was accompanied by an increase in farm family income.[4]

Despite this trend, in 1950 only 71 percent of farmhouses in the highest income group were reported to be in good structural condition and with all specified plumbing facilities; whereas, among nonfarm families at the same income level, 97 percent of the houses were similarly classified.[5] This lag may in part be a reflection of the conservative habits prevalent among farmers and in part a reminder that farming is, after all, a business requiring constant reinvestment of profits and energy alike. Furthermore, installation of facilities for running water and sewage disposal is apt to be less costly in built-up areas.

TABLE **15.**—PERCENT DISTRIBUTION OF DWELLING UNITS BY CONDITION AND PLUMBING FACILITIES, BY FAMILY INCOME IN 1949: 1950

Family income	Total	Not dilapidated				Dilapidated		
		Total	With private toilet, bath, and hot and cold running water	Lacking private toilet or bath, or hot running water	No running water	Total	With private toilet or bath, or hot running water	No running water
Total................	100	83	26	16	41	17	2	15
Under $1,000............	100	71	12	11	48	29	2	27
$1,000 to $1,999........	100	82	19	16	47	18	2	16
$2,000 to $2,999........	100	89	30	20	39	11	2	9
$3,000 to $3,999........	100	92	40	20	32	8	2	6
$4,000 to $4,999........	100	94	47	20	27	6	2	4
$5,000 to $5,999........	100	95	53	18	24	5	2	3
$6,000 to $6,999........	100	96	56	19	21	4	2	2
$7,000 to $9,999........	100	96	61	17	18	4	2	2
$10,000 and over........	100	97	73	13	11	3	2	1

Source: *1950 Census of Housing,* Vol. III, *Farm Housing Characteristics,* table 2.

Farm housing and farm economic levels

Before the 1950 Census of Housing little information was available as to the relationship between housing characteristics and the economic level of the farm operation. It was assumed that the higher a farm's produc-tivity, the more likely it is to support a good farmhouse; but before 1950 no national statistics existed to substantiate this observation. After the 1950 Censuses of Agriculture, Population, and Housing, the Bureau of the Census and the Department of Agriculture jointly undertook a study of the subject by correlating information taken on a sample basis from all

---

[4] See monthly release, "Farm Income Situation," U. S. Department of Agriculture, for income changes; and Chapter 1, p. 11, for general data dealing with farm family income.

[5] *1950 Census of Housing,* Vol. II, *Nonfarm Housing Characteristics,* Chapter 1, table A–4.

three censuses.   This study[6] provides extensive data on the housing and characteristics of the families of farm operators.[7]

Housing characteristics and the economic class of farm[8]

Tenure.   The Census-Agriculture study revealed that the economic class of a farm appears to have little effect on tenure of dwelling units occupied by commercial farm operators.   Operators of noncommercial farms, on the other hand, tend to own their houses.   Table 16 indicates that over 80 percent of these houses were owner occupied in 1950, as compared with 67 percent occupied and owned by commercial farmers.[9]

TABLE **16.**—TENURE OF DWELLING UNITS, BY ECONOMIC CLASS OF FARM: 1950

Economic class of farm	Number of farm-operator dwelling units	Percent by tenure			
		Total	Owner	Renter	Rent free
Total..............................	[1]5,341,190	100	72	17	11
Commercial.............................	3,769,059	100	67	20	13
Classes I and II.......................	481,386	100	68	21	11
Class III.............................	748,932	100	70	21	9
Class IV.............................	903,411	100	68	20	12
Class V.............................	912,664	100	66	18	16
Class VI.............................	722,666	100	66	18	16
Other farms...........................	1,572,131	100	82	11	7
Part time[2]..........................	618,915	100	81	11	8
Residential...........................	953,216	100	82	11	7

[1] The number of farm-operator dwelling units is not precisely the same as either the number of farm dwelling units or the number of farms; see footnote 7 to text.

[2] Includes operator dwelling units on abnormal farms.

Source: U. S. Bureau of the Census, *Farms and Farm People—Population, Income, and Housing Characteristics by Economic Class of Farm*, 1953, Chapter 5, table 3.

Explanations for the relatively larger number of owner-occupied dwelling units on noncommercial farms and, conversely, the fewer rented or rent-free dwelling units may be that (1) both part-time and residential farms are likely to be near other sources of employment, and their houses, therefore, may be occupied by families who have moved into the country to "have a place of our own"; and (2) noncommercial farms offer inducement to neither renter nor landlord as a source of income.

[6] U. S. Bureau of the Census, *Farms and Farm People—Population, Income, and Housing Characteristics by Economic Class of Farm*, 1953.

[7] Unfortunately, it was not feasible to include in these data the characteristics of farmhouses in which no farm operator lived (about 13 percent of all farm housing) because the houses were either vacant or occupied by families who did not operate the farms.   The tabulations include a few farm operators (less than 1 percent) who did not live on what was defined in the Census of Agriculture as a farm.   Furthermore, about 2 percent of the operators lived in urban areas, either on urban farms or as nonresident operators.   Strictly speaking, therefore, the housing discussed below should be referred to as farm-operator housing.   However, as only a relatively small part of the total occupied farm dwelling units (as defined by the Census of Housing) were excluded, farm-operator housing may be considered representative of all parts of the supply except those that are vacant.   For simplicity, the terms "farm housing" or "farm dwelling units" are used throughout this section.

[8] See Chapter 1, p. 8, for an explanation of the census classification of farms by economic level.

[9] See Chapter 1, table 4, p. 11, for figures relating to tenure and family income.

The commercial class VI farm obviously offers no greater rental induce-ment. Since over 90 percent of the renter and rent-free dwelling units of this class are in the South, most of the renters here are sharecroppers.

Size of farm-operator dwelling units. The size of a dwelling unit, as measured by its number of rooms, is directly correlated with a farm's economic class. The higher the economic class reported in *Farms and Farm People,* the more likely are the farms to have houses with 5 rooms or more. Table 17 shows 5 rooms or more for less than half of the dwelling units on class VI farms but for nearly 90 percent of the units on class I and II farms. Sizes of the units on other commercial farms fall between these extremes. On noncommercial farms more than half the units have 5 rooms or more.

TABLE 17.—ROOMS AND CONDITION, BY ECONOMIC CLASS OF FARM: 1950

Economic class of farm	Percent of all dwelling units, by rooms				Average number of rooms	Percent of all dwelling units, by condition	
	1 and 2 rooms	3 and 4 rooms	5 and 6 rooms	7 rooms or more		Not di-lapidated[1]	Dilapi-dated[1]
Total.....................	4	29	38	29	5.6	84	16
Commercial....................	3	26	38	33	5.8	86	14
Classes I and II............	1	11	36	52	6.8	97	3
Class III...................	1	14	37	48	6.6	95	5
Class IV....................	2	21	42	35	6.0	89	11
Class V.....................	4	35	37	24	5.4	81	19
Class VI....................	7	44	35	14	4.7	70	30
Other farms.................	5	35	40	20	5.2	80	20
Part time[2]................	5	31	41	23	5.3	84	16
Residential.................	6	36	40	18	5.1	77	23

[1] For definition of "dilapidated," see glossary, p. 187.

[2] Includes operator dwelling units on abnormal farms.

Source: Same as table 16.

Condition of dwelling unit. The physical condition of the farm dwelling unit accurately reflects the level of farm production. Most of the farm-houses in classes I and II are in good condition, i.e., in census terminology "not dilapidated"; only 70 percent of those on class VI farms are similarly classified, and class V farmhouses (with 81 percent) and houses on non-commercial farms (with 80 percent) are in much the same condition.[10]

Year built. The age of a farmhouse appears to be in almost inverse relationship to the economic class of the farm it serves. Generally speak-ing, the higher a farm's economic class, the less likely is its housing to be new. A relatively large volume of new dwelling units is obviously not an indication of high quality in farm housing. Much of the housing built on low-production farms is of poor construction or of a temporary nature which requires frequent replacement. Conversely, many of the good-quality houses were built years ago on better type farms.[11]

[10] See also table 15, p. 30, for condition and plumbing in farm dwelling units, by family income.

[11] More detailed discussion of this subject is provided in the section "Trend of residential construc-tion on farms," p. 38.

Plumbing facilities. Because the installation of plumbing facilities depends in large measure on water being easily available, it is not surprising to find that houses situated on farms should in general be equipped less adequately than houses elsewhere. The water main and sewer line is usually close at hand in most urban areas. But, as with other characteristics, the plumbing in houses on high-production farms and in houses on low-production farms is in marked contrast. Table 18 shows, for example, that only one-tenth of the farmhouses in class VI have hot and cold running water, compared with seven-tenths of the houses in the two upper groups. On the other hand, the table also shows that only a slightly greater proportion of noncommercial farmhouses than of class V farmhouses have the plumbing facilities specified by the census questionnaire. Since the 1949 family incomes of these two groups of farm operators were at about the same level, this similarity, in plumbing as well as other characteristics, is to be expected.[12]

TABLE **18.**—PLUMBING FACILITIES, BY ECONOMIC CLASS OF FARM: 1950

Economic class of farm	Percent of all dwelling units with facilities inside structure				
	Hot and cold running water	Cold water only	Flush toilet	Installed bath or shower	Kitchen sink
Total......................	31	12	30	33	58
Commercial..................	33	12	31	35	61
Classes I and II.............	70	10	65	70	88
Class III....................	48	14	44	47	82
Class IV.....................	32	14	29	33	68
Class V......................	22	13	22	24	50
Class VI.....................	10	8	11	14	26
Other farms..................	27	13	27	30	51
Part time[1].................	30	13	30	32	53
Residential..................	25	12	25	28	49

[1] Includes abnormal farms.
Source: Same as table 16.

Cooking fuel. The cooking fuel that a farm family uses is not wholly determined by the economic class of the family's farm. Electricity, for example, is not readily available on some isolated farms or may be too high priced for cooking use. Hence, substantial numbers of all farm households still use fuels such as coal or wood. According to the report *Farms and Farm People,* one-fifth of the households operating the farms in classes I and II used coal or wood in 1950. At the other end of the economic scale, three-fourths of the households on class VI farms and half of the households on noncommercial farms used coal or wood.

Refrigeration. Nearly all the houses on class I and II farms and more than half the houses on all other commercial farms, except those in class VI, were equipped with mechanical refrigerators in 1950. The proportion of refrigerators in class VI farmhouses is signficantly less than in the houses of either class V or noncommercial farms.

---

[12] See also table 15, p. 30, for condition and plumbing of farm dwelling units, by family income.

TABLE **19.**—COOKING FUEL AND REFRIGERATION, BY ECONOMIC CLASS OF FARM: 1950

Economic class of farm	Percent of all dwelling units using specified fuel				Percent of all dwelling units, by type of refrigeration	
	Coal or wood	Utility or bottled gas	Elec-tricity	Other or none	Mechanical	Other or none
Total....................	49	24	18	9	66	34
Commercial....................	46	25	19	10	69	31
Classes I and II..........	21	40	33	6	96	4
Class III..................	30	35	28	7	86	14
Class IV..................	44	26	20	10	74	26
Class V....................	55	20	12	13	59	41
Class VI..................	75	10	7	8	37	63
Other farms.................	55	20	17	8	59	41
Part time[1]...............	51	22	18	9	61	39
Residential...............	57	18	17	8	58	42

[1] Includes abnormal farms.

Source: Same as table 16.

Equipment on the farms. The study *Farms and Farm People* reports on a number of items of farm equipment enumerated by the 1950 Census of Agriculture. These items may not have occupied space in the farm-house, but they are reported as being present somewhere on the farm. Since most of them are electrically powered, figures on the availability of electricity are included with the equipment listed in table 20. They show a high rate of availability throughout all the economic classes. Even in class VI, well over half the farms are served by electricity, although only a small proportion list equipment that is electrically powered. However, it would be wrong to infer from the low percentage of electric washing machines reported for class VI that two-thirds of the families are without mechanical means of laundering. Gasoline or other fuel may be used to power their washing machines and also their water pumps and water heaters.

TABLE **20.**—EQUIPMENT ON THE FARM, BY ECONOMIC CLASS OF FARM: 1950

Economic class of farm	Percent of dwelling units with specified equipment on farm[1]					
	Elec-tricity	Home freezer	Electric washing machine	Electric water heater	Electric water pump	Telephone
Total....................	78	12	59	17	39	38
Commercial....................	80	14	62	19	43	43
Classes I and II..........	93	35	83	44	74	70
Class III..................	91	21	82	30	62	62
Class IV..................	83	11	67	17	44	45
Class V....................	74	8	54	10	30	31
Class VI..................	61	4	32	5	15	15
Other farms.................	73	9	53	12	29	28
Part time[2]...............	79	10	59	13	34	33
Residential...............	70	8	49	11	26	26

[1] Reported for the farm but not necessarily in the dwelling unit occupied by the operator.
[2] Includes abnormal farms.

Source: Same as table 16.

Housing quality

A review of the characteristics detailed above shows the same almost invariable pattern of relationship between a farm's economic class and its housing quality. "Year built" is the only characteristic failing to fit into this pattern: the age of a farmhouse obviously may have little to do with its quality.

It is reasonable to assume that as farm income becomes larger many farm operators do modernize their homes. But this does not mean that improvements are made uniformly within economic classes, nor, since low-production farms are geographically concentrated, are they uniform throughout the country as a whole.

How low-production farms influence the farm housing supply. In 1950 housing on part-time and residential farms constituted nearly one-third of all farm housing; houses on farms in classes V and VI were almost as large a part of the total. In view of these proportions, the characteristics of housing in the three groups greatly affect characteristics of all farm housing when averaged out across the Nation. Looked at statistically, then, the quality of the "average farmhouse" falls far below the standard of housing most people associate with a full-time farm. Few people think of farm housing as including the rural homes of city workers, on whose small acreages enough crops are raised or livestock kept to meet the current definition of a farm. Neither do they usually identify as typical the dwelling units on marginal farms in the coal regions of Pennsylvania and West Virginia and in the mountains of Virginia, Kentucky, and Tennessee, nor do they consider the sharecroppers' houses in the cotton- and tobacco-producing areas typical. For most people, the large rambling house on a dairy farm in the Northeast, the plain unadorned farmhouse in the Corn and Wheat Belts, or the age-mellowed plantation house in the South are much more likely to be regarded as typical.

Location of low-production farms. Houses on part-time and residential farms probably cover a wider range of quality than those of any other economic class. Some are found on elaborate country estates, whose products sell for less than the $1,200 limit which separates a noncommercial farm from a commercial farm. At the other extreme, the house may be nothing more than a tar-paper shack lacking all modern conveniences. Still others may be located on potentially high-production farms which, for one reason or another, produced nothing for sale in 1949 and thus are classified within the residential group.

Since part-time farms, by definition, and residential farms, often of necessity (they sell less than $250 worth of farm products annually), require other sources of income, these farms are usually situated near sources of nonfarm employment. Figure 4, p. 16, showing the general distribution in 1950 of part-time, residential, and commercial farms, indicates that very few part-time and residential farms are located in sparsely settled areas. They are usually most heavily concentrated in regions dotted with many small communities rather than close to large metropolitan areas. Even though other statistics[13] indicate that about 40 percent of these farms are in metropolitan areas or counties adjoining them, it is evident from figure 4 that the greatest concentration is in the southern Appalachians, in eastern Tennessee and adjoining States—a part of the General Farming Region where almost all farms are low in production. In economic subregion 33 (eastern Tennessee), 94 percent of the farms are either part-time, residential, or are in the low-production, commercial classes V and VI. In the adjoining subregion (31) of Virginia, West Virginia, and Kentucky, 97 percent of the farms are in these classes, although a relatively smaller number are part-time farms. The 76 low-production subregions where, in 1950, half or more of the farms produced less than $2,500 worth of products for sale, account for 86 percent of the residential farms and for 80 percent of the part-time farms.

Table 21 indicates the degree to which low-production farms of all types are concentrated in the same subregions. The 34 subregions in which 75 percent or more of the farms are low-production farms include more than half the total number of part-time and residential farms combined. On the other hand, the 8 subregions in which less than 25 percent of the farms are low-production, include only 1.5 percent of the part-time and residential farms, as opposed to 7 percent of all farms.

TABLE **21.**—Number of Economic Subregions and Percent Distribution of Farms by Percent of Low-Production Farms: 1950

Percent of low-production farms	Number of subregions	All farms	Part-time farms[1]	Residential farms
Total......................	119	5,386,210	640,882	1,026,865
Percent..................	...	100.0	100.0	100.0
Less than 25 percent............	8	7.2	2.0	1.3
25 to 49 percent................	35	27.7	18.3	12.7
50 to 74 percent................	42	28.8	31.7	29.0
75 to 89 percent................	23	23.8	30.0	31.7
90 percent or more..............	11	12.5	18.0	25.3

[1] Includes abnormal farms.

Source: Derived from special compilation of data on farms by economic class for economic subregions from *1950 Census of Agriculture*, Vol. I, *Counties and State Economic Areas*, economic area table 8.

Residential farms tend to be concentrated in the same subregions as part-time farms. The dividing line between part-time farms, which are part-time because they have a small annual production, and residential farms is based upon an insignificant difference in the amount produced for sale, that is, just under or just over the $250 annual value of products sold.[14] The operator of either type of farm may work more than 100 days a year off the farm. Consequently, a farm classified as residential one year may

---

[13] An unpublished analysis by the authors of economic class of farm by county.

[14] For definitions of commercial and noncommercial farms, see Chapter 1, p. 8.

well be part-time the next year, simply because the operator sells a little more produce.

Similarly, the dividing line between class VI farms and part-time farms is based only upon the number of days the operator works off the farm or upon the proportion of family income that is derived from off-farm sources. Thus, the same farm may change from one classification to another each year. It is logical, therefore, that concentrations of all three types generally appear in the same subregions, especially when the commercial farms in these subregions are largely low production.

The marginal quality of housing on low-production farms. In any event, whatever the type of low-production farm there is in a subregion, the effect on the housing characteristics of the area is much the same. There are apparently not enough part-time operators with large incomes to raise either the average quality of housing on low-production farms or the average family income from other sources.[15]

A classification of all subregions by the percentages of low-production farms dramatically demonstrates the relationship of low production to inadequate farmhouse facilities and equipment. Table 22 shows that in almost every instance the larger the percentage of low-production farms the larger is the percentage of houses lacking the specified characteristics. Exceptions to this general tendency may be noted in a comparison of the 8 subregions (corn, wheat, or cattle-raising areas) in which less than 25 percent of the farms are in the low-production group, with the 35 subregions containing 25 to 49 percent low-production farms. Houses in the 35 subregions seem to be slightly better as to condition, plumbing, and electric lighting than those in the 8 subregions. There is no ready explanation for these minor discrepancies.

TABLE **22.**—PERCENT OF OCCUPIED DWELLING UNITS WITH SPECIFIED CHARACTERISTICS, BY PERCENT OF LOW-PRODUCTION FARMS: 1950

Characteristic	All occupied dwelling units	Percent of low-production farms				
		Less than 25	25 to 49	50 to 74	75 to 89	90 or more
Percent dilapidated or lacking plumbing facilities[1]	88	69	65	72	89	92
Percent with no running water	56	48	40	47	74	78
Percent with less than 5 rooms	64	15	25	34	51	48
Percent built 1940 or later	15	8	11	15	19	22
Percent without electric lights	20	10	11	16	30	30
Percent in which wood was used for cooking fuel	38	12	22	36	62	63
Percent with 1.01 or more persons per room	22	10	14	20	32	33
Percent in which family income was less than $1,000	35	14	22	32	49	52

[1] Lacking hot or cold running water, private toilet, or bathing facilities.

Source: *1950 Census of Housing*, Vol. III, *Farm Housing Characteristics*, tables 1 and 2, and a special compilation of data on farms by economic class for economic subregions from *1950 Census of Agriculture*, Vol. I, *Counties and State Economic Areas*, economic area table 8.

[15] The section of Chapter 1 dealing with family income by economic class of farm (see p. 11) supports this hypothesis.

At the other end of the scale, in the 11 subregions where 90 percent or more of the farms are low in production, the houses, almost universally, lack plumbing facilities or are dilapidated. Half of them contain fewer than 5 rooms, and in a third of them there is an average of more than one person to a room. While a relatively large proportion were built between 1940 and 1950—and were not necessarily well built—an even larger proportion have no electric lights, and, in nearly two-thirds of these, wood is used for cooking fuel. Since none of the low-production farms in these 11 subregions, by definition, produced more than $2,500 worth of products for sale in 1949, it might be expected that family income would be supplemented from other sources. But the fact that the total income of over half the families amounted to less than $1,000 during 1949 indicates that very little supplemental income was earned from nonfarm work, at least by this half of the families.

Even though family income may have been underreported for the 1950 Census,[16] reasons for the low quality of housing on low-production farms are quite obviously related to low income. It is also obvious why, with about 60 percent of the farms in the low-production bracket, the average quality of farm housing in the United States is low.

Farm-nonfarm differences in high-quality housing. While it is true that the proportion of high-quality housing on farms (30 percent) is much less than that of all nonfarm housing (77 percent), the difference is much less significant when income levels are taken into account. At similar income levels housing on the farms that produce most of the Nation's agricultural goods is of much the same quality as all nonfarm housing; 79 percent and 93 percent high quality, respectively. Usually, it is as good, if not better, than nonfarm housing similarly located in open country. In other words, leaving aside such other factors as preferences and customs, which will be dealt with later in this study, income and location rather than occupation are the critical factors. Poor-quality housing on low-production farms is comparable to slum housing in urban areas in that it is associated with low incomes. There is even some question whether all low-production farms should be classed as farms, because of the ease with which they can slide from a farm to a nonfarm classification.

Trend of Residential Construction on Farms

It is an anomaly of the farm housing situation over the past 30 years or so that, while the number of farms and farmhouses has consistently decreased, construction of new houses appears to have gone on at a fairly high rate. Statistics provide only some of the clues to the number, characteristics, and location of these new farmhouses.

In the United States as a whole, over 15 percent of the farmhouses standing in 1950 were built after 1939. The total figure of 943,530 new

---

[16] Limitations of the reports on family income are described in Appendix C, p. 137.

units is, in fact, conservative, since it can safely be assumed that for one reason or another some new units fell into disuse during the 10-year period and thus were taken off the census inventory. Census data on year built provide an indication of the volume of construction for the decades 1930 to 1940 and 1920 to 1930. Overlooking, for the moment, differences in definition,[17] and assuming that the respondent's memory and the census method of determining the year a house was built did not vary greatly, the 1940 Housing Census figures are likely to provide a more accurate indication of how many farmhouses were built in the two decades from 1920 to 1940 than do data from the 1950 Census of Housing.

The 1940 Census reported that 1,289,881 farm units, or 18 percent of the estimated stock, had been built in the preceding 10 years—a number substantially above that reported for the decade 1940 to 1950.

For the years 1920 to 1930 the 1940 Census showed 1,262,349 new units, which amounted to about 17 percent of the 1940 stock and probably about the same proportion of the 1930 stock.

No precise estimates of either the 1930 or the 1920 inventories are available.[18] There were about 6.5 million occupied rural-farm dwelling units in both 1930 and 1920, and an estimate of the number of vacant units was added to this figure for the inventory estimates used in table 23. To make an estimate of vacant units some assumption had to be made. If the rural-farm vacancy rate in 1920 and 1930 had been similar to that of 1940, the total rural-farm inventory would have exceeded 7 million in each of these years. But different trends prevailed. In the United States as a whole, appreciable migration away from farms (at least to the extent that many farmhouses were left vacant) probably did not occur until nearly 1940. In fact, Department of Agriculture estimates of farm population show an increase in the midthirties.[19] From 1934 to 1940, the farm population decreased by 7 percent. Within regions, internal shifts of farm population were occurring throughout the thirties—migration from the "dust bowl," for example—and these shifts left vacant dwelling units in particular areas.[20]

The net effect of these shifts, even though some new units, probably

---

[17] The 1950 Census introduced minor changes in the way dwelling units in rural areas were identified as farm or nonfarm and changes in rural-urban classification, including urban annexations of rural territory. The procedure by which farm dwelling units are identified is discussed in detail in Appendix A, p. 121.

[18] The 1930 Census of Population obtained information on the number of private families on rural farms. In 1940 the number of these families was approximately equivalent to the number of occupied dwelling units. The 1920 Census count of families included both private families and quasi-family groups (institutions, etc.) in its count of occupied dwelling units, whereas the 1940 Census included some families living in lodginghouses and smaller quasi-family groups but did not include all institutions.

[19] Cooperative estimates made by the Bureau of the Census and the Bureau of Agricultural Economics and based on the 1950 definition of farm population, in Farm Population, Series Census-BAE, No. 16, 1953.

[20] See National Resources Committee, The Problems of a Changing Population, 1938, pp. 85–89 and 105–108.

shacks, were built, was to increase the number of vacant units in 1940 over the numbers in either 1930 or 1920. Farming was prosperous immediately following World War I, and it might be assumed that there were few vacancies in 1920. The total inventory figure for 1920 may, therefore, have been only a little greater than the number of families, or about 6.9 million units. Through most of the years from 1920 to 1928 or 1929, nonfarm employment was good. Although by 1930 net movement away from farms had undoubtedly left usable vacant dwelling units, it is probable that many people had in the meantime returned to the farm because of diminishing opportunities for employment elsewhere. Thus, there could very well have been a lower vacancy rate in 1930 than in 1940. If this assumption is correct, the inventory in 1930 should have been close to, or possibly a little more than, 7 million.

TABLE 23.—NEW CONSTRUCTION OF RURAL-FARM DWELLING UNITS AS PERCENT OF ESTIMATED INVENTORY, BY DECADES: 1920 TO 1950

[Numbers in thousands]

Decade	Rural-farm occupied dwelling units or families in first year of decade[1]	Vacancies in first year of decade	Inventory in first year of decade	New units added in decade	
				Number	Percent of inventory
1950................................	5,721	637	6,358	...	...
1940 to 1949......................	7,107	535	7,642	[2]954	12.5
1930 to 1939......................	6,605	[3]350	[3]6,955	[4]1,290	18.5
1920 to 1929......................	[5]6,684	[3]200	[3]6,884	[4]1,288	18.7

[1] Families, or private households, in 1920 and 1930 were roughly equivalent to occupied dwelling units in 1940 and 1950.

[2] Adjusted for not reporting by allocation of one-third of its proportionate share to the 10-year period.

[3] Estimated by methods discussed in text.

[4] Numbers adjusted for those not reported, as follows: 1930 to 1939, one-half of apportionate share for the period; 1920 to 1929, three-fourths of apportionate share for the period. It is assumed that, over and above the number unreported, new units were more accurately reported than older ones.

[5] Rural farm estimated on basis of relationship between total farm families and rural-farm families in 1930. Biases resulting from slight differences in definition of farm population and from changes in the proportion of urban to rural territory appear to offset one another.

Unfortunately, there is little other evidence to support the rough estimates of changes in the farm housing inventory described above. The number of farms cannot be related to the number of farmhouses from decade to decade because of differences in definition and changes in the farm economy. However, even if these very crude estimates are as much as 25 percent off, it is clear that new construction is still a highly important part of farm housing. Some questions are immediately suggested:

How much of the construction represented replacement of existing housing?

Why was there almost as much building during the depression years as in the 1920 decade?

What kind of housing is it?

Where was it built?

Was it actually housing for farm operators or extra housing built on operators' farms?

Since the farm housing inventory showed an increase in units only slightly over 10 percent from 1920 to 1940 and a decrease from 1940 to 1950, most of these new units must have meant replacement of some sort. Although they may not have replaced specific dwelling units, new units may have been built in one area to supply a need for additional housing while in other areas farmhouses may have been transferred to nonfarm users. Floods or fires sometimes destroyed units that were replaced. In some areas, particularly where a combination of mild climate and small returns from agriculture tends to encourage the use of inferior, short-lived structures, inadequate units were replaced by equally poor housing. In still other areas settled largely in the past 30 to 50 years, original temporary housing is still being replaced by permanent housing.

New construction related to various economic levels

In urban areas new construction usually implies increasing density of population. But in rural areas, and particularly on farms, many new dwelling units are only inadequate replacements of poorer ones, particularly if the family income is too low for a structurally sound, modern dwelling unit. Presumably, such new construction is not stimulated by market demand in the usual sense, but by the necessity for some slight improvement in shelter. Inadequate new construction is possible in most rural areas because it has to meet few of the minimum standards governing the type or quality of construction in and around urban areas.

The joint study,[21] from which much of the material used in this chapter has been drawn, deals with the age of the farm dwelling unit from two angles: (1) the economic level of the farm, and (2) family income of the farm operator. According to this report, two-thirds of the units built from 1939 to 1949 were on low-production farms (classes V, VI, part time, and residential). In 1949 nearly half of the farm-operator families living in these new houses had total family incomes of less than $1,000.

Table 24 shows that after 1944 proportionately more houses were built on class VI farms than on farms in any of the other economic classes; residential farms came next in order; and the smallest proportion were built on class IV farms.

In 1950 houses were more than 20 years old on 85 percent of the class III farms, but on only two-thirds or less of class VI, part-time, or residential farms.

While it is true that inadequate replacements of earlier housing account, to a great extent, for the large proportions of new houses to be found in the lower economic levels of farm operations, there is another contributing

---

[21] U. S. Bureau of the Census, *Farms and Farm People—Population, Income, and Housing Characteristics by Economic Class of Farm*, 1953.

factor. Some of the low-production farms, particularly in the noncommer-cial groups, are likely to have been quite recently established. Even though the total number of farms has been diminishing since 1930, many new, small suburban farms have been created in counties adjacent to metropolitan areas for families who depend primarily on urban centers for employment. (For example, the number of farm dwelling units in Prince William County, Virginia, near Washington, increased by 6 percent between 1940 and 1950.) A common practice in areas of this type is to divide relatively nonproductive farm land into small tracts for resale to urban workers. Normally, few zoning laws or construction standards exist in such counties, and the purchasers of these tracts are able to build what-ever type of house their financial resources and ingenuity permit.

TABLE 24.—PERCENT DISTRIBUTION OF DWELLING UNITS BY YEAR BUILT, BY ECONOMIC CLASS OF FARM AND FAMILY INCOME IN 1949 OF FARM OPERATOR: 1950

Economic class of farm and family income	Total	Year built				
		1945 or later	1940 to 1944	1930 to 1939	1920 to 1929	1919 or earlier
Total farm-operator dwelling units....................	100	9	6	14	14	57
ECONOMIC CLASS OF FARM						
Classes I and II....................	100	7	4	14	12	63
Class III..........................	100	6	3	6	13	72
Class IV...........................	100	5	6	13	14	62
Class V............................	100	7	5	14	15	59
Class VI...........................	100	14	4	17	15	50
Part time..........................	100	9	9	18	15	49
Residential........................	100	13	7	20	15	45
FAMILY INCOME IN 1949						
Under $1,000.......................	100	9	5	18	16	52
$1,000 to $1,999...................	100	9	6	16	13	56
$2,000 to $2,999...................	100	9	4	13	15	59
$3,000 to $3,999...................	100	5	6	14	13	62
$4,000 to $4,999...................	100	10	5	12	11	62
$5,000 to $9,999[1]................	100	9	3	9	11	68

[1] Data for incomes over $10,000 were not published, since the tabulation was based on a small sample and relatively few of the sample cases fell into this income group. The data probably would not differ materially from those applying to the $5,000-$9,999 income classes.

Source: U. S. Bureau of the Census, *Farms and Farm People—Population, Income, and Housing Characteristics by Economic Class of Farm*, 1953, Chapter 5, tables 3 and 4.

The distributions of dwelling units by "year built" are substantially alike for each income class. The relationship between income and new housing is much less pronounced than when distributions are taken by "economic class of farm." However, the proportions of new dwelling units built for farm operators with low incomes is again much larger than might be expected if they were of the type currently built in urban areas. For ex-ample, from 1940 to 1950 there were relatively and actually more new dwelling units built for families with incomes of less than $1,000 a year than for families whose annual incomes ranged from $5,000 to $9,999. A little over 47,000 units (12 percent of the total housing for that group) were built in this period for families in this higher income bracket.

During the same 10 years families in the lowest income group account for 155,000 new units, or 14 percent of their total housing, and over 164,000 new units were built for farm families with incomes of $1,000 to $1,999. Together, these two low-income groups account for 43 percent of the new farm construction, and all the income groups below $3,000 account for 60 percent.

When the cost of construction between 1940 and 1950 is considered, it is almost inconceivable that many of the new units for these low-income farm families could equal in quality even the most modest of the new homes in urban areas. Long-term credit assistance by Federal agencies would reach very few farm families at these income levels. Conventional credit arrangements for new homes, even if available, would be difficult for a family with a $2,500 income and practically impossible for one with an income of less than $1,000. It is possible, of course, that in many cases the farm families themselves provided most of the labor and that some farmers may have used their own lumber for the cost of the sawing only. Be that as it may, while some of these frugally built dwellings were no doubt structurally sound, many of them fell far below normal standards, and many were not provided with modern plumbing facilities.

Characteristics of the new construction

In the 1950 Census the only housing characteristics that were actually tabulated by "year built" were condition, plumbing, and number of rooms. Thus, it is not possible in one table to relate the three factors: family income, quality (condition and plumbing), and year built. However, the detailed cross-classifications which are tabulated in Appendix E and which provide the basis for discussion in Chapter 3, together with the data on new construction and family income examined above, can be regarded as a fairly sound basis for some deductions. It can be deduced, for example, that since 60 percent of the units built in 1940 or later were built on farms occupied by families with incomes of less than $3,000, and since 55 percent of these houses had no running water or were classified as "dilapidated," there is considerable likelihood that most of the 55 percent, at least, were occupied by low-income families. It is even more certain that the dilapidated new units were generally occupied by families in the lowest income class.

Similarly, the new dwelling units of 4 or fewer rooms were undoubtedly built largely on farms in the low-income groups. Over half of all the new units had fewer than 5 rooms. The number of rooms in a house may not of itself provide a criterion of quality, but there is evidence to show that it does have a bearing on quality. According to the 1950 Census of Housing,[22] relatively few (8 percent) of the new units which were without deficiencies in condition or plumbing contained fewer than 4 rooms. On

---

[22] *1950 Census of Housing*, Vol. III, *Farm Housing Characteristics*, table 2. (See also appendix table D–6, p. 142.)

the other hand, two-thirds of the units which either lacked running water or were dilapidated contained 4 or fewer rooms.

Construction prior to 1940 shows different characteristics. Of farm units built in this earlier period, 44 percent, as compared with 28 percent of the new units, were equipped with flush toilets and were not dilapidated. Nearly half of them contained 5 rooms or more. Almost as many new units were equally large, but the proportion of 1- or 2-room houses was far greater among the new units than among the old. Thus, it would seem that, from an over-all view, construction undertaken from 1940 to 1950 failed to raise the general level of farm housing quality.[23]

Location of new construction

A tabulation of farms according to economic subregion, from the 1950 Census of Housing, points up differential building rates from one part of the country to another (tables 25 and 26). In 20 of the 119 economic subregions, all 20 in the South or West, more than one-quarter of the dwelling units have been built since 1939. The new farmhouses in these subregions represent 27 percent of all new farmhouses in the United States, whereas farmhouses as a whole for the same areas form only 15 percent of the United States total.

TABLE **25.**—DISTRIBUTION OF ECONOMIC SUBREGIONS, BY PERCENT OF OCCUPIED DWELLING UNITS BUILT SINCE 1939: 1950

Percent of units built since 1939	Number of economic subregions	Percent of new units in all subregions	Percent of total units in all subregions
Total..........................	119	100.0	100.0
1 to 4 percent......................	6	0.7	3.1
5 to 9 percent......................	30	12.1	27.3
10 to 14 percent.....................	25	16.8	20.1
15 to 19 percent.....................	19	23.6	21.0
20 to 24 percent.....................	18	19.5	13.6
25 to 29 percent.....................	11	19.1	10.9
30 percent or more...................	10	8.2	4.0

Source: *1950 Census of Housing*, Vol. III, *Farm Housing Characteristics*, subregion table 1.

Thirty-six economic subregions, which are almost entirely located in the Northeast and North Central areas, are in marked contrast. Less than 10 percent of their occupied units have been built since 1939. These new units represent 14 percent of the new farmhouses built in the United States, but the sum of units in these regions forms over 30 percent of the total.

Characteristics of new housing in selected economic subregions

The five subregions discussed below are selected to show how the charac-

---

[23] Further details on the characteristics of new construction will be found in Chapter 3, pp. 62–64. Estimates of 1949 expenditures for new construction of and major improvements to (a) farmhouses and (b) service buildings appear in Chapter 7, table 63, p. 116.

teristics of new houses are related to the economic conditions of the sub-region in which they are built.[24]

The largest percentage of farm dwelling units built and occupied between 1940 and 1950 applies to subregion 99 in the southern tip of Texas where modern methods of refrigeration and rapid transportation have opened up the area to fruit and truck farming. In 1950 nearly half (45 percent) of the occupied farmhouses in the three counties comprising this subregion were under 10 years old. And in 1949 the median income per farm from sale of farm products was approximately $9,000. With this relatively high income one might expect the new houses to be built for new farmers or their helpers, or to be good-quality replacements for earlier temporary housing. But this is not always the case. A comparison of statistics for 1940 and 1950[25] for the subregion shows no improvement in the housing supply in terms of number of rooms per house. However, so far as running water and private flush toilets are concerned, the percentage of units with these facilities doubled.

TABLE **26.**—NUMBER OF ECONOMIC SUBREGIONS IN GEOGRAPHIC REGIONS, BY PERCENT OF OCCUPIED DWELLING UNITS BUILT SINCE 1939: 1950

Percent of units built since 1939	Total economic subregions	Northeast	North Central	South	West
1 to 4 percent....................	6	4	2	...	...
5 to 9 percent....................	30	9	19	2	...
10 to 14 percent.................	25	3	10	11	1
15 to 19 percent.................	19	...	1	16	2
20 to 24 percent.................	19	...	2	11	6
25 to 29 percent.................	10	...	...	8	2
30 percent or more..............	10	...	...	6	4

Source: *1950 Census of Housing,* Vol. III, *Farm Housing Characteristics,* subregion table 1.

The new units in subregion 99 were not as large, on the average, as those built prior to 1940.[26] Nearly 60 percent of them contained fewer than 4 rooms, and about 80 percent had no running water and therefore no modern toilet or bath. It is clear that a great part of the increase in the over-all proportion of houses with running water or flush toilet must have been occasioned by installation of these facilities in new larger houses (all but about 10 percent of these had such facilities) and in the older large houses. The statistics appear to show that the high building rate for the area was due to replacement of small temporary units with similar units rather than to their replacement with better units. The large numbers of small units, both new and old, may in part be attributed to the existence in

[24] In Chapter 4 (pp. 70–87) several typical subregions are discussed in further detail as to how the characteristics of their farm housing, both old and new, relate to type-of-farming regions. For location of economic subregions, see map, figure 1, p. 6.

[25] Obtained by totaling county statistics from *1950 Census of Housing,* Vol. I, *General Characteristics,* Chapter 43, tables 32 and 33; and *1940 Census of Housing,* Vol. II, *General Characteristics,* Part 5, tables 22 to 27 for Texas.

[26] *1950 Census of Housing,* Vol. III, *Farm Housing Characteristics,* p. 235.

this part of Texas of many rent-free farmhouses which may be occupied
by workers on the truck and fruit farms. In addition, the fact that nearly
one-fifth of the farms in this subregion are noncommercial points to the
possibility that these noncommercial farms may be owned or rented by
farm workers, or workers in nearby Brownsville who operate them to supplement their salaries.

There is another factor to be considered in examining subregion 99.
Although 45 percent of all the farmhouses in the subregion were built between
1940 and 1950, the number of occupied farm dwelling units for the same
period shows a net loss of about 12 percent; this is accompanied by a 20-
percent increase in the number of farms. Thus, despite the high rate of
building, farm units have been disappearing at an even greater rate. This
suggests that, at the very minimum, 7,000 of the 14,600 farm units occupied in 1940 were no longer standing in 1950, at least as farm units.
Some of them may have been reclassified as nonfarm units, since the increase in nonfarm dwelling units exceeded the number built during the
10-year period. In 1950, 22 percent of the nonfarm units were new, but
nonfarm dwelling units had increased 125 percent. This reclassification
of dwelling units occurred not only as a result of change in the way they
were used, but also because rural territory was annexed by almost all of
the urban centers in the subregion. In addition, new urban areas were
created from rural territory. This resulted in their exclusion from the count
of rural farmhouses in the newly created urban territory.

Another example of a subregion with a high proportion of new dwelling
units is economic subregion 115, covering eight southern California
counties. Here more than 30 percent of the total farmhousing was built
between 1940 and 1950. Although this subregion is subject to greater
metropolitan influence, the economic and social characteristics of subregions 115 and 99 are similar in many ways, as are the crops and type
of labor. Both have grown rapidly since the turn of the century, particularly in nonfarm areas, although the growth recently has been less pronounced in subregion 115. The two areas are similar as to economic class
of farm, and the average value of farm products sold in each area in 1949
was close to $9,000. However, if class VI and noncommercial farms are
combined, nearly 40 percent of subregion 115 farms are at the low end of
the production scale, while in subregion 99 less than 25 percent are in this
bracket.

The similarities do not carry over into farm housing characteristics. In
the California subregion, in 1950, 35 percent of the new units contained
fewer than 4 rooms, compared with over 50 percent in the Texas subregion.
Both new and old small farmhouses were of better average quality than
those in the Texas subregion, and in California a larger percentage of the
new houses than of the old (49 and 36 percent, respectively) were not
dilapidated and had all the plumbing facilities specified by the 1950
Census of Housing. For both areas condition and plumbing in houses of

4 rooms or more were far better than the national average for farm units. Nationally, about 25 percent of all farmhouses of this size were classified as being "not dilapidated" and as having all plumbing facilities; in subregions 99 and 115, the equivalent percentages were 64 and 84, respectively.

The high quality of the larger units and the relatively high quality of the small units in subregion 115, compared with houses of the same size in subregion 99, reflect the influence of the large metropolitan centers in the California area. The small-acreage, low-production farms are often worked on a part-time or residential basis. The owners or renters have sufficient income from other sources to support a good house.

Looking at a third type of subregion—one which includes only one small metropolitan area, where the population has been declining and where the farms all have a low production rate—still other reasons for the high rate of construction may be found. Economic subregion 31 is located in the Appalachian Mountain areas of Kentucky, Tennessee, Virginia, and West Virginia. Generally it supports small farms averaging from 30 to 40 acres, but the rugged terrain restricts the actual tillable acreage. The principal source of off-farm income is coal mining. In this subregion 97 percent of the farms are low production, and the 1949 median family income was about $1,200. Seventy-seven percent of all the farms were classified as residential.

The nearly 27,000 new units built in this area between 1940 and 1950 (26 percent of the occupied units in 1950) were of much the same quality as those built previously. About one-fifth were classed as dilapidated and less than 10 percent had all plumbing facilities; half of both the old and new units had fewer than 5 rooms. The over-all picture would indicate that the new units, whether large or small, made only insignificant improvements in the farm housing supply. Generally, it would seem that inferior old units were replaced by similarly inferior new ones. In view of the average income level for the subregion, this is to be expected.

By way of contrast, the new housing may be compared in more prosperous subregions of entirely different types. One of these, economic subregion 5, which includes the most highly urbanized section of the country (New York-Northeastern New Jersey metropolitan area), has a relatively large number of part-time and residential farms but relatively few low-production commercial farms. Here, the 1949 median farm family income of $2,900 undoubtedly resulted from nonfarm employment in the cities.

Although the subregion is a part of the Northeastern Dairy Region, poultry, mixed farming, and specialty crops predominate. The median value of products raised in 1949 for sale by commercial farm operators was approximately $8,000. While the new farm dwelling units in this subregion made up only 16 percent of the 1950 supply, they were of much higher average quality than those in the subregions discussed above: 86 percent had all plumbing facilities, and less than 4 percent were classed as dilapidated; over 80 percent were of 5 rooms or more. Compared with older farmhouses, the new units showed an improvement in everything but size. In this they followed a trend toward fewer rooms evident also in the nonfarm housing of the area.

In economic subregion 102 in western Texas, the quality of new housing is also in striking contrast to that of subregions where low-production farms predominate. In 1950 this subregion led all others in value of farm products: the median value was approximately $13,000. It is unlikely that the median farm family income of $3,700 is derived from any but farm sources, since the area offers little opportunity for nonfarm employment. However, there would be a greater disparity than usual between family median income and true income because nearly one-third of the dwelling units in the area are rent free and presumably are occupied by laborers on the large cotton and cattle ranches which predominate. Nearly 15 percent of the farmhouses in existence in 1950 were built between 1940 and 1950; 54 percent of the new units and 49 percent of the older units contained more than 4 rooms. But the new houses showed the greatest rate of improvement in the matter of plumbing facilities: 54 percent of the new units, as compared with 19 percent of the old, were equipped with all such facilities. Only 5 percent of the new units, as against 19 percent of the old, were classed as dilapidated.

It is clear from the foregoing examples that the quantity of new construction does not necessarily improve the over-all quality of housing. Where the new housing is of high quality, as in subregions 5 and 102, the quality appears to be the result of relatively high incomes from farm or nonfarm sources. But the economic and sociological factors are so closely interwoven that it is difficult to identify the influence of each. Certainly, if the patterns set by nearby nonfarm dwelling units were as important as income, new farm homes in the San Francisco and New York areas (subregions 115 and 5) should have shown somewhat similar characteristics, and if neighborhood traditions were more important than income, some similarities in new construction patterns might have been expected in subregions 31 and 102, both of which are relatively isolated from large metropolitan areas. On this rather speculative basis, it may be concluded that income is the critical factor in establishing the type of new dwelling units constructed in farm areas.

CHAPTER 3

A REGIONAL COMPARISON
OF FARM HOUSING CHARACTERISTICS

People engaged in the same type of farming make a living in similar ways.[1] The fact that they produce the same product dictates, to a considerable degree, the patterns of their everyday lives. For example, farmers engaged in dairying generally need a nearby urban area as a market for their fluid milk. Families on dairy farms then, together with those engaged in specialized farming like truck farming, are very likely to be influenced by urban living patterns to a greater degree than families engaged in the more "rural" types of farming, such as grazing or cotton and wheat production. The type of farming undertaken, then, has a strong bearing on the kind of housing occupied by farm families.

The income that a particular type of farming brings in also has a definite influence on the character of farm housing.[2] Levels of income are generally higher in the wheat, corn, dairying, grazing, and West Coast Miscellaneous areas than they are in the Cotton Belt, Tobacco Region, the East and Gulf Coast Miscellaneous, and the General and Self-Sufficing Farming Regions of the Nation. The classification of regions used here and elsewhere in this study was developed to take into account variations in climate, soil, or topography as well as differences in types of farming.[3] A list of the 12 type-of-farming regions with the percentage of farmhouses in each is given on the following page.

As these statistics show, in 1950 there were more farmhouses in the Cotton Belt than in any other region. This is an important point to remember when national statistics are reviewed, because the character of farm housing in this region is a strong influencing factor on the national picture. At the other extreme are the Northern and Southern Wheat Regions and the Upland Summer Grazing Region where the fewest farm-

---

[1] See Carl C. Taylor, *et al.*, *Rural Life in the United States*, Alfred A. Knopf, New York, 1949, especially Part IV.

[2] The distribution of farm family income for 1949, by type-of-farming region, is shown in table 35, p. 69.

[3] See Chapter 1, p. 5, for an explanation of the method of classification used in this study. For location of type-of-farming regions and the economic subregions of which they are composed, see map, figure 1, p. 6.

houses are found. When the broad geographic area covered by these three regions is compared with the number of houses in each, it is apparent how sparsely the area is settled.

Despite regional differences, however, there is to a considerable extent a close link connecting all housing characteristics with each other and with the characteristics of the occupying families. We usually expect a newly built house to be equipped with modern plumbing, although this is not always so in farm housing. The fewer the rooms in relation to the number of persons in a family, the more probable it is that the house may be in need of repairs. If family income is high, there is every reason to suppose that housing will be adequate both in structural condition and in facilities and equipment.

This type of relationship between farm housing and family characteristics provides useful guidelines when one analyzes, on a regional basis, the data collected by the 1950 Census of Housing.[4]

		Occupied dwelling units, 1950	
	Type-of-farming region	*Number*	*Percent*
	Total	5,659,570	100.0
I	Northeast Dairy Region	543,440	9.6
II	Great Lakes Dairy Region	447,355	7.9
III	East and Gulf Coast Miscellaneous Region	273,490	4.8
IV	General and Self-Sufficing Region	881,955	15.6
V	Tobacco Region	238,465	4.2
VI	Cotton Belt	1,426,550	25.2
VII	Corn Belt	954,360	16.9
VIII	Northern Wheat and Small Grains Region	125,685	2.2
IX	Southern Wheat and Small Grains Region	104,190	1.9
X	Year Long and Seasonal Grazing Region	306,110	5.4
XI	Upland Summer Grazing Region	115,380	2.0
XII	West Coast Miscellaneous	242,590	4.3

Number of rooms related to other housing characteristics and to family characteristics

The number of rooms in the average farmhouse varies from one region of the country to another. In general, farmhouses in the Northeast are larger than in other sections of the country. However, the picture changes somewhat when other characteristics are taken into consideration. The number of rooms in a house varies according to the year the house was built and the ages of the family members. The more people there are in

---

[4] For a summary of census findings, see *1950 Census of Housing*, Vol. III, *Farm Housing Characteristics*, pp. XXIV–XXXII. Detailed tables, showing the percentage relationships of housing characteristics for the 12 regions, appear in Appendix D (see appendix tables D–9 to D–16, pp. 144–171). These tables were prepared from a special tabulation of a 20-percent sample of schedules from the 1950 Census of Housing. They are, in effect, regional summarizations of data on the economic subregions tabulated in *Farm Housing Characteristics*. For convenience, the comparable United States tables from that volume are also reproduced in the appendix (see appendix tables D–1 to D–8, pp. 140–143). Because of the complex operation of showing all possible interrelationships, the cross-tabulations in the 1950 Census material are limited to selected characteristics only.

the family, the more rooms the dwelling unit is likely to have. The determining factor for other housing characteristics may be some third family characteristic, such as family income. The fact that small houses are frequently dilapidated or lack plumbing can, for example, be associated with the income level of families that live in small houses.

Condition and plumbing. Table D–10 in the appendix cross-classifies the number of rooms by condition and plumbing facilities for owner- or renter-occupied farmhouses and for those that are rent free. The significant data from these tables are drawn together in table 27 to show regional differences. Table 27 combines information on renter and rent-free dwelling units because there is relatively little difference in most categories. Such differences as there are generally involve the larger dwelling units in regions located in the North and West. Within each size[5] and tenure group of farmhouses, the largest proportions in good condition with all plumbing facilities are seen to be in the West Coast Miscellaneous Region (XII). Here, the percentages are strikingly larger than those for the United States as a whole. Comparisons with figures for the Nation show percentages of good quality[6] units in this West Coast Region ranging from nearly twice as large, for owner-occupied farmhouses of 7 rooms or more, to nearly eight times as large, for 3- or 4-room farmhouses in the renter and rent-free groups.

It would be natural to expect high family income to account for this large percentage of good houses. And it is true that the 1949 median income in the West Coast Region was higher than that in other regions. But it was not significantly higher than in the Corn Belt Region (VII), the Northern Wheat and Small Grains Region (VIII), and the Upland Summer Grazing Region (XI) (see appendix table D–16). Furthermore, there were more high-production farms in these regions as well as in the Southern Wheat and Small Grains Region (IX) and the Year-Long and Seasonal Grazing Region (X). Hence, family income is not the only explanation.

More significant than relative income may be the fact that most farms in the West Coast Region are close to metropolitan centers. The most remote inland parts are mountainous or desert areas ill adapted to farming of any kind. Farm families in this region are, consequently, likely to be in closer touch with city people than the families of region VIII where the median income was only slightly below that of region XII. The fact that farm families in region XII received relatively more of their 1949

---

[5] Size as measured by number of rooms only.

[6] The words "good quality" or "high quality" and their antonyms are used frequently instead of the more cumbersome census phrases "not dilapidated, with private flush toilet and bath and hot and cold running water," "no private flush toilet or bath, no hot running water, or dilapidated." This condensation is not intended to convey an appraisal different from that adopted by the census. If the terms "good quality" or "high quality" are used in this volume to mean something other than the descriptive phrases stated above, the reader will be so informed. Further, the terms "high" and "low" are used to describe the extremes rather than to divide all dwelling units into two groups. In between the high and low are units that are not dilapidated and have only some of the designated facilities.

incomes from nonfarm sources than did families in the high-income grain and cattle regions is another indication of their closer connections with urban areas.[7]

TABLE 27.—DWELLING UNITS IN GOOD CONDITION WITH ALL SPECIFIED PLUMBING FACILITIES AS PERCENT OF ALL DWELLING UNITS, FOR TENURE-SIZE GROUPS, BY TYPE-OF-FARMING REGIONS: 1950

[See glossary for definition of facilities]

	Owner				Renter and rent free			
Region	1 and 2 rooms	3 and 4 rooms	5 and 6 rooms	7 rooms or more	1 and 2 rooms	3 and 4 rooms	5 and 6 rooms	7 rooms or more
United States................	4	13	29	46	3	7	17	29
Northeast Dairy...................	9	26	44	53	10	30	38	38
Great Lakes Dairy.................	3	15	30	41	4	18	24	32
East and Gulf Coast Miscellaneous..	5	13	27	46	2	6	13	24
General and Self-Sufficing........	1	4	13	28	1	3	7	15
Tobacco...........................	2	4	13	31	1	1	3	10
Cotton Belt.......................	2	4	18	37	1	1	5	12
Corn Belt.........................	4	14	30	45	4	10	16	28
Northern Wheat and Small Grains....	2	12	25	34	3	13	21	28
Southern Wheat and Small Grains....	5	26	48	56	8	19	28	36
Year-Long and Seasonal Grazing.....	4	23	47	64	5	15	30	41
Upland Summer Grazing.............	4	32	61	75	5	28	48	58
West Coast Miscellaneous..........	17	61	81	85	14	54	73	77

Note: 100 percent equals the total number of units in each tenure-size group for the area, e.g., 9 percent of the 1- and 2-room owner-occupied dwelling units in the Northeast Dairy Region were in good condition with all specified plumbing facilities.

Source: Appendix table D-10.

In contrast to region XII, the proportion of farm homes in region IV (general and self-sufficing farming) and region V (tobacco) that are in the higher quality group is almost insignificant. Even among owner-occupied houses of 7 rooms or more the percentage of good houses is well below the national average.

In neither region can the poor quality of farm housing be attributed to distance from cities; many scattered small cities and metropolitan centers exist in both regions. Here, poor-quality housing appears to be largely an outcome of low income from small farms. Tobacco, for example, is a crop that is not produced in large quantities in proportion to the labor expended because its production cannot be readily mechanized. In addition, the tobacco-growing counties of Kentucky, North Carolina, Tennessee, and Virginia have a relatively large rural population resulting—prior to the last decade at least—in competition for jobs in nearby urban areas. Thus, supplementary nonfarm wages and salaries have tended to be relatively low.

In both regions, but particularly in region IV, where many of the farms lie in mountainous areas, the social stimulus for improving the farm dwelling is lacking. Hence, even families on high-production farms, of which there were some 230,000 in the two regions in 1950, may have felt

---

[7] Chapter 5, p. 88, treats more fully the influence of urban areas on the quality of farm housing.

little compulsion to modernize their homes while they compared well or favorably with the homes of neighboring families.

Regardless of tenure or region, however, the cross-classifications point to certain generalizations. They indicate, for instance, that as the number of rooms in a dwelling increases, the proportion of dwellings classed as "not dilapidated and with all plumbing facilities" also increases. This direct relationship between size of dwelling unit and condition and plumbing is understandable. A family occupying a 1- or 2-room farmhouse, or even one that contains 3 or 4 rooms, is unlikely to install modern plumbing before enlarging the inadequate house.

When farmhouses are looked at from the viewpoint of age, it is noticeable that fewer houses in the group of largest size (7 rooms or more) were built between 1920 and 1950, as compared with the group of houses containing 5 or 6 rooms. Clearly, the superior quality of the former group has little to do with recent construction. (See appendix table D–9.)

When related to tenure, the greatest variation in the regional proportions of units with all facilities and in good condition is shown in the 5-room-or-more group. The higher the family income in a region, however, the less variation appears in the quality of owner-occupied and renter-occupied dwellings in this group. The explanation for this relationship between income level, quality, and tenure may be in part one of relative magnitudes; when large numbers of units in both tenure groups are of good quality, differences by tenure become statistically less important than when both tenure groups have relatively small numbers of good-quality units. To the extent that the variations reflect more than differences in relative magnitudes, there may be a further explanation: that owner and renter families are more alike in their housing standards when their incomes are relatively high than where they are relatively low. Evidence to support such an assumption can be found in the regions where tenure differences are most pronounced—regions where sharecropping and similar tenure arrangements are extensively practiced. Arrangements of this nature are apt to imply a more marked class distinction between landlord and tenant than when there is a cash-rent relationship.[8] What the two groups may aspire to in the way of good housing may, therefore, differ fundamentally in both tradition and practice.

Year built. The 1950 data show how the proportion of good-quality dwellings is directly related to the number of rooms and how the income level of farms in a region indicates to a degree both housing quality and number of rooms. In contrast, the relationship of a farmhouse's age to the number of rooms it may contain shows regional variation that bears very little on income. It will be seen from tables 28 and 29, which are based on appendix table D–9, that the houses with the greatest number of rooms are likely to be the oldest. But in regions where family income is relatively

---

[8] For detailed discussion on this, see Taylor, Raper, *et al.*, *op. cit.*, Chapters XV and XVIII.

low, the proportion of old large dwellings is small. Proportions of new farmhouses, on the other hand, show an almost opposite relationship to number of rooms, even though they may have the same relationship to family income level in the regions. In every region, and in each tenure group, the proportion of small new dwellings is larger than the proportion of new dwellings with 5 rooms or more.

Almost without exception, the largest percentage of old farmhouses of all types (other than owner-occupied 1- or 2-room units and renter-occupied 5- or 6-room dwellings) occurs in the Northeast Dairy Region (I). This is a region, like regions II, VII, and VIII, in which farming operations have been carried on for many years, so that the farming areas are relatively stable. Severe winters made it necessary to build a permanent house soon after the farm was established. It is not unusual to find many such farmhouses that are well over 100 years old. Farmhouses in the northern grain States have not stood for as long a time, but apparently similarly sound construction methods were used when they were built to replace the original sod houses and log cabins. If the farms in these regions have been in continuous operation, the old houses located on them are usually still structurally sound. Rooms may have been added from time to time to meet the needs of larger families. It can be assumed that many of the old farmhouses with 7 rooms or more attained their size in this way.

The picture is different in farming areas of equal age but with more favorable climate. Here, there is usually a higher percentage of new dwellings. About two-thirds of the houses in the Cotton Belt (region VI) were built after 1920 as against only one-fourth of the houses in the Northeastern Dairy Region (I). Again, from a half to two-thirds of the farmhouses in the East and Gulf Coast Region (III) and in the General and Tobacco and Southern Wheat and Small Grains Regions (IV, V, and VI) were built after 1920, as compared with the rate of building in regions II, VII, and VIII, which was approximately one-quarter of the houses. The three far western regions, being more recently settled, are exceptions. Farming areas in these three regions (X, XI, and XII) have not been settled as long as they have in the East. In many parts new farms have been created by subdividing old, larger farms. In addition, new farming areas have recently been opened up as a result of irrigation. It is doubtful, however, if the development of new farms accounts for as many of the units built since 1919 as do two other factors. First, and probably most important, is the mild climate that prevails in much of regions X and XII. Second is the fact that in all three regions many dwellings are occupied by farm laborers and hence are likely to be built only to fill temporary needs.

It has already been indicated that regional differences in the percentages of old and new units appear to have little to do with family income. It is true that in region XII, where incomes are at relatively high levels and most of the farms are relatively close to urban areas, favorable incomes may have induced the farmers to build new houses. But this can be only an assumption since no cross-tabulations were made of family income by "year built." In other high-income regions there seems to be no such correlation between high income and new construction. Except in the case of region XII, the reverse, in fact, is indicated—the lower the income, the greater the percentage of new units.

TABLE **28.**—DWELLING UNITS BUILT IN 1945 OR LATER AS PERCENT OF ALL DWELLING UNITS, FOR TENURE-SIZE GROUPS, BY TYPE-OF-FARMING REGIONS: 1950

Region	Owner				Renter and rent free			
	1 and 2 rooms	3 and 4 rooms	5 and 6 rooms	7 rooms or more	1 and 2 rooms	3 and 4 rooms	5 and 6 rooms	7 rooms or more
United States................	32	17	12	4	17	9	5	1
Northeast Dairy....................	40	20	6	1	20	8	4	1
Great Lakes Dairy..................	31	18	7	2	18	10	3	1
East and Gulf Coast Miscellaneous..	39	21	16	8	14	11	8	2
General and Self-Sufficing........	27	15	12	6	22	10	6	1
Tobacco...........................	23	14	10	7	13	8	6	3
Cotton Belt.......................	31	19	18	10	11	8	7	3
Corn Belt.........................	27	13	6	2	19	9	2	1
Northern Wheat and Small Grains....	23	10	7	6	16	8	4	2
Southern Wheat and Small Grains....	37	13	10	7	19	10	6	2
Year-Long and Seasonal Grazing.....	31	16	14	12	17	10	6	5
Upland Summer Grazing.............	26	17	14	9	22	10	6	...
West Coast Miscellaneous..........	50	25	14	9	26	18	11	2

Note: 100 percent equals the total number of units in each tenure-size group for the area.

Source: Appendix table D-9.

TABLE **29.**—DWELLING UNITS BUILT IN 1919 AND EARLIER AS PERCENT OF ALL DWELLING UNITS, FOR TENURE-SIZE GROUPS, BY TYPE-OF-FARMING REGIONS: 1950

Region	Owner				Renter and rent free			
	1 and 2 rooms	3 and 4 rooms	5 and 6 rooms	7 rooms or more	1 and 2 rooms	3 and 4 rooms	5 and 6 rooms	7 rooms or more
United States................	25	38	49	74	31	42	62	85
Northeast Dairy....................	24	50	70	88	51	67	75	90
Great Lakes Dairy..................	25	40	61	78	29	56	73	86
East and Gulf Coast Miscellaneous..	13	24	32	57	22	36	47	73
General and Self-Sufficing........	30	39	48	63	21	44	60	80
Tobacco...........................	38	47	51	58	44	50	56	70
Cotton Belt.......................	21	30	31	48	32	36	46	65
Corn Belt.........................	40	61	73	82	45	66	82	88
Northern Wheat and Small Grains....	41	58	60	69	42	59	74	80
Southern Wheat and Small Grains....	37	49	51	65	26	47	64	79
Year-Long and Seasonal Grazing.....	20	32	34	45	18	32	44	59
Upland Summer Grazing.............	19	35	43	56	25	40	56	74
West Coast Miscellaneous..........	8	22	30	48	18	23	40	57

Note: 100 percent equals the total number of units in each tenure-size group for the area.

Source: Appendix table D-9.

Income does appear to be a factor in regional differences in terms of percentages of new units classified by tenure. In regions where income is relatively high the difference in the percentages of owner-occupied farmhouses and of renter-occupied farmhouses built after 1944 is greater than in regions where income is relatively low, e.g., regions III, V, and VI. In these regions only insignificant percentages of renter-occupied units with more than 5 rooms were built between 1945 and 1950. When consider-

ing houses built before 1920, the fact that the proportion of renter-occupied
is larger than that of owner-occupied units may reflect a landlord's tendency to replace his own dwelling more readily than he does the houses he
rents out.

Some other aspects of the regional differences in characteristics of
newly constructed dwellings are examined in the last half of this chapter,
where condition and plumbing facilities are cross classified with other
housing characteristics.

Type of cooking and heating fuel.   The fuel used by farm families
can give a partial indication of their level of living.   While a farmhouse
in which coal or wood is used for cooking may be quite adequate structurally, these fuels do entail more work for the family.   They are not as clean
nor as convenient as the cooking fuels commonly used in urban houses.
However, gas or electricity may not be available in all parts of all regions;
and their lack, therefore, is not necessarily an indication of low income.

Heating fuels are in much the same category, but with this distinction:
whether or not a farmhouse is equipped with central heating does not depend on the availability of oil, gas, or electricity.   Coal or wood can give
efficient service, and central heating equipment has been available for many
years.   If a farmhouse does not have central heating, the reasons may be
economic, sociological, or a combination of both influences.   Climate, too,
is an important factor.   The wood stove in the South is a different matter
from a similar type of heating in the North.

Wood is the fuel most commonly used for cooking in the Northeast
Dairy, Great Lakes Dairy, East and Gulf Coast Miscellaneous, General and
Self-Sufficing, Tobacco, and Cotton Belt Regions (I, II, III, IV, V, VI, see ap-
pendix table D–11).   A shortage of woodland appears to govern the habits
of farming families living in the Corn Belt and the Northern Wheat,
Southern Wheat, and Year-Long and Seasonal Grazing Regions (VII, VIII,
IX, and X).   Here bottled gas is the fuel most commonly used, with coal
running a close second in region VIII.   Coal, wood, and electricity each
account for almost one-third of the fuel used in the Upland Grazing Region,
(XI) while electricity is most popular in the West Coast Miscellaneous
Region (XII).

Regional differences in the type of cooking fuel used in varying sizes of
dwellings are equally insignificant.   In most instances, greater proportions
of large units than of small use such fuels as electricity.   But, with that
exception, no definite relationship can be traced in any of the regions between number of rooms in a dwelling unit and the type of cooking fuel used.

Considering the widespread use of electricity in farmhouses throughout
the country it is surprising that so few farm families use this fuel for cooking.
In 1950, 80 percent of the farmhouses in the Nation were equipped with
electric lighting.   Only in the Cotton Belt (VI) was the percentage less than
70, and in region XII on the West Coast it was as high as 95.   (See
appendix table D–14.)   Yet, electricity was used for cooking in only 15

percent of the Nation's farmhouses. Region XII is the only region which shows a higher proportion of electricity used for cooking than of any other fuel. Relative cost with the cost of other cooking fuels may undoubtedly be a major factor.

On the other hand, the Year-Long and Seasonal Grazing Region (X), where, in 1950, 80 percent of the farmhouses had electric lights, shows a higher use of bottled gas than of electricity for cooking. Because this region has a comparatively high income level, it is evident that in many cases availability and personal preference may play as large a part as income in the choice of cooking fuel.

The heating fuel predominating in farmhouses throughout the country is either coal or wood. Liquid fuel is the major fuel in the Southern Wheat and Small Grains Region (IX). Its use in nonfarm units has increased appreciably in recent years, and in five of the regions it runs second in importance to wood or coal.

In the cross-tabulations (appendix table D–11), the only heating fuels listed separately are coal, wood, and liquid fuel, since nationally a small proportion of all households use other types of fuel. However, in regions VI, IX, X, and XII large proportions of the farm dwellings appear in the group "other fuel, or not reported." Data from other sources[9] indicate that many of these houses are heated by bottled gas.

If the use of liquid fuel or gas in a central-heating system may be taken as evidence of modern equipment and facilities, it is possible to measure the relative housing levels of the regions in terms of tenure and number of rooms. This does not hold true, however, for regions substantial parts of which do not require central heating for comfortable living. In table 30, regions III–VI, which are of this type, are therefore shown separately, and the use of liquid fuels or gas in all types of heating equipment is provided as a substitute standard. Such a standard seems justified by the climatic differences within the regions; moreover, even in the deep South it is an unusual winter when some heat is not a necessity, or at least a comfort.

In the low-temperature regions the 1950 data show regions IX and XII to have the largest proportions of farmhouses with central heating by liquid fuel or gas, for most categories of tenure and by number of rooms. The fact that these two regions extend far south, and that region II, much of which is along the Canadian border, shows relatively low proportions of houses that are centrally heated with modern fuels, indicates that climate is not always the controlling factor. Income plus proximity to urban areas may well be the most significant factors in the West Coast Region. Income may also be an important factor in region IX (though the income level in this region, which has suffered from dust storms and low wheat prices, has not always been so high as in 1950).

---

[9] *1950 Census of Housing*, Vol. I, *General Characteristics*.

TABLE **30.**—DWELLING UNITS USING LIQUID FUEL OR GAS AS PERCENT OF ALL DWELLING
UNITS, FOR TENURE-SIZE GROUPS, BY TYPE-OF-FARMING REGIONS: 1950

[Percentages include a very small number of units which were not reported or which were heated by other fuels]

	Owner				Renter and rent free			
Region	1 and 2 rooms	3 and 4 rooms	5 and 6 rooms	7 rooms or more	1 and 2 rooms	3 and 4 rooms	5 and 6 rooms	7 rooms or more
ALL TYPES OF HEATING EQUIPMENT								
East and Gulf Coast Miscellaneous..	30	32	40	41	26	26	27	32
General and Self-Sufficing.........	7	8	13	17	7	8	12	16
Tobacco...........................	9	8	15	19	11	8	7	8
Cotton Belt.......................	15	19	30	35	7	9	16	23
CENTRAL HEATING								
Northeast Dairy...................	2	8	12	14	5	9	10	8
Great Lakes Dairy.................	2	4	7	8	3	7	6	6
Corn Belt.........................	2	5	8	11	3	3	4	6
Northern Wheat and Small Grains....	1	5	10	12	1	4	5	9
Southern Wheat and Small Grains....	(1)	9	18	27	2	6	12	15
Year-Long and Seasonal Grazing.....	1	3	7	14	1	1	4	7
Upland Summer Grazing.............	1	4	8	13	(1)	2	4	6
West Coast Miscellaneous..........	2	10	17	21	2	8	11	16

[1] Less than 0.5 percent.

Source: Appendix table D-11.

   In all the low-temperature regions, the 1950 data show that larger proportions of owner-occupied units with 5 rooms or more than of renter-
occupied and rent-free units of the same size use liquid fuel or gas for
central heating.

   Of the temperate regions, region III is shown as having the largest proportions of houses using liquid fuel or gas for any form of heating. This
region extends as far north as New Jersey and includes many urban areas,
so it is not surprising that fuels which provide more comfort with less work
are commonly used.   The very low proportions of houses in this heating
group shown for region IV is a reflection of both low income and the ready
availability of coal and firewood.   The region includes hardwood forest
areas in the Appalachians and coal-mining areas in West Virginia and
southern Illinois.

   Persons per room.   The average number of persons per room in a
house is a rough indication of a level of living. The mental and emotional
welfare of each member of a family is affected by the degree of crowding
in the family living quarters.   In cases of extreme crowding even physical
health may be affected.

   There can be no fixed standard for the desirable number of persons per
room.   Too many other factors bear upon it—size of room, for instance;
family composition and room arrangement; housing facilities and equipment.   Most analysts agree, however, that as a general rule an average of
one person to a room is a reasonable working standard.   Appendix table
D–12, therefore, presents a dichotomy of 1.00 or less and 1.01 or more
persons per room.   By comparing the percentages of farmhouses in each
of these groups, the differences by region, tenure, and number of rooms
can be evaluated.

As might be expected, farmhouses with more rooms show greater percentages with 1.00 or less persons to a room. This is so in every region and for all three tenure groups. All regions have almost identical patterns in that there is a regular progression in the 1.00-or-less-persons-per-room column from the 1- and 2-room units to the 7-room or larger units. Furthermore, this pattern is shown for all types of tenure.

The relationship of tenure to crowding differs from region to region, but the greatest variation appears between eastern and western rather than between northern and southern regions. The reasons are fairly clear why small rent-free units are more likely to be overcrowded. It is less easy to account for a reverse situation. In all but one (region III) of the eastern regions relatively more of the renter-occupied than of the rent-free units, especially those of 1 or 2 rooms, are shown to average 1.01 or more persons to a room. Possibly many of the units classified as farm dwelling units in 1950 were actually extra houses occupied by small families who did not actively participate in farm operations. If this is so, many of these 1- to 4-room units might be expected to show up in the next section as being occupied by families whose heads are in the older age group.[10]

Age of head of household. Appendix table D–13 lists for each region the number of farmhouses by age of the head of household. They also show the distribution of farmhouses in each group by tenure and number of rooms. Appendix table D–5 gives the same information for the United States.

Nearly half of the heads of farm households in the United States were less than 45 years old in 1950. Differences by type-of-farming regions are not very pronounced. The slightly higher proportions of household heads in the over-45 age group shown in the General Farming Region (IV) and the Northeast Dairy Region (I) may well be due to a migration of young people in these regions to urban areas. The relatively low farm income in region IV generally, and in the New England section of region I, has resulted in such a trend. It will be recalled that, in 1950, 82 percent of the farms in region IV were classed as either noncommercial or as producing less than $2,500 worth of farm products for sale in 1949.[11]

Tenure statistics for 1950 emphasize one self-evident fact: regardless of region, the older the head of a farm household the more likely it is that he owns his house. The proportions of owners in specific age groups vary from region to region, but these variations tend to reflect differences in tenure rather than in regional characteristics. In the United States as a whole and in all regions but two, one-half to two-thirds of the heads in the under-45 age group are shown to be owners. In the Tobacco and Cotton Regions (V and VI), where a substantial proportion of the farm households are share tenants, less than 40 percent of the heads in the under-45 age group are owners. In region VI this difference is noticeable for all age

---

[10] See p. 61.
[11] See Chapter 1, table 3, p. 10.

groups, but the difference between region V and the rest of the country is less marked for age groups over 45.

The East and Gulf Coast Region (III) and the Year-Long and Seasonal Grazing Region (X) show somewhat similar patterns; but while a high proportion of share tenants may be expected in region III, much of which lies in the southern States, the cattle-grazing type of farming dominant in region X does not to any great extent involve share tenancy. The high proportions of rent-free farmhouses occupied by young households in region X must derive from other kinds of farms (none of the type-of-farming regions are, of course, restricted wholly to one type of farming) on which sharecropping is practiced. In this region, too, houses on the farms may have been occupied either by farm laborers' families or by relatives of the operators. In 1950 this region reported at least 31,000 more farm dwellings than farms. Thus, it is quite conceivable that more than 30,000 of the 65,000 rent-free units were extra houses on farms. There is no way of determining in actual percentages the distribution of these extra houses by age of household head.

TABLE 31.—PERCENT DISTRIBUTION OF DWELLING UNITS BY AGE OF HEAD OF HOUSEHOLD, BY TYPE-OF-FARMING REGIONS: 1950

Region	Total	Age of head of household		
		Under 45 years	45 to 64 years	65 years and over
United States......................	100	44	40	16
Northeast Dairy.........................	100	39	42	19
Great Lakes Dairy.......................	100	41	43	16
East and Gulf Coast Miscellaneous........	100	44	40	16
General and Self-Sufficing..............	100	40	41	19
Tobacco.................................	100	47	38	15
Cotton Belt.............................	100	46	39	15
Corn Belt...............................	100	44	41	15
Northern Wheat and Small Grains.........	100	48	40	12
Southern Wheat and Small Grains.........	100	47	40	13
Year-Long and Seasonal Grazing..........	100	46	40	14
Upland Summer Grazing...................	100	46	41	13
West Coast Miscellaneous................	100	41	43	16

Source: Derived from appendix table D-13.

The age of the head of a household is correlated to some extent with the size of the household. Households whose heads are from 45 to 64 years of age have usually reached their maximum size, and hence in theory might be expected to need larger homes. In practice, however, the housing supply is not sufficiently flexible, particularly on farms, to make possible an easy adjustment between the number of rooms and the number of persons in the household. In general, the statistics for owner-occupied houses, both nationally and regionally, show the over-65 owner as being more likely than the younger owner to have a large house.

As might be expected, the renter and rent-free groups in the United States and most of the regions show relatively more of the household heads to be in the under-45 group, regardless of the size of their houses. But within this broad pattern there is a great deal of variation from region to region.

It was pointed out in the previous section[12] that in 1950 a relatively large number of 1- to 4-room rent-free units in some regions may have been occupied by small households whose heads were 65 years or over, and that this may have resulted in a relatively small average number of persons per room. This certainly was the case in the Great Lakes Dairy Region (II), where the rent-free units are not sharecropper houses. Almost 2,000 of the 1- to 4-room, rent-free units, or a little over 20 percent of the total houses in this class, were occupied by households with heads of 65 years and over. Nationally, the 1950 data show that only 11 percent of the rent-free units were occupied by households of this category. Lacking cross-tabulations for age of head by number of persons, no positive conclusions can be drawn, but it seems logical to suppose that these older, and probably smaller, households in region II represent an important reason why the average number of persons per room in rent-free 1- to 4-room dwellings is not greater.

Condition and plumbing facilities related to other housing characteristics and to family characteristics

The relation of the size of a farmhouse to its condition and plumbing has already been examined. But condition and plumbing in itself provides an excellent yardstick against which to measure other housing characteristics, such as year built, electric lighting, heating equipment, type of household, and income.

Year built. In Chapter 2 [13] it has been pointed out that the fact that farm-dwelling construction may be recent does not necessarily imply that it is of good quality. A regional cross-tabulation by age of house and by condition and plumbing provides a useful means of finding out where the bulk of the poor construction occurred prior to 1950 and whether, indirectly, the type of farming in that area was a contributory cause. In this instance, the type of farm per se could not be considered a factor in quality of construction, but differences in income yielded by various types of farms might obviously be expected to exert an influence.

Appendix table D–14 presents regional percentages; and appendix table D–6, the national numbers of farmhouses built between 1940 and 1950 that fall into the two categories "Condition" and "Plumbing facilities." The 853,500 occupied houses built since 1939 (appendix table D–6) represent 15 percent of the total number of occupied farmhouses. Of all the units that lack some or all plumbing facilities or are dilapidated, 14 percent are seen to be new. The new units thus have contributed relatively little to the over-all improvement of farm housing. Much the same situa-

---

[12] See p. 59.
[13] See pp. 41–44.

tion shows up in nonfarm housing (in 1950 new units were 20 percent of the total, and 16 percent of poor-quality units were new),[14] but since only 12 percent of all nonfarm units were classified in 1950 as dilapidated or as lacking plumbing facilities, against 57 percent of the farm dwellings if judged by the same standards, clearly farm housing stands in greater need of improvement.

The 1950 data show considerable variation from region to region in the ratio of new units to total farm dwellings. Percentages range from 6 percent in the Corn Belt (VII) to 25 percent in the West Coast Region (XII). Table 32 compares the plumbing facilities and quality of construction in old and new houses for each of the 12 regions.

TABLE 32.—PERCENT OF ALL DWELLING UNITS BUILT IN 1939 OR EARLIER AND 1940 OR LATER BY CONDITION AND PLUMBING FACILITIES, BY TYPE-OF-FARMING REGIONS: 1950

[Units with "all facilities" have private toilet, private bath, and hot and cold running water inside the structure; units with "some facilities" lack one or more of these facilities]

| Region | Not dilapidated | | | | No facilities or dilapidated | |
| | All facilities | | Some facilities | | | |
	Built 1940 or later[1]	Built 1939 or earlier[2]	Built 1940 or later[1]	Built 1939 or earlier[2]	Built 1940 or later[1]	Built 1939 or earlier[2]
United States...............	28	23	16	18	54	57
Northeast Dairy................	53	45	19	25	28	30
Great Lakes Dairy.................	39	31	20	25	41	44
East and Gulf Coast Miscellaneous..	24	20	22	18	54	62
General and Self-Sufficing.........	15	11	13	14	72	75
Tobacco..........................	14	9	15	13	71	78
Cotton Belt.......................	13	8	15	12	72	80
Corn Belt.........................	47	28	18	21	35	51
Northern Wheat and Small Grains....	39	21	14	17	47	62
Southern Wheat and Small Grains....	63	34	14	23	23	43
Year-Long and Seasonal Grazing.....	44	27	21	25	35	48
Upland Summer Grazing.............	49	43	17	21	34	36
West Coast Miscellaneous...........	68	70	16	14	16	16

[1] 100 percent equals total units built 1939 or earlier.
[2] 100 percent equals total units built 1940 or later.

Source: Derived from appendix table D-14.

Generally, farm housing in the regions which had the largest percentages of old dwelling units of good quality showed the smallest amount of improvement. While the West Coast Region leads all regions in the proportions of both old and new housing that are of good quality, the Southern Wheat and Small Grains Region (IX) comes close in proportions of new good-quality housing and, in addition, shows the greatest improvement in this category.

When housing quality, on the basis of age, is examined from the negative viewpoint, the picture looks more bleak. Nationally, in 1950, more than half of even the new units either had none of the specified plumbing facilities or were dilapidated. The only region in which the proportion of new farm dwelling units in this category was near that of new nonfarm

---
[14] *1950 Census of Housing*, Vol. II, *Nonfarm Housing Characteristics*, Chapter I, table A–4.

dwelling units in the United States was region XII. Twelve percent [15] of the new nonfarm units in the Nation and 16 percent of the new farm units in region XII had no facilities or were dilapidated—a low farmhouse percentage when compared with other regions.

The low level of income, which is the prime cause of the poor housing situation in regions IV, V, and VI (over 70 percent of the new dwelling units in these three regions were dilapidated or without plumbing in 1950) has already been discussed.[16] It may well be that the next decade or two may see changes in the quality of housing in these areas. Mechanization has already become more common for both cotton and tobacco farming. The introduction of new sources of electric power in much of region IV has provided greater opportunity for nonfarm employment, which gradually should drain off some of the excess farm population. Migration to more distant employment centers during the 1940 decade has already reduced the farm population in these regions.

These changes have been going on for the past 15 years or more and they have been reflected in farm housing more than the statistics show at first glance. The very fact that the rate of building in these regions was higher in 1950 than in others may reflect increases in income, even though large numbers of the new dwellings lack running water. This lack, rather than poor original construction, is the major reason why so many of the new units fall into the lowest category of quality. In region VI, for example, only 14 percent of the new units are in this category because they are classed as dilapidated, whereas nearly 35 percent of the old units are so classified. Similar comparisons in regions IV and V show percentages of 11 and 24, and 7 and 22, respectively. Thus, to the extent that better houses were being put up, the improvement in these regions is somewhat greater than table 32 indicates. If improvements in new dwellings continue, a greater prevalence of plumbing facilities may come next.

New dwelling units in good condition with all plumbing facilities were generally owner occupied. Nationally, in 1950, almost five times as many owners as renters (including rent-free households) occupied good-quality units built since 1939. The difference in the numbers of owners and renters who occupied old units was not as great. There were, however, some significant differences between regions (table 33).

It may be seen from table 33 that, in each region, owners in 1950 occupied more than a proportionate share of new good-quality farm dwellings, but that this was not necessarily the case for older houses of similar quality. In the low-income regions IV, V, and VI, the latter were to a great extent owner occupied, but in the higher income regions the percentages more nearly paralleled the over-all distribution by tenure.[17]

---

[15] *Ibid.*, table A–6.

[16] See p. 37.

[17] Owner-occupied units as percentages of total units in the United States and the 12 regions, for 1950, are as follows: U. S.–65, I–78, II–81, III–65, IV–77, V–55, VI–51, VII–62, VIII–74, IX–61, X–60, XI–75, and XII–72.

TABLE **33.**—PERCENT OF OWNER-OCCUPIED DWELLING UNITS BUILT IN 1939 OR EARLIER AND 1940 OR LATER BY CONDITION AND PLUMBING FACILITIES, BY TYPE-OF-FARMING REGIONS: 1950

[For explanation of plumbing facilities, see headnote, table 32]

Region	Not dilapidated, with all plumbing facilities		With no plumbing facilities or dilapidated	
	Built 1940 or later	Built 1939 or earlier	Built 1940 or later	Built 1939 or earlier
United States......................	84	80	68	36
Northeast Dairy.........................	86	83	76	72
Great Lakes Dairy.......................	90	83	82	78
East and Gulf Coast Miscellaneous......	92	68	68	67
General and Self-Sufficing.............	88	88	81	74
Tobacco................................	84	88	57	47
Cotton Belt............................	87	88	63	39
Corn Belt..............................	80	58	73	56
Northern Wheat and Small Grains........	85	77	80	70
Southern Wheat and Small Grains........	75	72	67	51
Year-Long and Seasonal Grazing.........	80	74	59	49
Upland Summer Grazing..................	86	70	78	70
West Coast Miscellaneous...............	78	78	61	53

Note: 100 percent in the total of each year-built group.

Source: Special tabulation from the 1950 Census of Housing.

At the other end of the quality scale, the percentages of owner-occupied old and new units also nearly paralleled the over-all distribution, although there are variations from this pattern in the lower income regions. The tenure figures suggest that there may have been greater inequality in distribution of income among owner and renter families in the low-income than in the high-income regions. Other figures dealing with the distribution of farm families by income give some corroboration.[18]

How large a proportion of the new farm units classified in 1950 as dilapidated or as having no plumbing facilities were small in size, i.e., of less than 5 rooms? Table 34 gives evidence that the new houses of low quality on the average had fewer rooms than those built prior to 1940. To a lesser degree, this is true also of high-quality units.

Differences between regions shown by the three-way cross-tabulation (year built, condition and plumbing facilities, and number of rooms) are similar to those shown for all farm housing without regard for age.[19] Differences in the percentages of new and old units with 5 rooms or more are generally greater, but perhaps this regional comparison is most striking in what it reveals for the southern regions. These regions, IV, V, and VI, for example, are seen to be in the group of regions containing the highest proportion of both high-quality and low-quality new dwelling units with 5 or more rooms.

---

[18] See table 35, p. 69.
[19] See table 27, p. 52.

TABLE 34.—PERCENT OF DWELLING UNITS WITH 5 ROOMS OR MORE BUILT IN 1939 OR EARLIER AND 1940 OR LATER BY CONDITION AND PLUMBING FACILITIES, BY TYPE-OF-FARMING REGIONS: 1950

[High-quality dwelling units—not dilapidated with private flush toilet and bath and hot and cold running water; low-quality dwelling units—lacking all the specified plumbing facilities or dilapidated]

Region	High-quality dwelling units		Low-quality dwelling units	
	Built 1940 or later[1]	Built 1939 or earlier[2]	Built 1940 or later[3]	Built 1939 or earlier[4]
United States......................	71	80	32	54
Northeast Dairy......................	72	94	31	80
Great Lakes Dairy....................	75	95	27	75
East and Gulf Coast Miscellaneous......	70	88	38	50
General and Self-Sufficing.............	77	92	39	52
Tobacco...............................	82	94	39	54
Cotton Belt..........................	81	89	36	35
Corn Belt............................	77	87	30	80
Northern Wheat and Small Grains........	78	90	42	67
Southern Wheat and Small Grains........	71	87	29	59
Year-Long and Seasonal Grazing.........	64	76	16	31
Upland Summer Grazing..................	60	75	16	29
West Coast Miscellaneous...............	53	50	12	37

[1] 100 percent equals total high-quality units built 1940 or later.
[2] 100 percent equals total high-quality units built 1939 or earlier.
[3] 100 percent equals total low-quality units built 1940 or later.
[4] 100 percent equals total low-quality units built 1939 or earlier.

Source: Special tabulation from the 1950 Census of Housing.

Electric lights. There is a high correlation between electric lights and housing quality. Nearly all (99 percent) of the United States farmhouses which in 1950 were classified as "having all plumbing facilities" and "not dilapidated" were equipped with electric lights. Three-fourths of the houses in good condition but with no running water or other plumbing facilities also had electric lights, as had slightly more than half of the dilapidated dwellings.

Regional percentages of farmhouses with electric lights vary somewhat from United States averages, the variations being more pronounced where dwellings were of low quality in 1950 (see appendix table D–14). In the West Coast Region (XII), for example, 88 percent of the dilapidated units are seen to be equipped with electric lights, compared with only 45 percent in the East and Gulf Coast Region (III). In all regions, units not dilapidated but lacking running water were more frequently equipped with electric lights than were dilapidated units.

The fact that in 1950 electric lights were present in about 75 percent of the farmhouses which were in good condition but without running water points to gradual improvement in the general quality of farm housing. Electricity for lighting the farmhouse can lead to electricity for water pumps, and hence to running water and adequate plumbing facilities. But these things come slowly, particularly where family incomes can support no better than dilapidated shelter.

Heating equipment. As the quality of farm housing improves, the proportion of dwellings with central heating increases. Nevertheless, the 1950 data show less than half of all farmhouses in the top-quality classification to have central heating. In some ways, however, the type of heating a farmhouse uses cannot provide an accurate yardstick for measuring its level of living. Whether central heating is basic to convenience and comfort depends upon climate and upon the heating practices general in an area. In regions where the climate is moderate, other home improvements may precede a central heating system. Even in severe climates the availability of cheap fuel, better adapted to noncentral heating methods, may deter some families from changing to a central heating system.

So climate is a factor, but not the only factor, in the extent to which central heating is used. Two of the northernmost regions, the Northeast Dairy Region (I) and the Great Lakes Dairy Region (II), are shown (appendix table D–14) to have the highest proportions of farm dwellings so heated—45 percent and 38 percent, respectively. However, in the Northern Wheat and Small Grains Region (VIII), which is located in one of the coldest parts of the country, only 32 percent of the farmhouses are centrally heated. And in the Upland Summer Grazing Region (XI), a large part of which lies in the northwestern mountainous area, the percentage is as low as 16. Against this, there is the Southern Wheat and Small Grains Region (IX), far to the south, where 20 percent of the farmhouses are centrally heated. There may, of course, be a difference in cost between the type of heating unit that is suitable for a southern area and one necessary for northern climates. The cost of installation also may be greater in the northern areas because of the type of construction in old houses. The element of cost, however, like that of climate, cannot provide all the explanations for a situation showing so many variations.

Cultural attitudes may have an important effect on a farm family's decision to install central heating. There seems to be some evidence to this in the fact that in 1950 central heating was used in more than half of the best-quality farmhouses in only four regions. In these regions, and particularly in the Northeast Dairy Region, central heat has long been traditional. Long before oil-burning, forced-air furnaces were available, the most prosperous farmers had pipeless or piped warm-air heating systems; some of them, it has been observed, had even installed steam heat, commonly using wood for fuel unless coal was readily available. Appendix table D–11 shows that coal and wood for central heating are still used extensively in these regions.

In view of the over-all low family income level in region IV, it is not surprising to find only 8 percent of the farmhouses there with central heating. The scattering of high-production farms, some of them with characteristics similar to those of farms in the two dairy regions, is likely to account for the greater part of this percentage. Here, tradition again influences the situation, since much of the eastern portion of the General

Farming Region was originally settled by families from New England, New York, and Pennsylvania.

It will be noted that in appendix table D–14 the sum of the percentages of units with central heat and with noncentral heat with flue does not equal 100. The balance of the units in 1950 either had heating equipment with no flue, such as electric heaters, old-fashioned oil heaters, and so forth, or were not heated. Obviously the proportions in these residual groups were small, particularly in the northern regions. In the East and Gulf Coast Miscellaneous Region (III), which includes most of Florida and practically all the Gulf Coast area, the residual groups included over one-quarter of the units, which were nearly equally divided between the high- and low-quality categories. Some of the high-quality units may have been heated by modern electric wall panels or electrically heated radiators.

Type of household. The principal reason for a cross-classification of type of household by condition and plumbing is to determine what type of household it is that usually occupies the largest proportion of dwellings that are in good condition and with all plumbing facilities, and whether there are differences in this respect from region to region. For example, can one-person households or families with only one parent at home afford to live in dwellings of the best quality?

The term "household," as it is used here, means the family and other related and unrelated persons living in one dwelling unit. Households are classified in appendix table D–15 as follows: (1) families consisting of a married couple and family members related by blood or marriage (over 80 percent of the households in the sample used for this analysis); (2) families with a household head, but no spouse, and one or more persons related to the head; (3) one-person households; (4) households in which there are persons not related by blood or marriage to the head—such persons as, for example, lodgers, foster children, wards, or resident employees.

The largest proportion of farmhouses classified in 1950 as "not dilapidated" were occupied by classifications (1) and (4). But within this "not dilapidated" category households in classification (4) occupied the largest percentages of farmhouses equipped with all plumbing facilities. The largest proportion of houses which either were dilapidated or had no plumbing facilities were occupied by one-person households.

Evidently, the presence of nonrelatives in a household (4) accounts for additional income which helped to install plumbing facilities. Also, it is usually an indication of a larger-than-average household, and it has been seen that the larger the farmhouse the more likely it is to have all plumbing facilities. If the nonrelatives were not lodgers but farm employees, their presence may indicate that the farm was productive enough to warrant employment of extra labor and prosperous enough, therefore, to provide for modern plumbing. In some instances, of course, the installation of plumbing facilities may have been for the purpose of attracting lodgers.

The types of households bear roughly the same relationship to each other in all the regions. The group of dwellings occupied by one-person households nearly always includes the smallest percentage of high-quality units, and the group occupied by households with nonrelatives generally includes the highest proportions.

Income. Detailed income distributions by type-of-farming regions are given in table 35. For purposes of analyzing housing standards by regions and by income, these are grouped in appendix table D–16 into four broader income classes.

The data in this chapter have led to the expectation that the relationship between average income level in a type-of-farming region and housing condition and plumbing is direct and can readily be predicted. The appendix tables clearly demonstrate that this is correct. In every region there is seen to be a direct relationship between high income and high-quality housing. It is equally clear that low income and low-quality housing are also directly related.

Appendix table D–16 also strengthens the impression that characteristics of housing—in this case, condition and plumbing facilities—are influenced by regional custom, practices, and attitudes. While it would be inaccurate to assume that the same customs and attitudes hold throughout an area the size of a region, it would seem that, where the type of farming is the same and families have been settled long, similarities in specific levels of housing quality should exist. This can be tested by comparing a specific income class in all regions. If local custom and tradition were of no importance and income were the only influencing factor, farmhouses occupied by families in that income class would be distributed in approximately every region in identical percentages in each category of condition and plumbing facilities. Since even differences in enumeration and other factors could change the distributions slightly, some minimum differences might be expected, possibly no more than 5 percentage points.

Such a comparison of the regions reveals that when units are divided into those dilapidated and those not dilapidated, the maximum variation in the percentages of units in the $4,000 to $5,999 income group, for example, is only 7 percent (between the Cotton Belt and the Corn Belt). Thus, so far as condition is concerned, it seems reasonable to assume that income is by far the most important factor in determining the proportions of houses in each category. But it is apparently less important in relation to plumbing facilities. The percentages of farmhouses not dilapidated and with all facilities in this same income class range from 33 percent in the Cotton Belt (VI) to 79 percent in the West Coast Region (XII). This large variation within one income class undoubtedly reflects the difference in attitudes between the rural South and the Pacific Coast, where farms tend to be clustered close to large cities. But even though income is held constant in this example, it may exert an indirect influence on attitude. The large numbers of high-income farm families dwelling in the West Coast

Region have set high standards of housing to which the lower income families of the region may have aspired. If in the process better housing on these levels was achieved, the whole level of housing quality has been raised.

The above comparison can be applied with similar results to other levels of housing quality as measured by plumbing facilities, or to other classes of income. It may be concluded that the matter of income is of less direct concern in determining whether farmhouses have plumbing facilities than in determining the condition of housing in an area. Apparently dilapidated housing is never acceptable in any income group, but housing without plumbing facilities may be widely accepted.

TABLE 35.—PERCENT DISTRIBUTION OF FAMILIES BY INCOME IN 1949, BY TYPE-OF-FARMING REGIONS: 1950

Region	Total	Under $1,000	$1,000 to $1,999	$2,000 to $2,999	$3,000 to $3,999	$4,000 to $4,999	$5,000 to $5,999	$6,000 to $6,999	$7,000 to $9,999	$10,000 and over	Income not reported
United States.........	100.0	32.9	22.5	16.2	9.9	5.2	3.1	1.7	2.2	1.6	4.7
Northeast Dairy...........	100.0	21.0	19.6	19.6	13.3	7.2	4.3	2.5	3.2	2.6	6.7
Great Lakes Dairy.........	100.0	23.1	22.0	19.5	13.3	7.1	4.1	2.3	2.6	1.2	4.8
East and Gulf Coast Miscellaneous................	100.0	36.4	25.2	13.9	7.8	4.0	2.4	1.2	1.5	1.6	6.0
General and Self-Sufficing................	100.0	40.2	24.5	15.2	7.6	3.4	1.7	0.9	0.9	0.6	4.9
Tobacco...................	100.0	34.4	27.3	16.3	8.0	3.7	1.9	1.0	1.0	0.7	5.7
Cotton Belt...............	100.0	50.7	23.5	10.9	5.0	2.3	1.1	0.6	0.7	0.5	4.7
Corn Belt.................	100.0	17.7	21.1	20.3	14.1	8.1	5.0	2.9	3.6	2.0	5.2
Northern Wheat and Small Grains...................	100.0	19.3	18.8	17.6	12.6	7.9	5.2	3.3	5.2	5.0	5.0
Southern Wheat and Small Grains...................	100.0	19.8	20.2	17.6	11.8	7.6	5.2	3.2	4.8	5.1	4.7
Year-Long and Seasonal Grazing.................	100.0	22.3	23.0	17.2	11.5	6.3	4.2	2.4	3.6	4.0	5.6
Upland Summer Grazing.....	100.0	23.4	19.6	19.1	13.2	6.9	4.0	2.1	2.8	2.2	6.6
West Coast Miscellaneous..	100.0	18.5	17.1	18.9	15.5	8.7	5.1	2.9	3.7	3.6	6.1

Source: Special tabulation from the 1950 Census of Housing.

CHAPTER 4

VARIATIONS OF FARM HOUSING
WITHIN REGIONS

The 10-year span between censuses provides a useful gauge with which to measure trends in farm housing. Despite the decline since 1940 in the total number of houses occupied by farmers, 1950 data show a distinct improvement in the condition and quality of the houses that were occupied by farmers. At a national level, this trend is analyzed in Chapter 2; while in Chapter 3 the way in which housing characteristics and family characteristics (as shown by the 1950 data) are interrelated is examined region by region.

To understand the differences among the regions is essential to an understanding of the farm housing situation of the Nation, because those differences are so great in many instances. This is not to say, however, that all farm housing within each of the regions is similar in many characteristics. On the contrary, the over-all regional figures already given represent averages. It is the purpose of this chapter to show what varied types of housing within each region make up those averages. By using this type of analysis a more detailed picture is obtained of the total farm housing situation of the Nation.

Subregional Characteristics of Farm Housing

In Appendix E (tables E–1—E–12), selected subregions,[1] regarded as

---

[1] Because statistics for economic subregions were not tabulated in 1940, extracting information for that year on a basis comparable with 1950 involves combining the statistics for all counties in each subregion. So massive a task seemed unjustified within the compass of this study. But an alternative technique was worked out which, on a sampling basis, provides general indexes to the occupancy and physical characteristics of farm housing in 1940 and 1950 for each region. 1940 statistics for the counties in each of 30 selected subregions were totaled, these subregions being considered representative of each of the type-of-farming regions in which they are located.

Each subregion was given a rating derived from the distribution of farms by economic class, as indicated by the *1950 Census of Agriculture* (Vol. I, *Counties and State Economic Areas*). In most cases three subregions, taken from the top, middle, and bottom of the scale of ratings, were selected to represent each region. The subregions at the top were, in effect, ones in which commercial farms with a relatively high gross income predominated, whereas in the subregions at the bottom of the scale a large majority of the farms were either commercial with a low gross income or were noncommercial.

Where regions were made up of only a few subregions, and where there was no significant deviation from the scale, either two subregions or one subregion were assumed to be typical of the region. The subregions selected for each region, and the counties of which they are composed, are listed in Appendix B, pp. 133–136.

typical of the variation shown in each of the 12 type-of-farming regions, are statistically analyzed according to their dominant characteristics—(1) physical, (2) occupancy, (3) facilities and equipment—in 1940 and in 1950. Here the emphasis is first on four of the regions which may be considered representative of farming areas in the South, Midwest, Northeast, and extreme West. Farm housing characteristics in the Northeast Dairy Region, the Cotton Belt, the Corn Belt, and the West Coast Miscellaneous Region show marked differences between selected subregions. In different degrees, similar variations are shown for each of the eight other type-of-farming regions analyzed in the appendix. Extremes of variation in farm housing characteristics between subregions of all of the 12 type-of-farming regions are noted in a summary at the end of this chapter.

The analysis in this chapter is based on data for a total of 30 economic subregions, selected on the basis indicated in footnote 1.

Region I.   Northeast Dairy[2]

Farming activities.[3]

Areas	*Dominant enterprises*
Central Northeast	Specialized dairy
Western New York (truck crops, fruit, wheat, potatoes, hay, and dry beans)	Dairy and cash crops
Southern New England (truck crops, potatoes, tobacco, and fruit)	Dairy, poultry, and mixed farming
Hudson River Valley (fruit and truck crops)	
Central Maine (fruit, truck crops, and potatoes)	
Central Pennsylvania (poultry, truck crops, fruit, potatoes, and wheat)	Dairy and general farming
Northern Piedmont (poultry, wheat, tobacco, fruit, and canning crops)	
Lake Erie border (wheat, and small grains)	
Southern Shore Lake Erie	Fruit, truck, dairy
Southern Shore Lake Ontario	
Northern New England—small-scale (poultry, potatoes, and truck crops)	Dairy and general farming
Allegheny Plateau, Pennsylvania—small-scale (poultry and truck crops)	

Physical characteristics of the farmhouses.

Age. Many of the oldest farmhouses in the United States are in this region. Of the 30 economic subregions selected, the highest percentages

---

[2] Selected for study: economic subregions 7, 10, 27. For detailed data, see appendix table E–1, p. 175.

[3] The source for the farming activities listed for this region and for others in the following pages is: Bureau of Agricultural Economics, "Generalized Types of Farming in the United States," *U. S. Dept. of Agr. Inf. Bul. No. 3*, February 1950. Enterprises specified within parentheses are those which are important in addition to the dominant enterprises.

of houses standing in 1950 and built before 1920—89 and 86 percent, respectively—were situated in subregions 7 and 10.[4]

Size. It has been seen that older farmhouses tend to be larger than their modern counterparts. The houses of the region generally follow this trend. The median number of rooms in the farmhouses located in each of the subregions, which include areas in New York, northern Pennsylvania, and Vermont, is unusually high amongst the 30 subregions. But in economic subregion 27, where farming in the West Virginia counties developed at a later date, the houses are neither as old nor as large as those in the two other subregions just discussed.

Data from the 1950 Census publications[5] show that the few farmhouses built recently in the northern area (subregions 7 and 10) are smaller than those built several decades ago; on the other hand, farmhouses recently built in West Virginia and Maryland (subregion 27) are of much the same size as those previously built there, and sometimes are larger.

Quality. The terms used by the 1940 and 1950 Censuses for the quality or condition of farmhouses in the United States are not the same.[6] The closest comparison that can be made is between 1940 data on houses "not needing major repairs" and 1950 data on houses "not dilapidated." Disregarding the slight discrepancies that may have arisen through differences in terms and in interpretation, the higher percentages in the latter category for each of the three subregions (appendix table E–1) are undoubtedly a result of the general prosperity and postwar availability of building materials.[7] In 1950 only one of every ten houses in economic subregions 7 and 10 and one of every six or seven in economic subregion 27 were considered dilapidated.

Occupancy characteristics.

Tenure. In the Northeast Dairy Region it appears that more than three of every four families owned the farmhouses in which they lived in 1950. The percentage distribution in each of the selected economic subregions is shown in appendix table E–1 which also shows, accompanying a decline in the number of farmhouses, a slight increase in the percentage of owner-occupied dwellings between 1940 and 1950.

Size of household. The median number of persons in a farm household

---

[4] An earlier study has indicated that the median age of farmhouses in the Northeast whose age was known is approximately 80 years. Had the age of the remaining houses—some one-fifth of the total—been known, the median figure undoubtedly would have been higher. See Glenn H. Beyer, *Farm Housing in the Northeast*, Cornell University Press, Ithaca, 1949.

[5] *1950 Census of Housing*, Vol. III, *Farm Housing Characteristics*, tables 2–7, 2–10, and 2–27.

[6] See glossary, p. 187.

[7] Quite frequently in this analysis the bases for the data (or their totals) for 1940 and 1950 are slightly different and therefore not strictly comparable, because different numbers and different houses may be involved. Nevertheless, the authors believe that in those instances where relationships are important it is permissible to show the data in comparative form. In such instances lack of strict comparability is of secondary importance to an over-all analysis of major general trends.

in 1950 ranged from 3.5 in subregion 10 to 3.7 in subregion 7, and in two of the three subregions the size of household declined over the decade.

Degree of crowding. Because the farmhouses in this region are larger, they are less likely to be crowded than those in other regions. The 1950 data show only 6 percent of the total occupied, and 13 percent of the tenant-occupied, farmhouses in economic subregion 10 to average 1.01 or more persons per room.

Facilities and equipment. Among the farmhouses of the Nation, those in this region rank fairly high in adequacy of facilities and equipment. Only the newer houses in the West Coast farming areas and in some of the wheat and grazing areas have more modern facilities. This emphasizes the influence not only of income and farm ownership, but also of proximity to urban areas.

Plumbing. In 1950 more than one of every three houses in economic subregion 27 still lacked running water, but in subregion 10 only one of every five houses showed this lack. In all three of the selected economic subregions, the percentage of farmhouses with running water increased considerably between 1940 and 1950 (appendix table E–1). Improvement in the percentages of farmhouses with private flush toilets or with private tubs or showers is not as marked: in 1950, 42 percent of the farmhouses in economic subregion 10 still lacked a private flush toilet, and in subregion 27 the percentage was as much as 64.5.

Heating. The heating equipment most commonly used throughout these economic subregions has been the heating stove. In 1950 approximately 57 percent of the farmhouses in economic subregion 27, 60 percent in subregion 10, and 67 percent in subregion 7, were still so heated. But these percentages show a large decline from those of 1940. During the decade the percentage of centrally heated houses increased, and by 1950 greater proportions of houses were heated by warm air in subregions 10 and 27 than in most of the other regions covered by this study.

Cooking fuels. In 1950 a high percentage of farmhouses in the region used fuels other than gas or electricity for cooking—three of every four in economic subregion 7, 58 percent in economic subregion 10, and half in economic subregion 27. Nevertheless, over the decade, gas and electricity had replaced wood to a considerable extent and, less markedly, had replaced coal. Subregions 7 and 10 show a marked decline in the proportion of dwelling units in which wood was used for cooking fuel. Similarly, subregion 27 shows a decline in the proportion using coal.

Electric lights. In line with the tremendous increase in the use of electricity in farmhouses across the Nation, the Northeast Dairy Region shows conspicuous improvement between 1940 and 1950. In 1940, close to half of the farmhouses in the selected economic subregions lacked electric lights. By 1950, this was reduced to 5 percent in subregion 10, to 7 percent in subregion 7, and to 12 percent in subregion 27.

Region VI.   Cotton Belt[8]

Farming activities.

Areas	Dominant enterprises
Texas Black waxy prairies	Specialized cotton
Deltas of Mississippi River and tributaries	
Mississippi and Tennessee clay hills and sand loams	
Sand Mountain-Alabama	
Southern Piedmont	
Upper Coastal Plains	
Central Coastal Plains, North Carolina-South Carolina	Cotton and tobacco
Lower Coastal Plains, Georgia-Florida	Cotton, tobacco, hogs, and peanuts
Alabama-Mississippi Black Belt	Cotton and livestock
Mississippi-Tennessee-Louisiana silt loam	
Post Oak Strip of Texas	Cotton and range livestock
Central Louisiana	Cotton and sugar cane
Rolling plains, Texas-Oklahoma	Cotton and general farming
Western sandy coastal plains, Texas-Arkansas-Louisiana-Oklahoma	
Arkansas River valleys and uplands	
Limestone valleys and uplands, Tennessee-Georgia-Alabama	
Piedmont of central Carolina	
Sandhills of the Carolinas and Georgia	
Gulf coast piney woods	Cotton and forest products
Texas-Louisiana cut-over	Forest products, truck crops, and cotton

Physical characteristics of the farmhouses.   Geographically, the Cotton Belt is the largest type-of-farming region in the United States, and it has the largest number of farmhouses—25 percent of the total for the Nation in 1950.

Age.   Although the region was among the first areas to be cultivated, the farmhouses for the most part are not old. Those that were built when the South was first settled are far outnumbered by small, comparatively new houses. The average age of the farm dwellings in the Cotton Belt ranks midway between those of houses in the Northeast Dairy Region and in the West Coast Region.

In economic subregion 35 half of the farmhouses in use in 1950 were built in 1919 or earlier. The equivalent percentage for subregion 97 is 26, and for subregion 43 it is 37. These data and comparable data for 1940 are shown in appendix table E-6.

---

[8] Selected for study: economic subregions 35, 43, 97. For detailed data, see appendix table E-6, p. 180.

Size. In terms of number of rooms, the farmhouses in the Cotton Belt are among the smallest in the Nation. This circumstance is directly related to the principal type of product from these farms. Cotton farming traditionally has involved a high degree of tenancy and generally low incomes. In 1950 farmhouses in economic subregion 43 had a median of 4.5 rooms and those in economic subregions 35 and 97, a median of 4.6 rooms. While these represent a slight increase over the medians for 1940, appendix table E–6 shows how high are the percentages of farmhouses with 4 rooms or less.

Quality. In condition, too, the houses of the Cotton Belt in 1950 were inferior to the farmhouses of any other region. Of the 30 economic subregions selected, subregion 35, with 36 percent of its farmhouses dilapidated, presents the least attractive picture, although the 1950 situation is apparently an improvement over that existing in 1940. Economic subregion 97, which includes the newer cotton sections of Texas-Oklahoma, has a higher level of quality with only 21 percent of its houses classified in 1950 as dilapidated. Here, the renter and rent-free dwelling units were on the average of better quality than in subregion 35 and thus raised the average for all farm dwelling units.

Occupancy characteristics.

Tenure. Though a high proportion of the farmhouses in the Cotton Belt are still tenanted by sharecroppers, the percentage has declined appreciably in recent years. Appendix table E–6 shows that between 1940 and 1950 the percentage of tenant-occupied dwelling units declined substantially in each of the three subregions.

Size of household. Households in the region as a whole are large in relation to farm households throughout the Nation. But they are smaller than they were in 1940. The high 1950 medians of 4.2 persons to a household in subregion 35 and 4.0 in subregion 43, are balanced somewhat by the median in economic subregion 97, which is only 3.2 persons to a household.

Degree of crowding. Naturally, the combination of large families and small farmhouses has led to overcrowding; there is more incidence of crowding in the Cotton Belt than in other regions. In 1950, 40 percent of the farmhouses in economic subregion 35 were occupied by households averaging 1.01 or more persons to a room. (This was equaled in only one other of the selected economic subregions: subregion 31 in the General and Self-Sufficing Farming Region. See appendix table E–4.) In areas where tenant-farming is common, the degree of crowding is usually higher. Some 53 percent of the farmhouses occupied by tenant farmers in economic subregion 35 averaged 1.01 or more persons to a room. The percentage was also high in subregion 43 but considerably lower in subregion 97, which is in Texas.

Nonwhite families live in many of the farmhouses of the Cotton Belt.

This is especially true of subregion 35, which contains counties in South Carolina, Georgia, and Alabama. Here, in 1950, 45 percent of the farmhouses were occupied by nonwhite families.

Facilities and equipment. A high proportion of the farmhouses in the Cotton Belt lack modern conveniences. It is true that the warm climate lessens the need for certain facilities such as central heating. More surprising is the fact that the farmhouses of some northern regions lack facilities other than central heating as frequently as farmhouses in some of the economic subregions of the Cotton Belt. And sometimes the incidence is even greater in the North.

Plumbing. A study of the appendix tables for this (E–6) and other regions indicates that although nearly three of every four farmhouses in economic subregions 35 and 43 were without running water in 1950, the proportions shown are not as high as the comparable proportions for several of the selected areas of other regions. Moreover, the third Cotton Belt subregion, 97, shows only 55 percent of its farmhouses to be without running water, and in each one of the three subregions a significant proportion of houses acquired running water between 1940 and 1950.

The scarcity of modern toilet facilities is more serious. Despite some improvement after 1940, in each of the three economic subregions more than four of every five farmhouses were without a private flush toilet in 1950.

Heating. Almost all the farmhouses in this region are heated by a heating stove or space heater—a fairly satisfactory method in this climate. Consequently, little change in type of heating equipment has taken place.

Cooking fuel. So far as cooking fuel is concerned, there have been considerable shifts. The 1950 figures for subregions 35 and 43 show that over the previous 10 years gas and electricity, especially the latter, had replaced wood in many farmhouses. A most impressive change took place in subregion 97. Here, in Texas, as natural gas became available, the proportion of families using wood declined from 57 percent in 1940 to 22 percent in 1950, while that of families using gas increased from 4 percent to 32 percent in that period.

Electric lights. The Cotton Belt is an area where many farmhouses still are without electric lights. Economic subregion 35, where nearly one of every three farmhouses in 1950 lacked such lighting, is a conspicuous example. Nevertheless, compared with 1940, all three subregions show an impressive rate of increase in the installation of electricity for lighting purposes.

Region VII.   Corn Belt[9]

Farming activities.

Areas	Dominant enterprises
Central Missouri Valley Eastern Iowa-western Illinois	Cattle feeding and hogs
Central Iowa East Central Illinois	Cash corn, oats, and soybeans
Central Indiana-southwestern Ohio Wabash and lower Ohio River Valleys	Hogs and soft winter wheat
Northwestern Ohio-northwestern Indiana	Livestock dairy, soy- beans, and cash grain
Northeastern Iowa-northwestern Illinois-southwestern Wisconsin	Hogs and dairy
Northwestern corn-livestock transition Southwestern corn-hard winter wheat transition Western Corn Belt fringe Northwestern Corn Belt fringe Northern Iowa-southwestern Minnesota	Livestock and cash grain
Western Missouri-eastern Kansas	Livestock, cash grain, and dairy
Southern Iowa-northern Missouri-west central Illinois Northwestern Indiana-southwestern Michigan	Livestock and pasture

Corn-Belt farm families usually depend almost entirely upon farm production as their source of income.   This is due in part to the type of farming, which requires long days of activity and some activity the year around, and in part to the location of the farms, which are not often close to large urban centers where supplementary employment can be found.

Physical characteristics of the farmhouses.

Age, size, and quality.   Among the 12 regions, farmhouses of the Corn Belt, with those of the Great Lakes Dairy Region, rank second to the Northeast Dairy Region in average age.   Appendix table E–7 shows 77 percent in economic subregion 92, 74 percent in subregion 86, and 69 percent in subregion 51 to have been built before 1920.   Perhaps because of their age, the farmhouses are also somewhat larger than the average for the Nation as a whole.   Economic subregion 86 is conspicuous for this characteristic.   This same subregion, with subregion 92, is also notable among the 30 economic subregions as having the fewest houses considered to be dilapidated.   The proportions for 1950 are as low as 4 and 5 percent.

Occupancy characteristics.

Tenure.   Farm tenancy in the Corn Belt is relatively common.   Half of the farms in economic subregion 86, 42 percent in subregion 92, and 25 percent in subregion 51 were operated by tenants in 1950.   But in this

---

[9] Selected for study: economic subregions 51, 86, 92.   For detailed data, see appendix table E–7, p. 181.

area tenant families have many of the characteristics of families who live on their own farms: their farms are often as highly mechanized, and their homes frequently are similarly equipped. The proportion of owner-occupied farmhouses is increasing. This is especially apparent in subregion 92, where the proportion of owner-occupied units changed from 41 percent to 58 percent between 1940 and 1950. (See appendix table E–7.)

Size of household and degree of crowding. The average-size household in the Corn Belt Region varied in 1950 from a median of 3.2 persons in economic subregion 51 to 3.6 in subregion 86. Because of their relatively large size, however, the houses are not overly crowded. In fact, in economic subregion 86 there were 1.01 or more persons per room in only 7 percent of the owner-occupied farmhouses and in only 9 percent of the houses lived in by tenants. This latter figure is the lowest shown for any of the 30 selected subregions.

Facilities and equipment. The percentage of houses with modern facilities in the Corn Belt, as represented by the three subregions, is at the middle of the range for all the houses in the 30 selected subregions. Since, on the average, family income is relatively high, it seems probable that much of it finds its way into other farm expenses, especially investments in farm machinery.

Plumbing. Even though facilities for running water have been added to a considerable number of farmhouses since 1940, almost two-thirds of the houses in economic subregion 51 and 46 percent in subregion 86 were still without running water in 1950. More than three of every four farmhouses in subregion 51 still lacked a private flush toilet, and subregion 86 was hardly better off, with 62 percent of its farmhouses lacking a private flush toilet.

Heating and cooking fuels. A heating stove is still the popular means of heating throughout the Corn Belt. In 1950 more than three of every four houses in economic subregion 51 were heated in this manner, and the percentage for subregion 92 is almost as high. In each of the three subregions, however, there is a noticeable trend toward warm-air heating, and between 1940 and 1950 the proportion of farmhouses heated with a stove substantially declined. There is a trend, too, toward the use of gas as a cooking fuel, and toward a decline in the use of coal and wood. Electricity has not, apparently, increased in use as much as gas.

Electric lights. So far as electric lighting is concerned, economic subregion 86 shows one of the lowest percentages in any of the 30 subregions: in 1950 only 4 percent of its farmhouses were still without electric lights. But the picture for the region is balanced by subregion 92, where more than one of every four farm homes in 1950 was without electric lights.

Region XII. West Coast Miscellaneous[10]

Farming activities.

Areas	Dominant enterprises
Central Washington area (deciduous fruit, hay, truck crops, and hops)	Fruit and mixed farming
Southwest Oregon (deciduous fruit and poultry)	
Sacramento Valley (deciduous fruit, rice, dry beans, hay, and sugar beets)	
San Joaquin Valley (deciduous citrus fruit, grapes, dairy, hay, cotton, and potatoes)	
Central California Coast (deciduous fruit, livestock, sugar beets, dairy, and poultry)	Fruit, truck, and mixed farming
Sierra Foothills	
Southern California and southwestern Arizona (citrus fruit, dairy, poultry, dry beans, and hay)	
Southern Yakima Valley (fruit, potatoes, and dairy)	Livestock and special crops
Kalamath Basin, Oregon-California (potatoes)	Special crops

Agricultural enterprises have been more recently developed in the West Coast Miscellaneous Region than in any other area in the Nation. One reason for this is the irrigation of semi-arid land which could not heretofore be used for agricultural purposes.

Physical characteristics of the farmhouses.

Age. Because agricultural development is relatively new, at least in some parts of the region, the majority of farmhouses also are relatively new. In economic subregion 115, which includes the southern counties of California, 78 percent of the farmhouses standing in 1950 had been built since 1919; and in subregions 116 and 119, 70 percent and 68 percent, respectively, of the farmhouses had been built during the same period. (See appendix table E–12.)

Size. These recently built farmhouses are modest in size, though not as small as those in the Year-Long and Seasonal Grazing Region (appendix table E–10) and in some of the southeastern farming areas of the Nation. In 1950 the median for farmhouses in economic subregion 115 was 4.8 rooms; that for subregion 116, 4.6 rooms; and that for subregion 119, 5.2 rooms.

Quality. The farmhouses of the region are in fairly good condition. In 1950 only 9 percent of all of the farmhouses in economic subregion 115 were found to be dilapidated. Corresponding percentages for subregions 116 and 119 are 13 and 10. In large part, this generally good condition may be attributable to the relatively high income of many of the farm families living in the region.

---

[10] Selected for study: subregions 115, 116, 119. For detailed data, see appendix table E–12, p. 186.

Occupancy characteristics.

Tenure. The farmhouses of the region are to a large extent owner occupied. This is especially true of economic subregion 119, which includes the Puget Sound and Willamette Valley. Here, in 1950, owners lived in 84 percent of the farmhouses. Only the three selected subregions of the Great Lakes Dairy Region (appendix table E–2) ranked higher in this respect. Appendix table E–12 shows a considerable increase in owner occupancy in each of the three West Coast subregions since 1940.

Size of household. The households in some parts of the region are among the smallest in the Nation. In 1950 the median size of household for economic subregion 115 was 2.9 persons—lower than for any other of the selected subregions. Ranking third among the 30 subregions is economic subregion 119, where the median size of household in 1950 was 3.1. In subregion 116 the corresponding median was 3.3.

Degree of crowding. Because households in general are small, overcrowding is not serious. In 1950, economic subregion 119 had an average of 1.01 persons or more per room in only 14 percent of its farmhouses. The comparable percentage in subregion 115 was 16, and in subregion 116 it was 21. The 1950 ratios of crowding for farmhouses occupied by tenants are somewhat higher. In subregion 119 approximately one of every five houses occupied by tenants averaged 1.01 persons or more per room; in subregion 115, the figure is 25 percent; and in subregion 116, it is 34 percent.

Facilities and equipment.

Since farm incomes in the West Coast Miscellaneous Region are relatively high, the number of farm families with extremely low incomes is not large enough to have an important effect on the average for the region as a whole. This, together with the fact that much of the housing is new, accounts for a predominance of modern facilities and equipment throughout the three selected subregions. In most of these recorded characteristics the farmhouses of at least one, and often all three, of the subregions outpace those of the other selected subregions across the Nation.

Plumbing. In economic subregion 115, for example, only 6 percent of the farmhouses lacked running water in 1950, and the proportions in subregions 116 and 119 were very similar, 9 and 11 percent, respectively. In all three cases, and particularly subregion 119, the improvement between 1940 and 1950 is remarkable. (See appendix table E–12.)

Again, in relation to private flush toilets in 1950, subregion 115 had the lowest percentage of farmhouses (17) reporting their lack, and the comparable percentages for subregion 116 (26) and subregion 119 (32) were not far behind. In all three subregions the percentages are considerably lower in 1950 than in 1940. Only 15 percent of the farmhouses in subregion 115 lacked a private tub or shower in 1950. The improvement between 1940 and 1950 is again especially significant in economic subregion 119.

Heating. A mild climate undoubtedly is responsible, at least in part, for the fact that four of every five farmhouses in each of the three subregions were still, in 1950, heated by means of a heating stove. While there was some change to warm air heating during the 1940–50 decade, improvements in this area were not as marked as were those made with other equipment and facilities.

Cooking fuels. In 1950 gas was the predominant type of cooking fuel used in the two California subregions; at least half of the families in each subregion were using this type of fuel. After gas, electricity was most widely used. The use of wood as a cooking fuel declined appreciably between 1940 and 1950 and, to a lesser degree, so did the use of kerosene or gasoline. In subregion 119 electricity, rather than gas, became a major cooking fuel for 41 percent of the farm families. But wood still ranked first with 46 percent of the families, though this percentage had declined from a high of 90 percent in 1940. While the figures for kerosene or gasoline are relatively small, a rather unusual increase in the use of kerosene or gasoline is noticeable in the subregion during the decade.

Electric lights. Practically all of the farms in the three subregions are electrified. This is demonstrated by the low percentages of farmhouses lacking electric lights in 1950—2 in subregion 116, 3 in subregion 119, and 4 in subregion 115.

Summary of Extremes Among Subregions, 1950

Ten-year trends in occupancy characteristics, physical characteristics, and modern facilities and equipment of the farmhouses in the selected subregions of four representative type-of-farming regions have been described in detail in the preceding pages of this chapter. The following pages summarize and tabulate the total data for 1950 for the 30 selected subregions of the 12 type-of-farming regions, in order to emphasize the extremes in farmhousing characteristics that exist across the Nation.[11]

Physical characteristics. The largest group of old farmhouses in the Nation is clearly in the Northeast Dairy Region. That of the Corn Belt closely follows. At the other extreme, the newer farm housing is generally located in areas that have been developed for agricultural purposes comparatively recently. These include the Year-Long and Seasonal Grazing Region, which was once made up of semidesert areas in Texas and the West Coast, and areas in Florida and along the Gulf Coast recently converted to the growing of truck crops.

It has already been pointed out in connection with overcrowding that the smallest farmhouses are generally located in the South. The greatest number of small houses are seen to be in two subregions of the Year-Long and Seasonal Grazing Region, both in the State of Texas; in a subregion of the

---

[11] Statistical data on which the summary, and preceding pages of this chapter, are based appear in Appendix E, pp. 175–186.

General and Self-Sufficing Farming Region, with counties in Missouri, Arkansas, and Oklahoma (economic subregion 82); and in subregion 31 in the southern Appalachians. The relatively small houses in economic subregion 97, in Texas, were built quite recently.

TABLE 36.—AGE—ECONOMIC SUBREGIONS WITH HIGHEST OR LOWEST PERCENT OF DWELLING UNITS BUILT IN 1919 OR EARLIER: 1950

Type-of-farming region and economic subregion	Percent built 1919 or earlier	Type-of-farming region and economic subregion	Percent built 1919 or earlier
Areas with highest percent:		Areas with lowest percent:	
Northeast Dairy, subr. 7................	89.0	Year-Long and Seasonal Grazing,	
Northeast Dairy, subr. 10..............	86.1	subr. 102...........................	7.2
Corn Belt, subr. 92....................	77.2	East and Gulf Coast Misc., subr. 39....	15.8
Corn Belt, subr. 86....................	73.7	West Coast Miscellaneous, subr. 115....	21.9
Northeast Dairy, subr. 27.............	72.8	East and Gulf Coast Misc., subr. 58....	23.0
Northern Wheat and Small Grains,		Year-Long and Seasonal Grazing,	
subr. 90............................	70.2	subr. 98............................	26.7
		General and Self-Sufficing, subr. 31...	27.7
		West Coast Miscellaneous, subr. 119....	31.8

Source: Derived from *1950 Census of Housing*, Vol. III, *Farm Housing Characteristics*, subregion table 1.

The largest farmhouses in the Nation are found in the Northeast Dairy Region, the Corn Belt, and the Great Lakes Dairy Region. Between farmhouses with the highest median number of rooms and those with the lowest there is a marked difference: an average of about two more rooms to a farmhouse may be noted in the economic subregions shown in the left-hand column when compared with the subregion in the right-hand column of table 37.

TABLE 37.—SIZE OF DWELLING UNIT—ECONOMIC SUBREGIONS WITH HIGHEST OR LOWEST MEDIAN NUMBER OF ROOMS IN DWELLING UNITS: 1950

Type-of-farming region and economic subregion	Median number of rooms	Type-of-farming region and economic subregion	Median number of rooms
Areas with highest median:		Areas with lowest median:	
Northeast Dairy, subr. 7..............	7.1	Year-Long and Seasonal Grazing,	
Northeast Dairy, subr. 10.............	7.0	subr. 102...........................	4.0
Corn Belt, subr. 86...................	6.6	Year-Long and Seasonal Grazing,	
Great Lakes Dairy, subr. 50...........	6.2	subr. 98............................	4.2
Corn Belt, subr. 92...................	5.9	General and Self-Sufficing, subr. 82...	4.3
Northeast Dairy, subr. 27.............	5.9	Cotton Belt, subr. 35.................	4.3
Great Lakes Dairy, subr. 88...........	5.8	General and Self-Sufficing, subr. 31...	4.4
Northern Wheat and Small Grains,		Cotton Belt, subr. 43.................	4.5
subr. 90............................	5.7	Tobacco, subr. 53....................	4.5
		Cotton Belt, subr. 97.................	4.5

Source: Same as table 36.

Considerable variation, too, is shown in the condition of farmhouses from region to region. It has been generally recognized that housing of the poorest quality is to be found in the South. But it has been less obvious how great is the contrast between the condition of farmhouses here and in northern farming regions. It will be seen from the data that in two of the selected Cotton Belt subregions one of every three farmhouses in 1950

was considered to be dilapidated. The comparable ratio for two of the
Corn Belt subregions selected is one farmhouse or better in every twenty.

TABLE **38.**—CONDITION—ECONOMIC SUBREGIONS WITH HIGHEST OR LOWEST PERCENT OF
DILAPIDATED DWELLING UNITS: 1950

Type-of-farming region and economic subregion	Percent dilapi-dated	Type-of-farming region and economic subregion	Percent dilapi-dated
Areas with highest percent:		Areas with lowest percent:	
Cotton Belt, subr. 35..................	35.6	Corn Belt, subr. 86....................	3.6
East and Gulf Coast Misc., subr. 58....	28.1	Corn Belt, subr. 92....................	5.4
East and Gulf Coast Misc., subr. 21....	26.3	Southern Wheat and Small Grains,	
General and Self-Sufficing, subr. 31...	26.1	subr. 94............................	6.1
Cotton Belt, subr. 43..................	25.6	Northern Wheat and Small Grains,	
Tobacco, subr. 24......................	23.6	subr. 90............................	6.8
		Upland Summer Grazing, subr. 112.......	7.1

Source: Derived from *1950 Census of Housing*, Vol. III, *Farm Housing Characteristics*, subregion table 2.

Occupancy characteristics. It is generally known that farm tenancy
is most common in the South. This is clearly confirmed by the data, which
show that of the 30 economic subregions selected for special study, five of
the six in which the lowest percentage of owner occupancy appears are
subregions in the Tobacco Region, the East and Gulf Coast Miscellaneous
Region, and the Cotton Belt.

At the other extreme, owner occupancy is most common in the Great
Lakes Dairy Region, where all three selected subregions show percentages
of owner occupancy higher than in any subregion elsewhere. Closest to
this group is a subregion on the West Coast and one in the Northeast Dairy
Region.

TABLE **39.**—TENURE—ECONOMIC SUBREGIONS WITH HIGHEST OR LOWEST PERCENT OF
OWNER-OCCUPIED DWELLING UNITS: 1950

Type-of-farming region and economic subregion	Percent owner occupied	Type-of-farming region and economic subregion	Percent owner occupied
Areas with highest percent:		Areas with lowest percent:	
Great Lakes Dairy, subr. 66............	90.2	Tobacco, subr. 24......................	37.2
Great Lakes Dairy, subr. 88............	86.4	Year-Long and Seasonal Grazing,	
Great Lakes Dairy, subr. 50............	83.9	subr. 102...........................	43.2
West Coast Miscellaneous, subr. 119....	83.7	East and Gulf Coast Misc., subr. 21....	45.0
Northeast Dairy, subr. 10..............	82.9	Cotton Belt, subr. 35..................	49.6
		Corn Belt, subr. 86....................	49.9
		Cotton Belt, subr. 97..................	51.9

Source: Same as table 36.

That farm families are largest in the South is also confirmed by the data
for the five subregions with the highest median number of persons to a
household. Four are southern.

The lowest median number of persons to a household is shown for subregions on the West Coast. In two of these, families in 1950 had a median
of 3.1 persons or less—well below the average for the Nation. The other
subregions with small families are fairly well scattered and include one of

the subregions of the Cotton Belt. Farming conditions in the highly mechanized cotton areas of Texas, in which this particular subregion is located, are very different from those common to the older cotton sections of Georgia, Mississippi, Alabama, and Louisiana.

TABLE **40.**—SIZE OF HOUSEHOLD—ECONOMIC SUBREGIONS WITH HIGHEST OR LOWEST MEDIAN NUMBER OF PERSONS IN DWELLING UNITS: 1950

Type-of-farming region and economic subregion	Median number of persons	Type-of-farming region and economic subregion	Median number of persons
Areas with highest median:		Areas with lowest median:	
East and Gulf Coast Misc., subr. 21....	4.5	West Coast Miscellaneous, subr. 115....	2.9
Tobacco, subr. 24......................	4.4	East and Gulf Coast Misc., subr. 39....	3.1
General and Self-Sufficing, subr. 31...	4.4	West Coast Miscellaneous, subr. 119....	3.1
Cotton Belt, subr. 35..................	4.2	General and Self-Sufficing, subr. 82...	3.2
Cotton Belt, subr. 43..................	4.0	Corn Belt, subr. 51....................	3.2
		Southern Wheat and Small Grains, subr. 94..............................	3.2
		Cotton Belt, subr. 97.................	3.2

Source: Same as table 36.

A comparison of the size of household with the number of rooms in the house results in a density ratio. The relatively small farmhouses of the South, combined with the large families that prevail there, give a basis for assuming that overcrowding is worse in the southern regions than elsewhere. The data support this assumption. Among the six subregions showing highest percentages of overcrowding, three are totally in the South and two, economic subregions 31 and 98, include counties in Virginia, Kentucky, West Virginia, Tennessee, and Florida.

TABLE **41.**—OVERCROWDING—ECONOMIC SUBREGIONS WITH HIGHEST OR LOWEST PERCENT OF DWELLING UNITS WITH 1.01 PERSONS OR MORE PER ROOM: 1950

Type-of-farming region and economic subregion	Percent of over-crowding	Type-of-farming region and economic subregion	Percent of over-crowding
Areas with highest percent:		Areas with lowest percent:	
General and Self-Sufficing, subr. 31...	40.7	Northeast Dairy, subr. 10..............	6.1
Cotton Belt, subr. 35..................	39.6	Corn Belt, subr. 86....................	7.1
Tobacco, subr. 24......................	36.9	Northeast Dairy, subr. 7..............	7.9
East and Gulf Coast Misc., subr. 21....	36.5	Southern Wheat and Small Grains, subr. 94............................	9.8
Year-Long and Seasonal Grazing, subr. 98............................	34.3	Great Lakes Dairy, subr. 50...........	10.2
Cotton Belt, subr. 43.................	34.1		

Source: Same as table 36.

The degree of overcrowding is greater in tenant houses than in farmhouses in general. The figures for tenant-occupied houses are shown below. Realizing that tenancy is common in the South, the figures in the column on the left are striking indications of the relationship between overcrowding and tenancy. Similarly, since there is little tenancy in such regions as the Northeast Dairy Region, the importance of the figures in the right-hand column diminishes.

This parallel between a high degree of tenancy and a high degree of overcrowding does not follow for all regions throughout the Nation. For example, there is much more tenancy in the Corn Belt than in the Northeast Dairy Region, but farmhouses of this class in economic subregion 86 of the Corn Belt are less overcrowded than similar farmhouses in any other selected subregion.

TABLE 42.—RENTER OVERCROWDING—ECONOMIC SUBREGIONS WITH HIGHEST OR LOWEST PERCENT OF RENTER-OCCUPIED DWELLING UNITS WITH 1.01 PERSONS OR MORE PER ROOM: 1950

Type-of-farming region and economic subregion	Percent of over-crowding	Type-of-farming region and economic subregion	Percent of over-crowding
Areas with highest percent:		Areas with lowest percent:	
Cotton Belt, subr. 35.................	53.3	Corn Belt, subr. 86..................	8.5
General and Self-Sufficing, subr. 31...	52.1	Southern Wheat and Small Grains,	
Year-Long and Seasonal Grazing,		subr. 94............................	11.6
subr. 98............................	49.8	Corn Belt, subr. 92..................	12.5
Tobacco, subr. 21.....................	49.3	Northeast Dairy, subr. 10............	12.6
Cotton Belt, subr. 43.................	49.1	Northern Wheat and Small Grains,	
		subr. 110...........................	13.6
		Northeast Dairy, subr. 7.............	14.4

Source: Same as table 36.

Facilities and equipment. Perhaps the greatest variation in farmhouses from region to region occurs in connection with plumbing. In several of the selected subregions in the South, more than three of every four farmhouses in 1950 lacked running water. At the other extreme is one of the subregions selected in the West Coast Miscellaneous Region, where only one of every twenty houses lacked running water.

In regions where few farmhouses are without running water, recent construction and relatively high income are two contributing factors. In other regions low income levels undoubtedly account for the high proportion of houses without running water.

TABLE 43.—RUNNING WATER—ECONOMIC SUBREGIONS WITH HIGHEST OR LOWEST PERCENT OF DWELLING UNITS WITHOUT RUNNING WATER: 1950

Type-of-farming region and economic subregion	Percent without running water	Type-of-farming region and economic subregion	Percent without running water
Areas with highest percent:		Areas with lowest percent:	
General and Self-Sufficing, subr. 31...	84.8	West Coast Miscellaneous, subr. 115....	5.6
East and Gulf Coast Misc., subr. 21....	78.5	West Coast Miscellaneous, subr. 116....	8.8
Tobacco, subr. 53.....................	78.4	West Coast Miscellaneous, subr. 119....	11.3
Northern Wheat and Small Grains,		Northern Wheat and Small Grains,	
subr. 90............................	76.8	subr. 110...........................	15.1
Tobacco, subr. 24.....................	75.6	Upland Summer Grazing, subr. 112.......	17.0
Cotton Belt, subr. 43.................	74.6		
Cotton Belt, subr. 35.................	73.5		

Source: Derived from *1950 Census of Housing*, Vol. III, *Farm Housing Characteristics*, subregion table 2.

Comparative regional percentages of farmhouses lacking a private flush toilet are similar, though less extreme. In 1950 more than five of every six farmhouses in several of the subregions in the South lacked a private flush toilet. On the other hand, less than one of every three houses in each of the subregions selected in the West Coast Miscellaneous Region were so lacking.

TABLE 44.—PRIVATE TOILET—ECONOMIC SUBREGIONS WITH HIGHEST OR LOWEST PERCENT OF DWELLING UNITS WITHOUT PRIVATE TOILET: 1950

Type-of-farming region and economic subregion	Percent without private toilet	Type-of-farming region and economic subregion	Percent without private toilet
Areas with highest percent:		Areas with lowest percent:	
General and Self-Sufficing, subr. 31...	93.0	West Coast Miscellaneous, subr. 115....	16.7
Tobacco, subr. 24......	90.0	West Coast Miscellaneous, subr. 116....	25.5
East and Gulf Coast Misc., subr. 21....	88.9	West Coast Miscellaneous, subr. 119....	31.8
Tobacco, subr. 53......	88.6	Northern Wheat and Small Grains, subr. 110......	34.4
Cotton Belt, subr. 43......	88.5	Northeast Dairy, subr. 10......	41.8

Source: Same as table 43.

Lack of central heating is not an adequate guide to regional levels of living. Climate is as important a factor as income affecting its installation.

The fact, therefore, that nine out of ten farmhouses in many of the subregions in the South were still, in 1950, heated by means of a heating stove, while only half the farmhouses in the colder northern regions were so heated, cannot of itself be taken as evidence of wide differences in income levels.

TABLE 45.—HEATING STOVE—ECONOMIC SUBREGIONS WITH HIGHEST OR LOWEST PERCENT OF DWELLING UNITS WITH HEATING STOVE: 1950

Type-of-farming region and economic subregion	Percent with heating stove	Type-of-farming region and economic subregion	Percent with heating stove
Areas with highest percent:		Areas with lowest percent:	
East and Gulf Coast Misc., subr. 21....	96.9	Great Lakes Dairy, subr. 50......	52.8
Tobacco, subr. 24......	95.1	Northeast Dairy, subr. 27......	56.5
Cotton Belt, subr. 43......	95.0	Northern Wheat and Small Grains, subr. 90......	58.8
Year-Long and Seasonal Grazing, subr. 98......	95.0	Northeast Dairy, subr. 10......	60.3
Cotton Belt, subr. 35......	94.8	Corn Belt, subr. 86......	60.4
East and Gulf Coast Misc., subr. 39....	94.4	Northeast Dairy, subr. 7......	67.0
General and Self-Sufficing, subr. 31...	94.4		

Source: Same as table 43.

Extremes shown in the percentages of farm households that did or did not in 1950 cook with electricity or gas are almost as significant a guide to levels of farm living as are the percentages dealing with running water. In five of the selected subregions in the South, for example, more than four of every five households used fuels other than gas or electricity for cooking. In economic subregion 31 in the southern Appalachian region, and in subregion 35 in the Cotton Belt, the comparable figures are as high as 88 percent.

On the other hand, by 1950, in the West Coast Miscellaneous Region and in certain of the other northern regions of the country, gas and electricity had come into common use.

TABLE 46.—COOKING FUEL—ECONOMIC SUBREGIONS WITH HIGHEST OR LOWEST PERCENT OF DWELLING UNITS WITH COOKING FUEL OTHER THAN GAS OR ELECTRICITY: 1950

Type-of-farming region and economic subregion	Percent with other than gas or elec- tricity	Type-of-farming region and economic subregion	Percent with other than gas or elec- tricity
Areas with highest percent:		Areas with lowest percent:	
General and Self-Sufficing, subr. 31...	88.2	West Coast Miscellaneous, subr. 115....	12.6
Cotton Belt, subr. 35..................	88.1	West Coast Miscellaneous, subr. 116....	15.7
East and Gulf Coast Misc., subr. 21....	86.3	Year-Long and Seasonal Grazing,	
Tobacco, subr. 24......................	81.4	subr. 102.............................	19.6
Cotton Belt, subr. 43.................	80.3	Great Lakes Dairy, subr. 50...........	33.6
		Southern Wheat and Small Grains,	
		subr. 94.............................	34.0
		Corn Belt, subr. 86...................	36.6

Source: Derived from *1950 Census of Housing*, Vol. III, *Farm Housing Characteristics*, subregion table 1.

The presence or absence of electric lights in farmhouses cannot be as directly related to climate and geography—or even income—as most of the other facilities that have been described. Three of the subregions where the percentages of farmhouses without electric lights are among the highest are in the North (90, 92, and 104), while the rest of the subregions with farmhouses in this category are in the South. The high percentages in these particular subregions can be generally attributed to the fact that rural electrification has not yet reached them. Once rural electrification has been extended to a region, the factor governing installation of electric lights is income.

TABLE 47.—ELECTRIC LIGHTS—ECONOMIC SUBREGIONS WITH HIGHEST OR LOWEST PERCENT OF DWELLING UNITS WITHOUT ELECTRIC LIGHTS: 1950

Type-of-farming region and economic subregion	Percent without electric lights	Type-of-farming region and economic subregion	Percent without electric lights
Areas with highest percent:		Areas with lowest percent:	
Year-Long and Seasonal Grazing,		West Coast Miscellaneous, subr. 116....	2.0
subr. 104.............................	43.5	Upland Summer Grazing, subr. 112.......	2.7
East and Gulf Coast Misc., subr. 21....	33.6	West Coast Miscellaneous, subr. 119....	3.3
General and Self-Sufficing, subr. 31...	33.5	West Coast Miscellaneous, subr. 115....	3.5
Cotton Belt, subr. 35.................	31.3	Great Lakes Dairy, subr. 50...........	4.0
Northern Wheat and Small Grains,		Corn Belt, subr. 86...................	4.4
subr. 90.............................	29.9	Northeast Dairy, subr. 10.............	4.8
Corn Belt, subr. 92.....................	28.6		
Tobacco, subr. 53.....................	28.1		

Source: Same as table 43.

C H A P T E R 5

IMPACT OF URBAN CENTERS
ON FARM HOUSING

There is little doubt that large urban centers do influence to some extent the characteristics of farmhouses in nearby rural areas. The "urban factor" has been noted many times in the preceding chapters when we analyzed the differences between farm housing characteristics of a region where large urban areas exist, and those of regions where there are few or no urban areas. Even in an age of television, radio, and mass production of printed matter, the physical distance a farming area is from an urban center appears to exert an influence on housing characteristics. What is the pattern of urban influence? To find answers to this question it is necessary to study an area considerably smaller than a type-of-farming region. In an area so large, many factors besides the proximity of urban centers may be important in determining the characteristics of farm housing. Even if an area the size of an economic subregion is studied, these variable factors cannot be expected to hold constant.

The closer a farmhouse is in time and distance to an urban area the more noticeable, presumably, should be the urban influence on its characteristics. One might expect this influence to radiate from the center in all directions, diminishing in intensity as distance increases. If the housing in relatively small, successive concentric circles around an urban center is compared, and if it is found that dwelling units in these circles differ distinguishably, the analyst has ground for drawing some conclusions about urban influence. Other factors, such as type of farming and cultural background of families, will be nearly constant for all circles of an urban area.

The limited statistics on farm housing in minor civil divisions, e.g., townships or election precincts, are inadequate for such an analysis. Therefore, since counties are the smallest type of geographical unit for which statistics on farm housing are available in sufficient detail for purposes of comparison, counties are used here as the only practicable means of forming concentric circles around an urban area.

Concentric circles of urban influence

Counties in the areas selected for study have been, for the most part, divided into three groups. The first group, or circle, contains the urban area or areas, and includes all the counties within the metropolitan area as defined by the Bureau of the Census. The second circle contains all the counties contiguous to the metropolitan area. The third circle contains the counties contiguous to those in the second circle. In some instances adjustments have been made so that more perfect circles might be formed. For example, if only a small point of a county touches the metropolitan area and the bulk of it is in the outermost circle, it has been considered to be part of the third, or outermost, circle. Only in rare instances could a complete fourth circle be formed without its coinciding with an urban center outside the area concerned. In some instances, even counties in the third circle have been excluded because they are too close to an urban center other than the one selected.

The urban centers selected are those urban areas having no serious overlap of their county circles with the circles around other urban areas. However, the selected areas are sufficiently diversified, both in size and location, to be considered representative of all areas except those that are in clusters, such as are located around New York City. No urban center that is not a part of a standard metropolitan area has been selected, on the grounds that a city of less than 50,000 inhabitants probably exerts relatively little influence on housing beyond the borders of the county in which it is located.

Hypotheses about urban influence on farm housing

Urban influences on farm housing are both social and economic. They are so complex and may overlap to such an extent that their precise effect on farm housing characteristics cannot be specifically stated. For example, the proximity of urban homes with modern facilities and equipment may persuade farm families to want similar features because they see their utility and convenience in use; but unless the farm family income is adequate, they will not be able to afford them. On the other hand, because of their proximity to urban employment, these families are able to add to their incomes. Desire for housing facilities similar to those enjoyed by urban families arises not only from direct personal relations with urban families, but also as a result of the influence of advertising—in newspapers and magazines, on radio and television, by house-to-house salesmen, and similar means. The results of these constant reminders, which are heightened by the proximity of outlets for consumer goods, might be expected to have an effect that is in direct proportion to the distance of a farmhouse from the urban center.

An urban center can also exert a harmful effect on nearby farm housing. The overflow of urban population into open country not subject to zoning and other regulations sometimes leads to the growth of a rural slum fringe extending along transportation lines well beyond the boundary of the metropolitan area. The new housing in these rural fringes is either in poorly planned developments or not planned at all. Under such conditions, the farms and farm dwellings usually tend to deteriorate in quality.

As pointed out earlier,[1] some farm land in these slum areas is frequently divided into small 5- or 10-acre farms that are not sufficiently productive or desirable as home sites to warrant good housing. The shacks on such tracts of land pull down the average quality of all farm housing in the affected county.

Hypotheses drawn from the above generalizations have been set up for testing by the use of the concentric circles of counties. These hypotheses, which cover most of the items that bear on farm housing and that can be measured by statistics available in the Censuses of Agriculture, Population, and Housing, are listed below:

1. That larger proportions of the farm dwelling units in the inner circles than in the outer circles have the following facilities: (a) electric lights, (b) mechanical refrigeration, (c) piped running water, and (d) heating equipment.

2. That between 1940 and 1950, changes in housing equipment and facilities have occurred at a more rapid rate in the outer circles than in the inner circles.

3. That the proportions of farm dwelling units in good condition in 1950 and 1940 get progressively smaller as one moves from the center to the outer circles.

4. That the proportion of dwelling units built in 1940 or later decreases as the distance from the urban center increases.

5. That the closer farm dwelling units are to the urban center, the higher will be the average family income, but the lower will be the average income derived from the farm alone.

6. That the loss of farm dwelling units between 1940 and 1950 has been greater (or the increase in number of units less) near the urban center than it has been farther out.

7. That the ratio of rural nonfarm units to farm units has increased more rapidly from 1940 to 1950 in the inner circles than in the outer circles.

8. That the proportion of part-time and residential farms decreases as one moves out from the urban center.

Testing the hypotheses. Table 48 shows the results of tests, given the first two hypotheses. Percentage figures for both 1940 and 1950 are included.

Hypothesis 1. Totals for the 15 areas show that in 1950 the proportion of dwelling units with the first four facilities listed, i.e., electric lights, mechanical refrigeration, piped running water, and heating equipment have decreased successively from the first circle through the third. This is substantially true for each of the urban centers with few exceptions.

Hypothesis 2. Generally, the relative differences in proportions from circle to circle show up as being somewhat greater in 1940 than in 1950.

[1] See Chapter 2, p. 42.

The principal exceptions in this respect are Miami and Spokane where, in 1940, a larger proportion of the units in the third circle than in the second had electric lights, mechanical refrigeration, piped running water (in Miami only) and central heating (in Spokane only). The farmhouses in the third circle of counties in these two areas are apparently subject to special influences. In the third circle of Miami, for example, more than three-fourths of the houses are in Palm Beach, which is a resort area. And around Spokane the early development of electric power as a by-product of irrigation projects may account for the higher proportions of facilities in 1940 in the farmhouses of the third circle.

The percent change between 1940 and 1950 is based on a change in the number of farmhouses with the specified facilities rather than on a change in percentages. The change in the number of dwelling units with such facilities is usually relatively less than the change in proportions. This is because the total number of farm units in most areas was reduced during the decade while, during the same period, many more farmhouses were being equipped with these facilities. It is not possible to determine whether the units that disappeared from the farmhousing inventory between 1940 and 1950 were equipped with these facilities or not. In some counties the decrease in the total number of farm units was so great that there were actually fewer units with a specific item of equipment in 1950 than there had been in 1940.

In general, the percent change in proportion of farmhouses with these facilities is greater in the second circle than in the first, and greater in the third than in the second. This suggests that because the dwellings in the close-in counties were better equipped in 1940 than units in the outer counties, there was less opportunity for marked increases. The more remote counties were catching up, although in only two or three instances did the third circle of counties contain a greater proportion of farm dwellings equipped with these facilities than did the second circle.[2]

This rapid rate of change in the outer counties is rather a measure of the backwardness of the outer counties than an indication that direct urban influence has been greatest in these counties. The fact that the improvements reached the outer counties at a later date points to the gradual influence of urban centers, at least as a major contributing factor.

Hypothesis 3. In table 49 the first two columns show the percentages of farm dwelling units with "all plumbing facilities" and those that were "not dilapidated" in 1950 or were "not needing major repairs" in 1940. Since there were some differences between the two censuses in the terms used to define "condition," small differences in the proportions are not significant.[3] It is the opinion of most housing economists that interpretation of "dilapidation" resulted in a smaller number of dwelling units being

---

[2] Since the farm dwelling units equipped with all the facilities under discussion, except piped running water, are taken from sample areas only, very small differences in proportions may not be significant.

[3] See glossary, p. 187.

TABLE 48.—PERCENT OF DWELLING UNITS WITH SPECIFIED EQUIPMENT, BY CONCENTRIC CIRCLES OF COUNTIES AROUND SELECTED URBAN CENTERS: 1950 AND 1940

Urban center and circle	Electric lighting			Mechanical refrigeration			Piped running water			Central heating		
	1950	1940	Percent change, 1940 to 1950[1]	1950	1940	Percent change, 1940 to 1950[1]	1950	1940	Percent change, 1940 to 1950[1]	1950	1940	Percent change, 1940 to 1950[1]
Total of 15 areas:												
First circle	92	58	+19	73	31	+75	67	37	+37	24	16	+18
Second circle	81	32	+108	60	13	+276	45	18	+102	14	7	+57
Third circle	74	22	+108	54	10	+341	37	13	+122	10	5	+68
Atlanta, Ga.:												
First circle	89	44	+38	61	19	+122	51	14	+145	7	3	+86
Second circle	81	18	+237	46	6	+483	28	3	+599	2	⋮	+280
Third circle	76	8	+226	42	7	+347	27	4	+428	2	⋮	+299
Dallas–Fort Worth, Texas:												
First circle	94	51	+15	76	24	+98	70	38	+17	2	(1)	+166
Second circle	78	24	+132	57	10	+296	46	21	+61	1	(1)	+216
Third circle	76	17	+206	57	8	+390	41	16	+71	2	(1)	+262
Denver, Colo.:												
First circle	92	59	+8	70	20	+146	70	43	+12	28	18	+10
Second circle	84	37	+101	63	14	+306	52	22	+106	14	8	+57
Third circle	71	27	+115	57	9	+448	56	21	+111	16	7	+94
Houston—Galveston—Beaumont—Port Arthur, Texas:												
First circle	91	52	–28	68	36	–22	76	45	–29	7	1	+374
Second circle	74	16	+208	53	15	+133	45	16	+81	2	(1)	+252
Third circle	63	8	+428	45	7	+333	35	12	+104	1	(1)	+311
Louisville, Ky.:												
First circle	89	57	+32	74	32	+95	47	22	+82	26	18	+23
Second circle	80	27	+169	61	11	+395	24	5	+308	9	3	+147
Third circle	78	25	+180	58	10	+409	23	5	+328	9	3	+187
Miami, Fla.:												
First circle	89	59	+32	67	34	+71	89	51	+52	1	2	–49
Second circle	90	18	+292	45	12	+189	73	17	+230	1	⋮	+500
Third circle	78	32	+146	35	13	+179	48	24	+102	1	⋮	+2,400
Minneapolis–St. Paul, Minn.:												
First circle	90	63	+3	75	26	+112	62	33	+35	39	34	–17
Second circle	83	36	+110	69	11	+465	49	20	+118	32	23	+28
Third circle	84	35	+123	65	10	+523	45	15	+172	29	22	+31

[1] Based on the change in number of units.

TABLE 48.—PERCENT OF DWELLING UNITS WITH SPECIFIED EQUIPMENT, BY CONCENTRIC CIRCLES OF COUNTIES AROUND SELECTED URBAN CENTERS: 1950 AND 1940—Cont.

Urban center and circle	Electric lighting			Mechanical refrigeration			Piped running water			Central heating		
	1950	1940	Percent change, 1940 to 1950[1]	1950	1940	Percent change, 1940 to 1950[1]	1950	1940	Percent change, 1940 to 1950[1]	1950	1940	Percent change, 1940 to 1950[1]
Nashville, Tenn.:												
First circle	93	55	+23	74	34	+58	50	23	+59	17	9	+32
Second circle	76	23	+181	53	12	+278	24	7	-216	3	1	+129
Third circle	69	17	+242	50	10	+319	20	5	+247	3	1	+200
Oklahoma City, Okla.:												
First circle	76	34	+57	58	22	+86	53	25	+52	8	2	+164
Second circle	65	20	+137	54	13	+195	35	10	+150	5	1	+235
Third circle	64	15	+188	54	10	+247	31	9	+129	5	1	+193
Portland, Oreg.:												
First circle	93	79	+15	69	28	+144	82	58	+38	16	12	+29
Second circle	93	72	+20	63	21	+172	78	55	+32	12	7	+52
Third circle	92	47	+96	60	16	+267	72	51	+41	8	6	+36
Richmond, Va:												
First circle	86	51	+27	72	39	+41	60	32	+43	16	9	+31
Second circle	68	21	+160	50	14	+188	35	11	+152	7	3	+120
Third circle	61	15	+208	44	10	+229	25	7	+166	3	1	+112
Rochester, N. Y.:												
First circle	97	90	-1	85	43	+81	83	49	+55	71	58	+11
Second circle	92	70	+16	74	24	+176	65	27	+115	52	35	+32
Third circle	88	44	+80	62	14	+290	63	33	+72	27	16	+52
St. Louis, Mo.:												
First circle	98	46	+66	85	26	+155	59	22	+102	45	24	+42
Second circle	81	26	+187	65	10	+496	36	7	+361	19	8	+114
Third circle	70	18	+247	55	7	+585	27	5	+415	12	4	+153
Spokane, Wash.:												
First circle	99	57	+4	76	22	+109	79	50	-4	19	14	-19
Second circle	85	37	+83	64	16	+216	73	46	+27	14	6	+91
Third circle	85	46	+58	59	23	+117	68	44	+31	14	7	+85
Washington, D. C.:												
First circle	86	54	+34	71	38	+56	62	37	+40	32	24	+11
Second circle	81	36	+96	65	21	+174	54	25	+86	19	11	+55
Third circle	76	33	+99	58	17	+188	44	20	+97	15	10	+30

[1] Based on the change in number of units.

Source: Derived from 1950 Census of Housing, Vol. I, General Characteristics, Parts 2 to 6, table 33, and 1940 Census of Housing, Vol. II, General Characteristics, Parts 2 to 5, tables 22 and 23.

TABLE **49.**—PERCENT OF DWELLING UNITS WITH SPECIFIED HOUSING CHARACTERISTICS, 1950 AND 1940, AND MEDIAN FAMILY INCOME AND AVERAGE VALUE OF FARM PRODUCTS SOLD, 1949, BY CONCENTRIC CIRCLES OF COUNTIES AROUND SELECTED URBAN CENTERS

Urban center and circle	Percent of dwelling units--			Median income of farm families[2] (dollars)	Average value of farm products sold, 1949 (dollars)
	Not dilapidated, with all plumbing facilities		Built 1940 or later		
	1950	1940[1]			
Total of 10 areas:					
First circle........................	(3)	(3)	(3)	3,057	4,187
Second circle.......................	(3)	(3)	(3)	1,761	4,310
Third circle........................	(3)	(3)	(3)	1,564	3,462
Total of 15 areas:					
First circle........................	43	22	21	(4)	(4)
Second circle.......................	23	9	12	(4)	(4)
Third circle........................	17	5	14	(4)	(4)
Atlanta, Ga.:					
First circle........................	25	9	21	1,731	1,331
Second circle.......................	8	2	14	893	1,586
Third circle........................	9	2	16	964	1,500
Dallas-Fort Worth, Texas:					
First circle........................	41	20	29	2,385	3,336
Second circle.......................	16	4	14	1,708	3,918
Third circle........................	12	3	16	1,479	3,039
Denver, Colo.:					
First circle........................	46	24	22	3,103	8,131
Second circle.......................	28	10	10	2,522	13,277
Third circle........................	33	10	13	2,513	9,858
Houston--Galveston--Beaumont-Port Arthur, Texas:					
First circle........................	47	25	33	2,566	4,376
Second circle.......................	21	7	25	1,649	3,944
Third circle........................	11	3	24	1,331	2,803
Louisville, Ky.:					
First circle........................	27	17	20	(4)	(4)
Second circle.......................	10	3	12	(4)	(4)
Third circle........................	10	3	12	(4)	(4)
Miami, Fla.:					
First circle........................	56	38	46	3,118	14,756
Second circle.......................	43	12	50	2,192	28,592
Third circle........................	25	12	35	1,608	23,767
Minneapolis-St. Paul, Minn.:					
First circle........................	38	21	13	2,727	4,827
Second circle.......................	26	10	5	2,162	4,769
Third circle........................	22	7	7	2,148	4,693
Nashville, Tenn.:					
First circle........................	30	16	20	2,341	1,765
Second circle.......................	11	4	13	1,283	2,030
Third circle........................	7	2	14	1,141	1,751
Oklahoma City, Okla.:					
First circle........................	37	17	22	2,207	2,027
Second circle.......................	18	5	11	1,742	2,988
Third circle........................	15	4	13	1,666	3,196
Portland, Oreg.:					
First circle........................	58	31	25	(4)	(4)
Second circle.......................	52	26	22	(4)	(4)
Third circle........................	48	23	22	(4)	(4)
Richmond, Va.:					
First circle........................	39	23	14	(4)	(4)
Second circle.......................	19	8	14	(4)	(4)
Third circle........................	13	5	15	(4)	(4)
Rochester, N. Y.:					
First circle........................	62	34	7	3,181	5,279
Second circle.......................	39	16	3	2,374	5,337
Third circle........................	36	15	4	2,203	3,932
St. Louis, Mo.:					
First circle........................	34	14	16	2,824	4,347
Second circle.......................	16	4	10	2,210	4,281
Third circle........................	11	3	11	1,896	3,102

See footnotes at end of table.

TABLE **49.**—PERCENT OF DWELLING UNITS WITH SPECIFIED HOUSING CHARACTERISTICS, 1950 AND 1940, AND MEDIAN FAMILY INCOME AND AVERAGE VALUE OF FARM PRODUCTS SOLD, 1949, BY CONCENTRIC CIRCLES OF COUNTIES AROUND SELECTED URBAN CENTERS—Cont.

| Urban center and circle | Percent of dwelling units— | | | Median income of farm families[2] (dollars) | Average value of farm products sold, 1949 (dollars) |
| | Not dilapidated, with all plumbing facilities | | Built 1940 or later | | |
	1950	1940[1]			
Spokane, Wash.:					
First circle......................	54	26	14	(⁴)	(⁴)
Second circle.....................	48	18	13	(⁴)	(⁴)
Third circle......................	42	19	22	(⁴)	(⁴)
Washington, D. C.:					
First circle......................	45	27	21	(⁴)	(⁴)
Second circle.....................	32	15	11	(⁴)	(⁴)
Third circle......................	27	13	11	(⁴)	(⁴)

[1] The 1950 and 1940 data on condition are not entirely comparable; see glossary for explanation of differences.
[2] Based on number of rural-farm families of 2 persons or more.
[3] Totals included in the 15-area totals.
[4] Income and value of products sold not tabulated for these areas.

Source: Derived from *1950 Census of Housing*, Vol. I, *General Characteristics*, Parts 2 to 8, tables 32 and 33; *1940 Census of Housing*, Vol. II, *General Characteristics*, Parts 2 to 5, table 22; *1950 Census of Population*, unpublished data; and *1950 Census of Agriculture*, Vol. I, *Counties and State Economic Areas*, county table 7.

classified as poor housing than the interpretation of the 1940 term "needing major repairs." Nevertheless, since the figures for both censuses show that in 1940 and 1950 the major portion of farm housing in poor condition also lacked running water, there is basis for believing that the change in definition has little effect on the percentages shown in table 49.

In all areas, each census shows a greater difference between the first and second circles than between the second and third. Thus, the third hypothesis—that the proportion of farm dwelling units in good condition decreases as one moves away from the urban center—is not precisely borne out. The effect of the proximity of an urban center on the condition of farm housing does not seem to be particularly important beyond the first circle of counties. On the other hand, it is possible that there is some urban influence; this is indicated by the fact that whenever the proportion of good-quality units is high in the first circle, the proportions in the other circles of that area are also likely to be relatively high.

Hypothesis 4. Figures showing the proportions of farmhouses built since 1940 are usually significantly different only between the first and second circles. The second and third circles most often show similar proportions of new dwelling units.

Hypothesis 5. Because they require extensive computation, the last two items in table 49—median income of farm families and average value of farm products sold, 1949—have been computed for only 10 of the areas. On this basis, the hypothesis that the closer farm dwelling units are to an urban center, the higher will be the average family income, but the lower will be the average income derived from the farm alone, proves to be only partially correct. The table shows that the closer the farm units were to the urban center, the higher was the family income; but average farm income, as measured by value of products sold in 1949, was not always lower in the inner circles than in the outer ones. In seven of the ten areas, the average value of products sold from farms in the innermost circle was lower than that from farms in the second circle. But only in one area was the value in the second circle lower than the value in the third. In view of this, it may be assumed that the influence of the urban area did not adversely affect farm production beyond the first circle of counties. To demonstrate beyond doubt that there is a decrease in farm production on farms close to an urban area (where members of a farm family are likely to have nonfarm sources of income) it would probably be necessary to use a unit smaller than a county.

While differences from circle to circle in median family income were not pronounced, the expected relationships between circles were present in each of the ten areas. Differences in median family income were more significant between the first and second circles than between the second and third, as were differences of most of the characteristics being studied.

Hypothesis 6. This pattern is repeated when the test is applied to the hypothesis that farm dwelling units near urban centers have disappeared from the inventory more rapidly than those located farther out.[4] Table 50 shows a greater contrast in percent loss between the first and second circles than between the second and third. Only in the Portland, Rochester, and Miami areas did the second circle of counties lose more farmhouses than the first. Explanations for this departure from the normal pattern must be confined to speculation without more data than are available. All three cities expanded into adjacent areas during the 1940–50 decade and farms might therefore quite naturally have disappeared. It is possible that inner-circle farms that were large in 1940 were later split into smaller farms while second-circle small farms were merged into large farms. Statistics on size of farms[5] seem to support this theory. Disappearance of farms in the third circle may have resulted from a composite of many factors, such as the combination of small farms into larger ones, the abandonment of farms in submarginal farming areas, the growth of small urban areas, and the development of new sources of nonfarm income leading to a cessation of farm operations. Consequently, it is not surprising to find that the decrease in the number of farms in the third circle frequently exceeded that in the second circle, or differed little from it.

Hypothesis 7. Whenever there is a loss of rural-farm dwelling units, an increase in the number of rural-nonfarm units is to be expected because many of the farm units are lost by a change in use from farm to nonfarm. In addition, the overflow of an expanding urban area results in the building of many new nonfarm units in what was originally a predominantly farm area. In other words, the ratio of rural-nonfarm units to farm units

---

[4] See Chapter 1, pp. 4 and 5.
[5] *1950 Census of Agriculture*, Vol. 1, *Counties and State Economic Areas*, Parts 18 and 32.

increases faster close to a large urban center than it does at a distance from it. The column in table 50 showing the percent change in rural-nonfarm units for each circle attempts to demonstrate this point. But here again it has been found that the hypothesis is not supported by simple comparison, in this case, comparison of the decrease in farm units with the increase in nonfarm units.

TABLE 50.—PERCENT CHANGE IN NUMBERS OF RURAL-FARM AND RURAL-NONFARM DWELLING UNITS, 1940 TO 1950, AND PERCENT NONCOMMERCIAL FARMS, BY CONCENTRIC CIRCLES OF COUNTIES AROUND SELECTED URBAN CENTERS

Urban center and circle	Percent change in number of rural dwelling units, 1940 to 1950		Percent non-commercial farms	Urban center and circle	Percent change in number of rural dwelling units, 1940 to 1950		Percent non-commercial farms
	Farm	Nonfarm			Farm	Nonfarm	
Total of 15 areas:				Nashville, Tenn.:			
First circle........	-25	-3	47	First circle........	-27	-27	66
Second circle........	-17	+41	31	Second circle.......	-15	+67	32
Third circle........	-20	+40	30	Third circle........	-18	+74	30
Atlanta, Ga.:				Oklahoma City, Okla.:			
First circle........	-31	+13	70	First circle........	-29	+109	61
Second circle........	-23	+96	50	Second circle.......	-29	+35	33
Third circle........	-22	+71	49	Third circle........	-34	+23	28
Dallas-Fort Worth, Texas:				Portland, Oreg.:			
First circle........	-38	+2	59	First circle........	-3	+17	52
Second circle........	-28	+60	28	Second circle.......	-7	+71	43
Third circle........	-31	+33	29	Third circle........	-1	+70	42
Denver, Colo.:				Richmond, Va.:			
First circle........	-31	(¹)	36	First circle........	-25	-2	75
Second circle........	-12	+21	10	Second circle.......	-19	+57	51
Third circle........	-19	+20	13	Third circle........	-23	+83	39
Houston--Galveston--Beau-mont-Port Arthur, Texas:				Rochester, N. Y.:			
First circle........	-59	-8	60	First circle........	-9	-6	29
Second circle........	-35	+76	53	Second circle.......	-12	+31	27
Third circle........	-33	+28	45	Third circle........	-10	+36	30
Louisville, Ky.:				St. Louis, Mo.:			
First circle........	-15	+16	51	First circle........	-23	-39	27
Second circle........	-10	+42	24	Second circle.......	-8	+25	23
Third circle........	-11	+52	31	Third circle........	-12	+22	30
Miami, Fla.:				Spokane, Wash.:			
First circle........	-13	-40	38	First circle........	-40	+28	41
Second circle........	-23	+103	24	Second circle.......	-22	+27	30
Third circle........	+1	+50	40	Third circle........	-16	+26	32
Minneapolis-St. Paul, Minn.:				Washington, D. C.:			
First circle........	-28	+65	29	First circle........	-17	-9	49
Second circle........	-9	+33	11	Second circle.......	-13	+62	34
Third circle........	-6	+30	9	Third circle........	-13	+72	38

¹ Less than 0.5 percent.

Source: *1950 Census of Housing,* Vol. I, *General Characteristics,* Parts 2 to 6, tables 32 and 33; *1940 Census of Housing,* Vol. II, *General Characteristics,* Parts 2 to 5, table 22; and *1950 Census of Agriculture,* Vol. I, *Counties and State Economic Areas,* county table 7.

In some instances, the redefinition of what constitutes urban territory may account for a part of this.[6] For example, the number of rural-nonfarm units in the first circle decreased in eight of the areas. Most of these houses may not have gone out of existence; they were simply reclassified as "urban." In each of these eight circles a much greater increase in the

[6] The classification of housing (and population) in built-up areas around cities and in unincorporated areas with 2,500 inhabitants or more was changed in 1950 from "rural" to "urban." See glossary, p. 190, for more detail.

total number of urban units took place than can be accounted for by new construction or new conversions. No statistics are available from the Housing Census to determine the effect of the change in definition of urban territory, though some evidence of its effect on housing statistics may be obtained by examining the results of the population census. In Dade County (Miami), for example, the urban population was 23 percent greater in 1950 by the new definition than by the old. The number of urban dwelling units outside of Miami and Miami Beach, the largest cities in the area and those with the most stable boundaries, increased during the same period by about 950 percent. It is therefore quite understandable that rural-nonfarm units should have decreased 40 percent.

A similar situation prevailed in all the areas where there was either (a) a decrease in rural nonfarm units in the first circle or (b) an increase that was similar to or less than that in the second circle. Only two areas, Minneapolis-St. Paul and Oklahoma City, differed. In these two areas proportionally more of the urban expansion was within the urban limits as defined in 1940. The balance of the increase in nonfarm dwelling units in the metropolitan area, or first circle, was reflected therefore in relatively large increases in the number of rural nonfarm dwelling units. From an examination of the foregoing, it is apparent that the original hypothesis (7) does not allow for the effect of substantial urban growth in the first circle and for the change in definitions of what constitutes an urban area. The hypothesis should be restated in these terms: The ratio of total nonfarm units (both urban and rural nonfarm) to farm units increased more rapidly from 1940 to 1950 in the inner circles than in the outer circles.

Hypothesis 8. Computations for the final hypothesis—that more of the farms near an urban center than away from it are noncommercial— demonstrate that it is correct in all the areas selected, so far as the first and second circles are concerned. In half of the areas in 1950 the third circle contained slightly smaller proportions of these part-time and residential farms than the second circle. Since these differences were small and since in the other areas there were somewhat greater proportions of noncommercial farms in the third circle than in the second, it is doubtful whether the urban effects on farms of this type extend beyond the second circle of counties. There may be exceptions when the land in all three circles is potentially of approximately equal productive capacity.[7] This is so, for example, in the counties around Minneapolis-St. Paul or Richmond, Virginia.

Factors in urban influence

The results of the analysis of the extent of urban influence on the characteristics of farm housing clearly are not conclusive. Nevertheless,

---

[7] A study of Schuyler County, New York, undertaken in 1948, tended to confirm the theory that people living on poor agricultural lands are more likely to take an industrial job than those living on better land. See Leonard P. Adams and Thomas W. Mackesey, *Commuting Patterns of Industrial Workers,* Research Publication No. 1, Housing Research Center, Cornell University, Ithaca, 1955, p. 38.

they do serve to emphasize the economic and social factors associated with proximity to urban areas. Some consideration of what these factors are may help explain the differences from circle to circle observed in tables 48 to 50.

General economic factors. There appear to be three economic factors worthy of consideration: (1) off-farm employment opportunities, (2) marketing advantages, and (3) land values.

There are obviously greater opportunities for off-farm employment in counties close to a large urban center than there are in more distant counties. These opportunities may vary with general employment conditions, but throughout the 1940–50 decade the demand for labor in most urban centers was generally greater than the supply. The farmer, or members of his family, who wanted to supplement the farm income, consequently were in an advantageous position if they lived within commuting distance of an urban center. The close-in farmer had greater diversity of choice than the farmer in a more rural county and thus would be more likely to find employment suited to his ability. No doubt, some commuting was possible from distant counties. Adams and Mackesey found in their survey of five New York areas in 1951 that an average of 9 percent of the long-distant commuters, i.e., those driving over 20 miles to their work, were also farm operators. The primary reason for this low percentage undoubtedly is the time and cost of such travel. This conclusion is borne out by the findings of these authorities that the percentage of long-distance commuters was higher where the head of the household worked in a small community and lower where he worked in a large community.[8]

The higher income near urban areas may be due to nonfarm work. Table 49 shows fairly constant differences from circle to circle in income levels in all the areas studied. But it should be remembered that the total effect of income added by nonfarm jobs may not be fully reflected. It has already been pointed out that farm family income may have been under-reported in 1950.[9] The greater opportunity for additional income enjoyed by farm families near an urban center might also show up in higher percentages of houses with modern equipment. Furthermore, to the extent that high off-farm income encouraged the cessation of farming operations, dwelling units on this land probably would have been reported as "nonfarm" and thus would have contributed to the decrease in farm units.

With rapid transportation, the marketing advantage of being close to an urban area is of less importance today than it used to be. Therefore, this factor can be dismissed, generally, as one unlikely to increase the income of large numbers of families. But looking at the farmer as a consumer, the marketing factor may be quite important. Urban producers and distributors of household equipment may well concentrate on the close-in market before turning to the more distant counties. This may be one

---

[8] Adams and Mackesey, *op. cit.*, pp. 61, 111.

[9] See Chapter 1, p. 11.

reason why greater percentages of farm houses in the inner circles than in the outer ones are modern and well equipped.

In the concentric circle analysis the third economic factor, land values, probably is significant only for areas smaller than counties. Urban growth along transportation lines brings about a more intensive use of land and, thereby, higher values as well. These changes in use involve only relatively small areas and are thus hidden in county statistics.

Social factors. The social factors are somewhat less clear cut than the economic factors. Three seem to be most obvious: (1) urban social values, (2) desire to acquire greater home comforts, which may also be symbols of status, and (3) migration from urban areas to suburban areas. They are to some extent interdependent, and they also depend upon economic factors.

Urban social values are related to standards of housing quality and equipment. We assume that farm families in the inner circles have greater opportunity for contact with their nonfarm and urban neighbors. If their nonfarm neighbors live in houses of high quality, the farm families will eventually adopt this standard as their own. If and when family income is sufficient, they will probably improve their own houses to meet this standard. Where the rural fringes around an urban area are settled by rootless, low-income urban families, the effects on neighboring farm housing will be debatable.

Whenever the standards of housing in an area are raised to a higher level, the impetus is likely to come from the families' desire to acquire symbols of status in the form of greater home comforts. The example of neighboring families or nearby families in the same social stratum cannot help but lead to a certain amount of emulation. In this connection, the increasing migration of urban families to suburban and rural areas exerts a far-reaching influence. It can be assumed that the migrating families bring new housing values with them. If they are not low-income migrants, they generally move into new, modern houses, equipped with the latest facilities. New streets and roads are built. The changes demanded by the newcomers may create conflicts for a time, but eventually their standards of what is necessary in the way of community facilities prevail. As the area fills up, many of the farmhouses disappear and the urban influences spread still farther. As farm families associate with the newcomers in community activities, the farm family standards probably change. The data in table 48 suggests that the first of these changes involves the installation of equipment and facilities for electricity and running water. But, to some extent, the increase in use of electricity may be related to the fact that, in general, the more dense the settlement, the lower is the cost of electric power. In such situations it is difficult to separate the social from the economic factors affecting changes in farm housing characteristics.

CHAPTER 6

THE HOUSING OF NONWHITE FARM FAMILIES

Approximately 12 percent of the 5,660,000 farmhouses in the United States—a total of 663,800 units—were occupied by nonwhite farm families in 1950. While this group represents a relatively low proportion of the Nation's farm housing, its characteristics have an important bearing on the average standards of the farm housing for the country as a whole.

It is generally acknowledged that the housing of the nonwhite population, which includes Indians and Orientals as well as Negroes, is poorer in condition, more crowded, and served with fewer modern facilities and equipment than is the housing occupied by white families throughout the Nation. Before we analyze the data below in support of this statement, it may be well to look into some of the reasons for these conditions.

Obviously, one of the primary reasons for poor-quality housing is the income levels of nonwhite families, which are generally lower than those of white families. Another important reason is the high percentage of nonwhite families occupying tenant houses; and it is usually the case, although there are some exceptions, that tenant housing does not meet the standards of housing occupied by owners.

Beyond these two basic reasons for the condition of housing of nonwhite farm families, there are several others applicable to farm housing in general and to housing of nonwhite farm families in particular. One of these is that much of this farm housing is located in remote areas where facilities like running water, usually provided by municipalities, are not available. Because a farmhouse is located in a rural area and because the house occupied by a nonwhite family is frequently a tenant house, the assistance of a contractor in the construction or remodeling of such a house is not usually sought, nor is it often available. Such a farmhouse is usually constructed to meet only minimal needs for shelter, and county codes or regulations seldom affect the type of construction. The relatively high degree of mobility among nonwhite families also discourages tenants from remodeling or rehabilitation of their houses, even if materials are provided by the landlord.[1]

The impoverished families, whether white or nonwhite, living in the farming regions of the Nation might be compared with their counterparts in the slum areas of our cities. In both instances incomes are low and

---

[1] See Chapter 1, p. 24.

there is little incentive to repair or rehabilitate the family house. But it should be possible to attack the slum problems of urban areas more effectively because the houses are concentrated within a limited area. In contrast, "slum" farmhouses are widely scattered over broad areas. Furthermore, most of the slum clearance and urban redevelopment in our cities is encouraged by government participation and assistance. It is seldom that condemnation of a city dwelling drastically affects the means of livelihood of its occupants. But the farmhouse is part of a farm, and it is difficult, if not impossible, to place an economic value on a farmhouse apart from the value of the other structures and of the farm land.

Characteristics of Nonwhite Family Farm Housing

Although in 1950 almost two of every three of the farmhouses in the Nation were occupied by their owners, only one of every three farmhouses occupied by nonwhites was owner occupied. This points up one of the basic differences between farm housing for whites and nonwhites mentioned on p. 27: among the nonwhite families proportionately more of the farmhouses are renter occupied than among the white families. The comparisons are shown in table 51.

TABLE **51.**—Occupancy Characteristics of All Occupied Dwelling Units, 1950, and of Nonwhite-Occupied Dwelling Units, 1950 and 1940

Characteristic	All occupied units, 1950	Nonwhite-occupied units	
		1950	1940
Number.................................	5,659,570	663,800	1,004,600
Percent by tenure....................	100.0	100.0	100.0
Owner..................................	65.4	33.1	23.1
Renter and rent free..................	34.6	66.9	76.9
Percent by number of persons in household.........................	100.0	100.0	100.0
1 person..............................	4.7	5.4	6.3
2 persons.............................	23.7	19.1	19.3
3 persons.............................	20.3	15.0	16.7
4 persons.............................	18.2	13.0	14.0
5 persons.............................	12.8	11.0	11.4
6 persons or more.....................	20.3	36.5	32.3
Median number of persons in household......	3.6	4.3	4.1
Percent by type of household.........	100.0	100.0	(1)
Husband-wife families, no nonrelatives.....	82.1	77.7	...
2 persons.............................	19.8	15.6	...
3 persons.............................	17.2	11.8	...
4 persons.............................	16.0	10.4	...
5 persons or more.....................	29.1	39.9	...
Other family groups, no nonrelatives.......	8.9	12.6	...
One-person households.....................	4.7	5.4	...
Households with nonrelatives..............	4.3	4.3	...
Percent by income in 1949.............	100.0	100.0	(1)
Under $1,000..............................	32.9	64.6	...
$1,000 to $1,999..........................	22.5	21.8	...
$2,000 to $2,999..........................	16.2	6.0	...
$3,000 to $3,999..........................	9.9	1.8	...
$4,000 and over...........................	13.8	1.4	...
Income not reported.......................	4.7	4.4	...

[1] Data not available.

Source: *1950 Census of Housing*, Vol. III, *Farm Housing Characteristics*, tables 1 to 4, and *1940 Census of Housing*, Vol. II, *General Characteristics*, table 9.

Nonwhite farm households are generally larger than those of whites. For example, in 1950 nonwhite households had a median of 4.3 persons, an increase from 4.1 in 1940. The 1950 median size of household for all farm families, including nonwhites, was only 3.6 persons. More than one out of every three nonwhite households had a total of 6 persons or more in 1950; the comparable ratio for all farm households is one out of every five.

Nonwhite households are generally of the same types as other farm households in the Nation; that is, they usually consist of husband, wife, and children in a household without nonrelatives. Incidentally, percentages of households including some nonrelatives in 1950 were the same for both nonwhite farm families and all farm families in the Nation.

The housing occupied by nonwhite farmers is generally not as old as other farm housing throughout the Nation. In fact, 62 percent of the houses occupied by this population group were built in 1920 or later. The comparable percentage for all farmhouses in the Nation is only 46 percent.

Almost two of every three nonwhite families had money income of less than $1,000 in 1949, but only one in three of all farm families had an income as low as this. This is probably the most important single factor affecting the kind of housing occupied by nonwhite farm families. The low income level and rate of tenancy account for the conspicuously small size of units generally occupied by nonwhite households. It can be seen from the data in table 52 that in 1950 more than one out of every three of these houses had 3 rooms or less and one of three had only 4 rooms. Thus, only one out of every three of the farmhouses occupied by nonwhites in 1950 had 5 rooms or more. On the other hand, the situation in 1950 shows some improvement over that of 1940, when approximately 54 percent of the farmhouses occupied by nonwhites had 3 rooms or less, and another 28 percent had only 4 rooms.

The poor quality of farm housing occupied by nonwhite households is widely recognized. In 1950 approximately 46 percent of the houses occupied by nonwhites were considered to be dilapidated. In the Nation as a whole, only 18 percent of the farmhouses were classified as dilapidated. While the data for 1950 and 1940 on the quality of housing are not strictly comparable,[2] it is quite evident that there had been little, if any, improvement since 1940 in the condition of farm houses occupied by nonwhite families.

Houses occupied by nonwhite farm families are almost entirely lacking in modern facilities. In 1950, approximately 93 percent of them were without running water, 97 percent were without private toilet, and 96 percent were without bathtub or shower—far higher proportions than are shown for farmhouses in general. (See table 53.)

---

[2] For 1940 and 1950 definitions of "condition," see glossary, p. 187.

TABLE **52.**—PHYSICAL CHARACTERISTICS OF ALL OCCUPIED DWELLING UNITS, 1950, AND OF
NONWHITE-OCCUPIED DWELLING UNITS, 1950 AND 1940

Characteristic	All occupied units, 1950	Nonwhite-occupied units	
		1950	1940
Number....................................	5,659,570	663,800	1,004,600
Percent by year built................	100.0	100.0	(1)
1920 or later.............................	46.3	62.0	...
1919 or earlier...........................	53.7	38.0	...
Percent by rooms.....................	100.0	100.0	100.0
1 to 3 rooms.............................	15.5	36.5	54.5
4 rooms..................................	21.0	33.0	28.0
5 rooms..................................	19.1	15.5	9.7
6 rooms or more.........................	44.4	15.0	7.7
Median number of rooms.....................	...	3.9	3.3
Percent by condition[2]................	100.0	100.0	100.0
Not dilapidated...........................	82.5	53.7	56.3
Dilapidated...............................	17.5	46.3	43.7

[1] Data not available.
[2] The 1950 and 1940 data on condition are not entirely comparable; see glossary for explanation of differences.

Source: *1950 Census of Housing*, Vol. III, *Farm Housing Characteristics*, tables 1 to 4; and *1940 Census of Housing*, Vol. II, *General Characteristics*, Part 1, U. S. Summary, tables 6c and 8e.

TABLE **53.**—FACILITIES AND EQUIPMENT OF ALL OCCUPIED DWELLING UNITS, 1950, AND OF
NONWHITE-OCCUPIED DWELLING UNITS, 1950 AND 1940

Characteristic	All occupied units, 1950	Nonwhite-occupied units	
		1950	1940
Number....................................	5,659,570	663,800	1,004,600
Percent by water supply..............	100.0	100.0	100.0
With running water......................	44.1	7.1	1.9
Without running water...................	55.9	92.9	98.1
Percent by toilet facilities.........	100.0	100.0	100.0
With private toilet......................	28.3	2.6	0.7
Without private toilet...................	71.7	97.4	99.3
Percent by bathing facilities........	100.0	100.0	100.0
With private bath........................	30.1	3.7	0.6
Without private bath.....................	69.9	96.3	99.4

Source: *1950 Census of Housing*, Vol. III, *Farm Housing Characteristics*, tables 2 and 4; and *1940 Census of Housing*, Vol. II, *General Characteristics*, Part 1, U. S. Summary, table 6c.

Characteristics of housing in the selected subregions

The data given so far have dealt with housing for nonwhite families in
the Nation as a whole. Not all of this farm housing is as poor as the national
picture represents. It varies considerably, especially between the deep
South, where Negroes predominate, the West Coast, where Orientals predominate, and the Indian areas in the Mountain States.

Five economic subregions are selected for analysis here, not necessarily
because they are typical, but because they show the variations in the housing
of nonwhite farm families in the Nation in 1950. They are economic subregion 21 (with some counties in Virginia and North Carolina) in the East
and Gulf Coast Miscellaneous Region, economic subregion 24 (with some
counties in North Carolina) in the Tobacco Region, economic subregion 57
(with some counties in Alabama and Mississippi) in the Cotton Belt,

economic subregion 109 (with some counties in Colorado, Idaho, Montana, New Mexico, Washington, and Wyoming) in the Upland Grazing Region, and economic subregion 116 (with some counties in California) in the West Coast Miscellaneous Region.

Physical characteristics.   The dwelling units of nonwhite families in the subregions selected from the East and Gulf Coast and Tobacco Regions are generally older than those located in subregions selected from the Cotton Belt and the West Coast Miscellaneous Region (table 54).   Nearly all of the housing occupied by nonwhite families in the Upland Grazing Region was built after 1920, and much of it, after 1940.

TABLE **54.**—PHYSICAL CHARACTERISTICS OF DWELLING UNITS OF NONWHITE HOUSEHOLDS, FOR SELECTED ECONOMIC SUBREGIONS: 1950

Characteristic	Subregion 21	Subregion 24	Subregion 57	Subregion 109	Subregion 116
Number of occupied units.............	16,770	23,870	36,200	3,710	4,090
Percent by year built............	100.0	100.0	100.0	100.0	100.0
1920 or later......................	48.4	47.9	65.5	86.0	67.3
1919 or earlier......................	51.6	52.1	34.5	14.0	32.7
Percent by rooms.................	100.0	100.0	100.0	100.0	100.0
1 to 3 rooms.........................	30.3	20.0	57.6	85.3	47.4
4 rooms.............................	27.3	36.9	27.5	6.7	13.2
5 rooms.............................	8.1	21.1	9.7	4.0	22.7
6 rooms or more.....................	34.3	22.0	5.2	4.0	16.7
Median number of rooms..............	4.2	4.3	3.3	2.3	3.7
Percent by condition[1]............	100.0	100.0	100.0	100.0	100.0
Not dilapidated.....................	62.7	62.0	42.8	73.6	66.8
Dilapidated.........................	37.3	38.0	57.2	26.4	33.2

[1] The 1950 and 1940 data on condition are not entirely comparable; see glossary for explanation of differences.

Source: *1950 Census of Housing*, Vol. III, *Farm Housing Characteristics*, subregion tables 3 and 4.

Probably because they are older, the houses in the first group of subregions, on the whole are somewhat larger than houses of nonwhites elsewhere.   In 1950 these farmhouses in the subregions of the East and Gulf Coast Miscellaneous Region and the Tobacco Region had a median of 4.2 rooms and 4.3 rooms, respectively.   Nonwhite households in the subregions of the Cotton Belt and West Coast Miscellaneous Region, on the other hand, lived in farmhouses which had a median of only 3.3 rooms and 3.7 rooms, respectively.   The median for the subregion in the Upland Grazing Region was only 1.9.   The most significant difference in the distributions upon which these medians are based is the difference in the proportions of farmhouses of 3 rooms or less: the proportions range from 20 percent in the subregion of the Tobacco Region to 82 percent in the subregion of the Upland Grazing Region.   In a later section it will be shown that these small units were of both recent origin and poor quality.

A much higher percentage of farmhouses of nonwhite families in subregion 57 in the Cotton Belt than in the other subregions of the selected group were dilapidated in 1950.   The lowest percentage of farmhouses in this condition was in subregion 116, in the West Coast Miscellaneous Region.

Occupancy characteristics. Tenancy is most common in subregion 24, in the Tobacco Region, where four of every five of the farmhouses occupied by nonwhites in 1950 were renter occupied. Three out of every four such houses in subregion 57, in the Cotton Belt, and approximately two out of every three in the subregion selected from the East and Gulf Coast Miscellaneous Region were tenant occupied. As might be expected, the lowest proportion (12 percent) of tenant-occupied dwelling units shows up in economic subregion 109, where Indians predominate. (See table 55.)

TABLE **55.**—OCCUPANCY CHARACTERISTICS OF DWELLING UNITS OF NONWHITE HOUSEHOLDS, FOR SELECTED ECONOMIC SUBREGIONS: 1950

Characteristic	Subregion 21	Subregion 24	Subregion 57	Subregion 109	Subregion 116
Number of occupied units..................	16,770	23,870	36,200	3,710	4,090
Percent by tenure......................	100.0	100.0	100.0	100.0	100.0
Owner...	31.7	19.4	25.0	86.0	38.1
Renter and rent free......................	68.3	80.6	75.0	14.0	61.9
Percent by number of persons in household.............................	100.0	100.0	100.0	100.0	100.0
1 person....................................	3.1	2.2	5.8	2.4	12.1
2 persons...................................	10.3	11.8	20.0	9.2	23.3
3 persons...................................	12.8	12.4	15.4	8.6	16.3
4 persons...................................	13.5	13.4	12.9	17.0	15.3
5 persons...................................	11.7	12.3	10.5	15.1	11.5
6 persons or more..........................	48.6	47.9	35.4	47.7	21.5
Median number of persons in household.....	5.4	5.3	4.2	5.3	3.4
Percent by type of household..........	100.0	100.0	100.0	100.0	100.0
Husband-wife families, no nonrelatives....	79.3	82.1	74.9	77.9	62.2
2 persons...................................	8.7	10.3	15.4	6.2	15.4
3 persons...................................	10.2	10.4	11.7	6.3	11.2
4 persons...................................	11.1	11.0	9.9	13.6	11.0
5 persons or more..........................	49.3	50.4	37.9	51.8	24.6
Other family groups, no nonrelatives......	11.7	10.1	15.5	17.7	12.6
One-person households......................	3.1	2.2	5.8	2.4	12.1
Households with nonrelatives..............	5.9	5.6	3.8	2.0	13.1
Percent by income in 1949..............	100.0	100.0	100.0	100.0	100.0
Under $1,000..............................	56.7	57.7	79.5	58.6	31.9
$1,000 to $1,999..........................	25.5	23.6	13.7	16.6	23.4
$2,000 to $2,999..........................	8.8	8.3	2.2	7.4	17.7
$3,000 to $3,999..........................	2.9	3.1	0.7	3.1	9.0
$4,000 and over...........................	1.7	2.2	0.4	4.6	12.0
Income not reported.......................	4.4	5.1	3.5	9.7	6.0

Source: *1950 Census of Housing,* Vol. III, *Farm Housing Characteristics,* subregion tables 3 and 4.

The data indicate that perhaps the largest nonwhite farm households in the Nation are to be found in subregions of the East and Gulf Coast Miscellaneous Region, the Tobacco Region, and the Upland Grazing Region, which had medians of 5.4, 5.3, and 5.3 persons, respectively. The fact that nonwhite households in subregion 109, of the Upland Grazing Region, also lived in houses with an extremely low median number of rooms, indicates very crowded living conditions. The median of 3.4 persons to a household in subregion 116 in the West Coast Miscellaneous Region is close to the average size of farm household for the Nation as a whole, but it should be pointed out that 12 percent of the households in subregion

116 consisted of one person only, and a relatively high percentage consisted of two persons.

The distribution of types of household varies considerably in the five subregions. For example, the data in table 55 show that the percentage of households made up of husband, wife, children, and no nonrelatives was approximately one-third greater in subregion 116 in California than in subregion 24 in the Tobacco Region. The proportion of households including nonrelatives was considerably higher in subregion 116 than in the other four subregions. Perhaps many of the "nonrelatives" in this California area were extra workers on the fruit and truck farms.

In this group of five subregions, incomes were highest in subregion 116 in California and lowest in subregion 57 in the Cotton Belt. In the California subregion, 32 percent of the nonwhite families had incomes in 1949 of less than $1,000, but in subregion 57, with counties in Alabama and Mississippi, as many as 80 percent of the nonwhite families had incomes at this low level.

Facilities and equipment. The farmhouses of nonwhite families in subregions 21, 24, and 57, in the deep South, were almost all without running water, private flush toilet, and bathtub or shower in 1950. But nonwhite families in California's subregion 116 had farmhouses which were much better equipped: more than two of every three had running water in the house; at least one of every three had private flush toilet; and nearly half had a bathtub or shower. A higher level of income and a higher percentage of owner occupancy in this subregion as compared with the others, no doubt accounts for much of this situation. (See table 56.) However, it should be noted that while almost all the housing occupied by the Indians in subregion 109 was owner occupied, facilities there were much poorer than in subregion 116—once again giving evidence to the prime importance of income among factors affecting the housing of nonwhite households.

TABLE **56.**—FACILITIES AND EQUIPMENT OF DWELLING UNITS OF NONWHITE HOUSEHOLDS, FOR SELECTED ECONOMIC SUBREGIONS: 1950

Characteristic	Subregion 21	Subregion 24	Subregion 57	Subregion 109	Subregion 116
Number of occupied units.............	16,770	23,870	36,200	3,710	4,090
Percent by water supply..........	100.0	100.0	100.0	100.0	100.0
With running water..................	5.3	5.3	3.8	10.1	67.8
Without running water...............	94.7	94.7	96.2	89.9	32.2
Percent by toilet facilities......	100.0	100.0	100.0	100.0	100.0
With private toilet.................	1.4	1.0	0.9	4.8	37.8
Without private toilet..............	98.6	99.0	99.1	95.2	62.2
Percent by bathing facilities....	100.0	100.0	100.0	100.0	100.0
With private bath or shower.........	2.9	2.3	1.9	5.6	44.8
Without private bath or shower.......	97.1	97.7	98.1	94.4	55.2

Source: *1950 Census of Housing*, Vol. III, *Farm Housing Characteristics*, subregion table 4.

Analytical tabulations of characteristics of housing occupied by nonwhite households

Perspective on the over-all quality of farm dwelling units occupied by nonwhites can be obtained by cross-tabulating some of the basic characteristics. Most of the cross-tabulations below have been published for the 1950 Census of Housing.[3]

Characteristics of new housing by tenure and number of rooms. For the United States as a whole, in 1950, large proportions of the units were renter occupied. But when "tenure" is cross-tabulated with "year built," some striking differences are apparent. Well over half of all the new houses built were for owner occupants. Furthermore, these new units were almost one-third of all the units occupied by nonwhite owner households, whereas only a tenth of the nonwhite renter-occupied units were built after 1940. The new farm units occupied by owners, white and nonwhite combined, were almost one-sixth of all owner-occupied units.

In 1950 larger proportions of all owner-occupied than of renter-occupied new units had 5 rooms or more—54 percent as compared with 25 percent. Thus, as far as number of rooms is concerned, owners, on the average, had new housing of better quality than had renters. New, nonwhite owner-occupied units of 5 rooms or more as a proportion of all new units for nonwhite owners was a little higher than the proportion of houses of this size built for white owners—55 and 47 percent, respectively. The proportions of similarly sized, new renter-occupied units occupied by nonwhite and white households were not as close since 25 percent were occupied by white families; and only 16 percent, by nonwhites.

TABLE **57.**—Percent of Dwelling Units Occupied by Nonwhite Households Built in 1940 or Later, by Tenure and Rooms: 1950

Rooms	Owner	Renter
Total..............................	29	11
1 and 2 rooms..........................	38	15
3 and 4 rooms..........................	28	11
5 rooms or more........................	30	8

Source: *1950 Census of Housing,* Vol. III, *Farm Housing Characteristics,* table 3.

By using selected subregions again, it is possible to get some perspective as to geographic differences in the proportions of dwelling units built after 1940 to all units occupied by nonwhites and in the proportions of these new units having 5 rooms or more. (See table 58.)

In this group of subregions the largest proportions of new units in 1950 had been built in the Upland Grazing Region, where practically all of the nonwhite population is Indian. The fact that very few of these units had

---

[3] *1950 Census of Housing,* Vol. III, *Farm Housing Characteristics.*

5 rooms in 1950, together with the fact that, as tables 54, 55, and 56 indicate, all the units in this subregion were of poor quality, suggests that many
of the new units were simple temporary shelters of a type that must be
replaced at frequent intervals. In all five of the economic subregions,
owners are more likely to have new dwelling units than are tenants, and
a considerably larger proportion of owners than renters in 1950 had units
with 5 rooms or more. In economic subregion 116, part of the West Coast
Miscellaneous Region, the proportion of owners with new units was not as
large as it was in the East Coast and Tobacco Regions, despite the income
differential observed in table 54. An explanation for this apparent anomaly
may well be that on the West Coast the housing for nonwhite farm families
has always been of better quality than elsewhere, with the result that less
replacement has been necessary.

TABLE **58.**—NEW CONSTRUCTION AS PERCENT OF TOTAL DWELLING UNITS, AND NEW
CONSTRUCTION WITH 5 ROOMS OR MORE AS PERCENT OF TOTAL NEW UNITS, FOR NONWHITE-
OCCUPIED DWELLING UNITS, BY TENURE, FOR SELECTED SUBREGIONS: 1950

Economic subregion	Type-of-farming region	Percent built since 1940		Percent of new dwelling units with 5 rooms or more	
		Owner[1]	Renter[2]	Owner[3]	Renter[4]
21....................	East and Gulf Coast Misc.........	23	10	57	25
24....................	Tobacco..........................	29	9	56	23
57....................	Cotton Belt......................	29	9	34	8
109...................	Upland Summer Grazing............	40	43	6	...
116...................	West Coast Miscellaneous.........	28	17	31	16

[1] 100 percent equals subregion total of nonwhite owner-occupied dwelling units.
[2] 100 percent equals subregion total of nonwhite renter-occupied dwelling units.
[3] 100 percent equals subregion total of new nonwhite owner-occupied dwelling units of 5 rooms or more.
[4] 100 percent equals subregion total of new nonwhite renter-occupied dwelling units of 5 rooms or more.
Source: *1950 Census of Housing*, Vol. III, *Farm Housing Characteristics*, subregion table 3.

Other characteristics, by number of rooms in the dwelling unit.
While no other cross-tabulations have been made by "year built," cross-
tabulations of other characteristics add something to the knowledge of the
kind of housing occupied by nonwhite households. The number of persons per dwelling unit and the number of persons per room indicate, when
related to the number of rooms, the relatively greater degree of crowding
in the small farmhouses and in those occupied by nonwhite households as
compared with all households.

Table 59 seems to show that in 1950 small, renter-occupied units were
very crowded. Even though nearly one-fifth of the nonwhite households
living in renter-occupied dwelling units of less than 5 rooms had only 1 or
2 rooms, the average number of persons in those households was 4. Only
one-sixth of the white households in small, renter-occupied units lived in
1- or 2-room units, yet the median number of persons in these white families was smaller. The differences between white and nonwhite households
in the number of persons per dwelling unit were even greater for units

with more than 5 rooms. Thus, the considerable differences in the distribution of units by number of persons per room shown in table 60 are to be expected.

TABLE **59.**—MEDIAN NUMBER OF PERSONS IN ALL HOUSEHOLDS AND IN NONWHITE HOUSEHOLDS, BY TENURE AND ROOMS: 1950

Tenure and rooms	Median number of persons		Tenure and rooms	Median number of persons	
	All households	Nonwhite households		All households	Nonwhite households
Total..................	3.6	4.3	Renter.....................	3.9	4.5
Owner.....................	3.4	4.0	1 to 4 rooms............	3.7	4.0
1 to 4 rooms...........	3.1	3.5	5 rooms or more.........	4.1	5.6
5 rooms or more........	3.5	4.5			

Source: Derived from *1950 Census of Housing*, Vol. III, *Farm Housing Characteristics*, tables 1 and 3.

In 1950 nonwhite households in the small dwelling units of 1 to 4 rooms were generally young families. Where heads of households were under 45 years of age, 75 percent of the households lived in dwelling units with less than 5 rooms; this compares with 63 percent in the case of households whose heads were 45 years or older. There is some indication that the older the head of the household, the more likely it is that the dwelling unit was owned and had 5 rooms or more. Twenty-four percent of the households with a head of 65 years and over owned houses of 5 rooms or more, whereas only 9 percent of the households whose head was under 45 years of age owned houses of this size.

TABLE **60.**—PERCENT OF DWELLING UNITS WITH 1.01 PERSONS OR MORE PER ROOM, BY NUMBER OF ROOMS AND COLOR OF OCCUPANTS: 1950

Rooms and color of occupants	1.01 persons or more per room	Rooms and color of occupants	1.01 persons or more per room
White households..............	18	Nonwhite households............	49
1 to 4 rooms......................	32	1 to 4 rooms......................	53
5 rooms or more....................	10	5 rooms or more....................	40

Source: Same as table 59.

Condition and plumbing facilities as related to other characteristics. When condition and plumbing facilities are cross-classified with the number of rooms, the 1950 picture of housing for nonwhite farm households is fairly clear. Not only did this housing lack plumbing facilities, but very large proportions were dilapidated. This is particularly true of dwelling units with less than 5 rooms, of which half were dilapidated and almost all lacked plumbing facilities of any kind. In contrast, only one quarter of the farm units of this size occupied by white households were dilapidated, and over 40 percent, as compared with 5 percent of the units occupied by nonwhite households, had all or some of the specified plumbing facilities, i.e., hot or cold running water, private flush toilet, and bath.

Since so many units occupied by nonwhites were dilapidated or lacked all plumbing facilities, it can be safely assumed that many of those built since 1939 were inadequate. It has been pointed out that 54 percent of all new units fell into this category.[4] From appendix table D–6 it can be determined that 10 percent were classified as dilapidated, that is, they were of inadequate original construction. With these proportions of all new farm housing reported as dilapidated or lacking plumbing, presumably much larger proportions of the new units occupied by nonwhites were so classified, since both old and new combined were of poorer quality.

TABLE **61.**—PERCENT DISTRIBUTION OF DWELLING UNITS OCCUPIED BY NONWHITE HOUSEHOLDS BY CONDITION AND PLUMBING FACILITIES, BY ROOMS: 1950

Condition and plumbing facilities	1 and 2 rooms	3 and 4 rooms	5 rooms or more
Total reporting......................	100	100	100
Not dilapidated.........................	46	50	65
All facilities.....................	1	1	4
Some facilities....................	3	3	6
No facilities......................	42	46	55
Dilapidated............................	54	50	35
All or some facilities...............	2	1	2
No facilities......................	52	49	33

Source: Derived from *1950 Census of Housing*, Vol. III, *Farm Housing Characteristics*, table 4.

The quality of any farm dwelling unit has been found to be closely related to the income of the family occupying it.[5] This is undoubtedly equally true for the units occupied by nonwhite households; however, so few nonwhite families on farms reported incomes of over $1,000 in 1949 that it is difficult to demonstrate the relationship, even by the use of median incomes. The 1949 median income of all nonwhite farm families was only $740. Analyzed by condition and plumbing facilities, the median incomes of these families were as follows:

Not dilapidated units........................	$ 790
All facilities............................	1,580
Some facilities...........................	1,020
No facilities.............................	760
Dilapidated units..........................	690

Since less than 10 percent of the units occupied by nonwhites were not dilapidated and also were equipped with all or some of the plumbing facilities, the number of dwelling units at this level of median income is small. Even so, it indicates that income is a factor in the quality of housing as measured by condition and plumbing. The rest of the medians ($760 and $690) are so close together that the quality differences between them, as far as the relation of income to dwelling unit is concerned, are not significant. In any event, most of all farm housing classified as dilapidated also

[4] See Chapter 3, table 32, p. 62.
[5] See Chapter 3, p. 68.

lacked all facilities; thus it is to be expected that nonwhite median incomes for these two groups would be similar.

The relation between family income and condition and plumbing facilities of the dwelling unit differs from one part of the country to another. In economic subregion 57 incomes in 1950 were lowest and the differences between the medians were smallest. Only 2 percent of the dwelling units in that area were not dilapidated and had all or some plumbing facilities. The percentages of the farmhouses in these categories in the other subregions were: subregion 21, 4 percent; subregion 24, 5 percent; subregion 109, 9 percent; subregion 116, 55 percent. In this last West Coast region, therefore, not only were median family incomes higher, but a majority of the dwelling units were conspicuous in having at least some, if not all, of the specified plumbing facilities.

TABLE **62.**—MEDIAN FAMILY INCOME IN 1949 BY CONDITION AND PLUMBING FACILITIES, FOR SELECTED ECONOMIC SUBREGIONS: 1950

[In dollars]

Condition and plumbing facilities	Subregion 21	Subregion 24	Subregion 57	Subregion 109	Subregion 116
Not dilapidated......................	918	868	643	828	1,917
All facilities....................	2,000	1,375	804	2,500	2,227
Some facilities...................	1,017	1,214	678	1,286	2,076
No facilities.....................	906	852	640	786	1,115
Dilapidated..........................	745	763	581	683	1,288

Source: Derived from *1950 Census of Housing*, Vol. III, *Farm Housing Characteristics*, subregion table 4.

Outlook for Housing of Nonwhite Families

Obviously, there is plenty of room for improvement in the housing conditions of nonwhite farm families. How can this improvement occur?[6] If it is assumed that farms containing the poorest housing are the first to be abandoned, then migration from farms may provide some of the answers. Already, in 1949, a trend of this description was noticeable. In that year the figures show that slightly greater proportions of nonwhite males moved away from farms than did white males. In areas where there are the greatest concentrations of nonwhite households (region III, East and Gulf Coast Miscellaneous; region V, Tobacco; and region VI, Cotton Belt) about one in four of the farm-to-nonfarm male migrants was nonwhite. The 1940 and 1950 figures on the number of farmhouses occupied by nonwhite families offer further indication of this trend. Table 51 shows that during the decade these farmhouses decreased by 33 percent, as compared with a decrease of 17 percent in the over-all farm housing of white and nonwhite families.[7]

---

[6] See also Chapter 7.

[7] A part of the decrease in each group was due to changes in the definition of a farmhouse. See Chapter 1, p. 3.

To the extent that this type of migration creates a shortage of farm labor, the incomes of those remaining on farms will increase. Figures showing increases in the income of nonwhite farm families between 1940 and 1950 are not available, but in view of the over-all rise in both wages and farm income (which has been greater than the cost-of-living increase), it is likely that nonwhite family incomes have also risen. Over a short period, however, increases in income may not be reflected to any great extent in quality of housing. This lag may well be greater for nonwhite families than for white families. Restrictions on units available and preferences for other types of consumer goods rather than better housing may contribute to the delay in housing improvements when the income level of nonwhite farm families rises.

Governmental aids to the financing of new farm housing were on a relatively small scale during the 1940–50 decade. In addition, restrictions on granting credit to farmers who fail to meet certain production levels are likely to eliminate nonwhite renters from the group to whom aid is available. These renters would tend to be eliminated because of their low-average production as indicated by income. Even among the nonwhite owners, the large numbers that are part-time or residential farmers would not qualify.

Improvements in nonwhite farm housing characteristics, taking place as a result of a rise in income level and also as a result of abandonment of the worst-type dwellings, may be expected to be very gradual. Housing is not a flexible commodity; furthermore, the number of houses reported to be in poor condition is a large proportion of the whole.

Improvements between 1940 and 1950 certainly were not dramatic, as can be observed by examining tables 51 to 53. There was a smaller proportion of renter occupancy. The median number of rooms rose slightly. There were only small gains in plumbing facilities. Although the terms used in the two censuses to define condition are not strictly comparable, the more restrictive 1950 definition of good condition resulted in a slightly larger proportion of units classified as being in good condition. The only notable improvement in nonwhite housing between 1940 and 1950 occurred in the percentages of units with electric lights, which rose from 4 percent in 1940 to 44 percent in 1950. All in all, the improvement in nonwhite farm housing during the 1940–50 decade was inconsiderable when compared with the improvement in all farm housing discussed in Chapter 4.

So far as the present decade is concerned, it seems probable that, with continued increases in income, greater improvements will be evident in 1960 than were evident in 1950. Furthermore, by that time the lag between rises in income and improvement in housing may be partially overcome.

CHAPTER 7

THE FUTURE OF FARM HOUSING AND
THE NEED FOR RESEARCH

During the last four decades America's population increased by nearly 60 million persons to a total of 151 million in 1950.[1] While the population as a whole was increasing, the farm population was declining. In 1910 there were approximately 32 million persons on farms, compared with only slightly over 24 million in 1950. Proportionately, our farm population represented 35 percent of the total population in 1910, but only 16 percent in 1950.

Meantime, despite the decline in farm manpower, the Nation's total farm product was expanding. The farm population of 1950, approximately one-fourth smaller than in 1910, produced two-thirds more food and fiber than in 1910. This apparent paradox was brought about by greater individual output as a result of the tremendous progress made in farm mechanization and by improvements in farm practices. According to Johnson,[2] "The effect of technological change on the physical productivity of labor in agriculture may be summarized in this way: In 1945 one farm worker produced enough to provide himself and about 14 other persons with agricultural products. In 1920 he produced enough for himself and 9 other persons. About 100 years earlier, or in 1820, one farm worker produced enough for himself and only a little more than 3 other persons."

In line with this increased productivity, the average-sized farm is becoming larger. In 1880 the average-sized farm was only 134 acres; in 1950 the average was 210 acres.

An interesting comparison of urban and rural growth trends is provided by Bean.[3] "In 1860, we had around 2 million farms and only about 400,000 business firms, or five farms for each firm. This proportion has declined over the past nine decades so that 5,382,000 farms in operation in 1950 represent only 1.35 farms for each business firm. A continuation of this trend would mean a ratio of about one to one by 1970—5 million

---

[1] As of April 1, 1956, the Bureau of the Census estimated the population of the United States at 167,440,000, including Armed Forces overseas.

[2] Sherman E. Johnson, "Technological Changes and Rural Life," *Journal of Farm Economics*, Vol. XXXII, No. 2, May 1950, p. 231.

[3] L. H. Bean, *The Agricultural Situation*, monthly publication of the U. S. Department of Agriculture, July 1952, p. 7.

firms, 5 million farms, or a change of balance from five farms to one business in 1860 to one farm for each enterprise in 1970."

The cities are reaching out and absorbing a part of the Nation's farm land. Transportation facilities now make it possible to live some distance away from a place of work.[4] According to Woodbury,[5] "The population trends in metropolitan areas seem well established, for the short term at least. They seem likely to gain in momentum. Suburbanization will continue. Its most extreme form, growth in the rural rings, will become more, rather than less, significant. Commercial and industrial suburbanization also will continue—the former possibly more rapidly than the latter."

An understanding of the implications of this movement toward cities and away from farms is obviously important to sound agricultural production programs and land policies that will maintain or raise levels of farm income. Fortunately for this Nation, efforts are being made to place agriculture and agricultural production on a sound economic basis. That these efforts should continue appears to be essential not only for the welfare of farmers, but for the benefit of the farming industry, if it is to maintain progress parallel to that of nonfarm industries. Government policy in this direction and the growing trend toward the higher education of young farm men offer encouraging signs.

The commercial farm

Of the 5.4 million farms in the United States in 1950, 3.7 million were defined by the Census of Population as "commercial." Commercial farms accounted for 97.5 percent of total farm sales in 1949. The kind of housing that serves the operators of these farms is therefore of major importance to an understanding of farm conditions and farm population trends.

Farm and nonfarm housing in the Nation are not yet equal in terms of quality and facilities, and they are not likely to be in the near future. Where there is a constant demand for new machinery, improved service buildings, and, perhaps, additional land, these expenses compete for the share of income that might otherwise be spent on improving the family house.

But there is evidence that the gap between the quality of farm and nonfarm housing is narrowing. In 1949, the last year for which these data are available, a greater expenditure was made in the Nation as a whole on farm housing than on farm service buildings—$935 million compared with $690 million. However, the expenditure in the two instances differed

---

[4] For detailed study of this aspect of rural-urban development, see Samuel W. Blizzard and William F. Anderson, II, *Problems in Rural-Urban Fringe Research: Conceptualization and Delineation*, Progress Report No. 89, Pennsylvania State College, November 1952; and Leonard P. Adams and Thomas W. Mackesey, *Commuting Patterns of Industrial Workers*, Research Publication No. 1, Cornell University Housing Research Center, 1955.

[5] Coleman Woodbury, "Suburbanization and Suburbia," *American Journal of Public Health*, Vol. 45, No. 1, January 1955.

considerably in kind.   Because there was no shortage of farmhouses, more *new construction* of service buildings was undertaken than of houses.   On the other hand, there was a greater volume of *major improvements* to dwelling units than to service buildings.   (See table 63.)

TABLE 63.—ESTIMATED NUMBER OF BUILDINGS AND CASH EXPENDITURES FOR DWELLING UNITS AND SERVICE BUILDINGS, BY TYPE OF CONSTRUCTION: 1949

Type of construction	Farms reporting (thousands)	Number of buildings (thousands)	Contract work (millions of dollars)	Cash expenditures (millions of dollars)		
				Total	Material	Labor
DWELLING UNITS						
Total......................	2,946	3,036	...	935	...	...
New construction.............	81	83	57	294	169	68
Major improvements...........	796	807	136	442	234	72
Repairs......................	2,069	2,146	...	199	...	...
SERVICE BUILDINGS						
Total......................	1,767	2,350	...	690	544	146
New construction.............	678	840	...	459	368	91
Major improvements...........	286	323	...	99	77	22
Repairs......................	803	1,187	...	132	99	33

Source: U. S. Department of Agriculture, *The Agricultural Situation*, by R. K. Burroughs, January 1952, p. 7.

The farm home reflects to a large degree the economic level of the family. It was pointed out in Chapter 4 that farmhouses in the higher income regions, such as the two dairy regions and the Corn Belt, contain many modern conveniences.   For example, in 1950 practically all of the families in such regions had electric lights and radios as well as telephones.   Refrigeration, running water, and even central heat, which is difficult to install in sturdily built old houses, were becoming more prevalent on commercial farms in the higher income group.

The subsistence farm

Farms that yield little income or are worked on a part-time basis represent but a small portion of the Nation's total farm sales in any one year. Nevertheless, their operators contribute to the farming industry and their families constitute a major economic problem of this industry.

Cooper,[6] in a reference to small commercial as well as subsistence farmers, has said, "Many persons consider our small-scale farms to be of little economic value and therefore of little importance to the Nation.   It is true that in 1949 these three and one-third million farms, where family gross incomes from farming were less than $2,500 in 1949, produced only 11 percent of our agricultural production for sale.   But it is true also that these small farms produce much of the food used by the 13 million people who occupied them and enough additional food and fiber to support about

[6] M. R. Cooper, *The Agricultural Situation*, monthly publication of the U. S. Department of Agriculture, April 1954, pp. 1 and 2.

15 million off-farm persons at average consumption rates. And, while we must admit that these so-called farms as a group are low on the scale of efficient agricultural production, we cannot overlook their great value as places to live for millions of low-income persons." Many authorities differ with Cooper's point of view. Since the quality of farmhouses on low-income farms is below most accepted standards, the question is: What is the best solution to the housing problem of these families?

In recent years two different approaches toward a solution have been suggested. One would invoke the use of direct governmental housing assistance; the other would attempt to work out the socio-economic problems of low-income farm families so that they themselves might improve their levels of living.

One of the principal proponents of public relief has been Charles Abrams.[7] Appearing at a time when to many economists a postwar depression appeared inevitable, his writings still hold some significance today as an approach toward the solution of the subsistence farmer's housing problem. Abrams acknowledges that the rural housing problem is secondary to the greater problems arising from farm mechanization and unsalable surpluses. But, he says, "It is indefensible to contend that because other problems of the rural economy must persist, we should therefore postpone housing reform." He suggests that the housing program of these families should be organized and supervised by county housing authorities in the Department of Agriculture and that houses should actually be built. He feels that the government "should make loans at reasonable interest to those who can pay it and provide loans free, or partly free, of interest to others. Where principal must be waived it should be charged to the national cost of rural relief."

Another approach to the problem of the subsistence farmer, much different from subsidized housing and direct relief, is frequently advanced by agricultural economists. They would encourage some subsistence farmers to give up farming for nonfarm occupations in which they would have the opportunity to earn a decent living. This would help to solve not only their problems of shelter, but other problems involved in earning an income adequate for the necessities of life.

On this, Johnson[8] states, "The biggest part of the job of helping those who are disadvantaged by technological changes will consist of aid and encouragement to those who are likely to find their best income opportunities in nonfarm occupations. Many today are ill-prepared for such transfers because of low educational attainment, health handicaps, or lack of training and special skills for specific types of nonfarm work. Because of strong resistance to change, a program of public investment in these fields probably should begin with education and health services for the

---

[7] Charles Abrams, *The Future of Housing*, New York, Harper and Brothers, 1946, pp. 385–387.

[8] Sherman E. Johnson, *op. cit.*, pp. 238–239.

children who are growing up on small-scale farms, or in the families of hired laborers. . . . From the standpoint of economic benefits to the people who remain on farms, public investments to aid those who are no longer needed in farming are likely to return higher dividends over a period of years than direct aids to agriculture. Migration of workers from farm occupations is necessitated by both the increase in farm population above replacement needs and by the release of workers as a result of technological change. It is only possible to maintain high production and high income per worker when those who are not needed in farming find the road open to nonfarm employment. . . . The need for public investments in land conservation is now widely recognized. But the need for similar investment in human conservation is not so generally understood."

Migration from farms is likely to continue, even without government intervention. This trend may reduce the number of subsistence farms and thus eliminate some housing problems.

Suggestions for further research

This monograph has raised many questions, some of which it could only partially answer and some not at all. It is hoped that even these latter will serve to underscore the need for further research in the field of farm housing. Among the problems for which further study might provide additional answers are the following:

1. What is the actual rate of change of farm to nonfarm housing? More precise data than those made available in the census are required. It would be desirable to have this information for the various regions. Other breakdowns also would be desirable, especially with regard to the proximity to urban areas.

2. While a considerable amount of study was given to the matter of redefining rural housing during the preparation of this monograph, the recommendations, which are set forth in Appendix A, are not considered final. Further studies of this problem would be extremely useful.

3. Related to point 1 above is the need for obtaining a better understanding of the urban influence on farm housing. For example, where is this influence exerted most effectively? How rapidly does it become effective? What is the nature of this influence during its initial and later stages?

4. Research is needed concerning the economic value of farmhouses in relation to the value of the farm land. Do any patterns exist? What changes are there in the value of the dwelling unit when it shifts from farm to nonfarm use, or vice versa?

5. What is the relationship between the quality of the dwelling unit on a farm and the quality of the land and service buildings? Some indication has been given in earlier chapters that the quality of housing is not always directly related to the economic classification of farms. Research on this subject would provide a better understanding of the economic and social implications involved.

6. What is the relationship between residential expenditures and nonresidential expenditures of farm income? Much has been written about the priority that is given to improving the farm in general, including service buildings, before the farmhouse. While there seems to be general agreement concerning this hypothesis, a more comprehensive and detailed study should be made in order that the problem might be better understood. Yet, since this research has been spotty for the different regions, and inadequate, more research is needed to determine the real functional requirements of farmhouses, especially if these requirements are different from those of urban dwellings.

7. The two subjects on which most research in farm housing probably has been undertaken (especially in our land grant colleges) are house design and the physical characteristics of farmhouses.

8. Finally, it has been pointed out (on p. 62) that while only 12 percent of all nonfarm houses were found to be dilapidated in 1950, the comparable figure for farmhouses was 57 percent—well over half. This monograph has indicated quite conclusively that these dwellings, for the most part, are on low-production and, accordingly, low-income farms. Many of them are in the temperate climate regions. The real problem then, for the greatest proportion of our farmhouses, is that of finding a type of construction that, on the one hand, is low in cost (including both construction labor and materials) and, on the other, meets a decent standard of living. In other words, it is essential to obtain more housing value per dollar invested.

Further research on the kinds of problems listed above would contribute greatly to a better understanding of the complex social and economic problems related to farm housing.

APPENDIX A

NEED FOR NEW DEFINITIONS AND CONCEPTS[1]

Throughout this book we have been dealing with a universe that has been labeled "farm housing." Such a term is a convenient label, but it must be admitted that as a means of describing the housing of people who operate farms, it lacks precision. A farmhouse may mean different things to different people. Does "farm housing" imply a specific type of housing or is it merely a generic term? What are the limits of the universe? In what terms can the universe be defined?

If the term implies a specific type of housing, such housing should have characteristics which distinguish it from all other classes of housing. If, on the other hand, farm housing is a general term for housing located on farms, its characteristics would not necessarily differ from the characteristics of other housing. The limits of the universe would be determined by the definition of a farm. This raises still another question. Is there a specific definition of a farm that will clearly distinguish the housing on it from all other housing? Among the current dictionary definitions the most applicable is, "any tract devoted to agricultural purposes." But such a definition does not solve the problem for the housing analyst, because there are too many divergent interpretations of "agricultural purposes."

Some evidence of the confusion that can stem from varying interpretations of what constitutes a farm is indicated in Chapter 1, when statistics based on the United States Population and Agriculture Censuses are compared.[2] In brief, the Census of Population depends largely on the respondent's opinion of what constitutes a farm residence, while the Census of Agriculture definition of a farm depends on information collected in that census. The confusion is compounded by other Federal agencies. There is no standard definition of farm housing used by all Federal housing agencies, neither does Federal housing legislation provide a standard definition of farm and nonfarm housing, even though separate agencies are authorized to deal with farm and nonfarm housing programs. It is doubtful that State and private agencies concerned with either farms or farm housing use definitions that are any more uniform.

---

[1] The recommendations and conclusions represent the opinions formed by the authors on the basis of statistics presented or referred to herein. They do not in any way reflect an official position of either the Bureau of the Census or the Social Science Research Council.

[2] See p. 13.

Census of Population classification

Before evaluating the advantages and disadvantages of the classifications used in the 1950 Census, it is necessary that we review the definitions used and the way in which they were interpreted in the enumeration of the Housing Census.

In 1950 urban housing consisted of all dwelling units in (a) all places of 2,500 inhabitants or more that were incorporated as cities, boroughs, and villages; (b) incorporated towns of 2,500 inhabitants or more, except in New England, New York, and Wisconsin, where "towns" are simply minor civil divisions of counties; (c) the densely settled urban fringe around cities of 50,000 or more inhabitants including both incorporated and unincorporated areas; and (d) unincorporated places of 2,500 inhabitants or more outside any urban fringe. All other dwelling units were either rural-nonfarm dwelling units or rural-farm dwelling units. The rural-nonfarm units consisted of a variety of residences, such as isolated nonfarm units in the open country, dwelling units in villages and in fringes of metropolitan areas, and units in areas around urban places of fewer than 50,000 inhabitants.

Enumerators were specifically instructed to classify a rural dwelling unit as nonfarm or farm according to the respondent's answer to the question, "Is this house on a farm?" The classification may not therefore depend on the occupation of the members of the household but, rather, on the respondent's concept of what a farm is.

Should the respondent reply that his house was on a farm, the enumerator was instructed to classify it as a nonfarm house if cash rent was being paid for the house and yard only. The enumerator was not asked to record any answer about cash rent. Thus, it is possible that the question may have been omitted by some enumerators after they received a positive answer to the "on a farm" question.

Nevertheless certain steps in the census procedure modify total dependence on the respondent's answers, and provide the enumerator with the opportunity for determining whether cash rent is paid for a house. The enumerator for the 1950 Census was instructed to complete an agricultural questionnaire if the place was reported by the respondent to be a farm or ranch, or if specific agricultural operations were carried on at the place. On all other places of three or more acres the enumerator was requested to complete at least section I of the agricultural questionnaire.[3]

---

[3] Item 7 of this section reads as follows:

7. Were there in 1949 or will there be in 1950 on this place—(a) 25 or more chickens? ducks? geese? pigeons? or other poultry. . . . . ☐ No ☐ Yes
(If you have checked "Yes" for this question, skip to question 8 and fill the remainder of the questionnaire; likewise, as soon as you check "Yes" for any of the questions (b) through (f), skip to question 8 and complete this questionnaire.)
(b) Any hogs? cattle? sheep? horses? goats? domestic rabbits? fur animals? other livestock? or bees? . . . . ☐ No ☐ Yes
(c) Any crops grown, such as corn, oats, cotton, etc. . . . . ☐ No ☐ Yes

If any of the questions in item 7 received an answer of "Yes" the enumerator was required to complete the agricultural questionnaire. If all of these questions were answered in the negative, no further work was required. Because of this variation in treatment, an enumerator might develop a tendency to report a place as a farm if he believed that the answer "Yes" would be obtained to any part of item 7. Similarly, he might not report a place as a farm if he believed that all parts of item 7 would be answered in the negative.[4]

Despite these modifying influences, so flexible a procedure clearly places the responsibility for classification upon local decisions. The variation between what was considered farm and nonfarm property was probably greatest in areas where part-time and residential farms predominate.

Evaluation of the urban, rural-nonfarm, and rural-farm classifications for housing[5]

So far as housing is concerned, there are serious disadvantages in the urban, rural-nonfarm, and rural-farm classifications; there are also disadvantages in definitions and concepts, as well as disadvantages inherent in the classifications themselves.

The word "farmhouse" implies an occupational distinction in housing which certainly is not associated with any other occupation. It can be logically argued that a few decades ago the usual isolation of farmhouses was a justification for setting them apart. With the increased use of the automobile and the resultant spread of nonfarm dwelling units into open country, this argument is less conclusive.

The most impressive justification for an occupational distinction for farm dwelling units is that the farmer frequently does use his house as his business headquarters. This is very effectively described in Taylor's biography of several generations of a farm family in the Catskill Mountains of New York State:

"The fact that a farmer's business headquarters is his home, and also the fact that his home is in the midst of his business, makes it difficult to disassociate

---

(d) Any hay cut? or land pastured or grazed?........................... ☐ No ☐ Yes
(e) Any fruits? nuts? or nursery and greenhouse products?................ ☐ No ☐ Yes
(f) Any vegetables or berries grown for sale?........................... ☐ No ☐ Yes
(If you have checked "No" for all questions 7 through 7 (f), do not fill the remainder of this questionnaire.)

[4] It is necessary to realize that many respondents would not give a definite answer to all questions. When the enumerator asks if a place is a farm, the respondent is likely to indicate the nature and extent of the agricultural operations and leave the determination to the enumerator. Thus, the reports on farm residence in the Population and Housing Censuses may adhere more closely to the treatment in the Census of Agriculture than strict interpretations of the instructions might imply. It should be noted that after the 1950 agricultural questionnaires were received in Washington, any such questionnaires were rejected if examination indicated that the annual value of agricultural products was less than $150. The enumerator did not know of this practice and may have reported such places as farms in the Population and Housing Censuses. (See p. XXXII of Vol. II of the *1950 Census of Agriculture* for details of the over-all effect of this editing process.)

[5] The definitions of urban, rural-nonfarm, and rural-farm classifications are based on those given in the *1950 Census of Housing*, Vol. II, *Nonfarm Housing Characteristics*, Part 1, Chapter 1.

one from the other. The activities of the entire combined enterprise are the common concern of all the family and are often the subject of common discussion." [6]

Though the farmhouse is the business headquarters of the farmer, his is not the only occupation in which the family house is used for that purpose. Many professional people as well as small businessmen either conduct their business from an office in the home or at least do the office work at home. In both rural and urban areas, small stores combined with the owner's dwelling are commonplace.

Economic factors provide further justification for a classification of farm dwelling units that distinguishes them from other units similarly located in the open country.

For example, the value of a farm dwelling unit depends much more on the farm's potential productive capacity than on its competitive position in the housing market as a place to live. Except in metropolitan areas, relatively few farms are purchased for the house alone. In contrast, every nonfarm dwelling unit for sale or rent is in competition with all other nonfarm units in the same neighborhood and in approximately the same price class. [7]

There are also the disadvantages that are inherent in the classifications themselves. Data are usually classified according to their distinguishable characteristics or, to put it another way, similar data are combined in the same group. In housing there are clearly basic differences between urban, rural-nonfarm, and rural-farm units. [8] But the rural-nonfarm group includes characteristics of both of the other two classifications. It is not a clearly defined classification in its own right. [9]

Another minor disadvantage of the present classification arises when persons who are not entirely familiar with census terminology interpret "rural-nonfarm" to mean all nonfarm dwelling units in open country. From time to time, as a result of this misunderstanding, the Bureau of the Census has had inquiries for statistics based on a classification that does not exist. A classification set up for open-country dwelling units apparently would fill a statistical need.

Census of Agriculture definition of a farm

The 1950 Census of Agriculture did not depend upon the respondent's opinion as to whether his was a farm or not. Being essentially the census of an indus-

---

[6] George D. Taylor, *These Hills Are Not Barren*, Alfred A. Knopf, New York, 1945, p. 11.

[7] There is also inconsistency in the present classification of farm-nonfarm units. While farm dwelling units in urban areas are identified in the enumeration, they are rarely tabulated separately. The number of urban farm units is so insignificant (less than 100,000 throughout the Nation), that even though there were important conceptual differences between farm and nonfarm units in urban areas, separate tabulations would be of little value.

[8] This can be verified by consulting the *1950 Census of Housing*, Vol. II, *Nonfarm Housing Characteristics*, Part 1, Chapter 1, tables 2 to 13.

[9] Later in this appendix statistics are presented which demonstrate that rural-nonfarm dwelling units (defined according to the Census of Population) in open country are of the same or a little poorer quality than the rural-farm dwelling units. The rural-nonfarm dwelling units in communities of less than 2,500 inhabitants (below the urban level in size) are, on the average, of about the same quality as urban dwelling units.

try, it was necessary that the definition used should be more clear cut and objective. Places of 3 acres or more were counted as farms if the value of agricultural products, excluding home gardens, amounted to $150 or more in 1949. The products included those raised for both sale and home use. Places of less than 3 acres were counted as farms only if the value of sales of agricultural products in 1949 amounted to $150 or more. Places operated in 1949, but on which the value of agricultural products in 1949 amounted to less than $150 because of crop failure or other unusual circumstances, and places operated in 1950 for the first time, were included as farms if they could normally be expected to produce these minimum quantities of farm products. These uniform criteria were applied in processing the schedules in Washington.[10]

Investigations of present concepts and new classifications

Because of these differences in definitions, the Bureau of the Census explored the possibility of finding a definition of farm housing that would take into account all the various purposes for which the data might be used.[11] A large part of the research, which was undertaken to develop better techniques and methods for conducting intercensal housing surveys for the Housing and Home Finance Agency, was devoted to concepts and definitions. A number of different definitions of farm housing were tested, as were methods for determining more objectively the differences between farm and nonfarm housing. On the basis of these tests, it was recommended that new definitions or new classifications be used. The two major classifications recommended were (1) community housing and (2) open-country housing. In order to retain at least partial comparability with earlier statistics, new statistics could be classified as follows:

1. Urban housing
2. Rural community housing
3. Open-country housing
   a. Nonfarm
   b. Farm

Both the old and the new classifications were tested on a small scale to find out what similarities and differences in housing characteristics there were within each classification and between classifications. Other evidence from work in the Housing Research Center at Cornell [12] supported the findings of these small-scale tests.

It was felt, however, that still more evidence was needed before these recommendations could be widely accepted. Therefore, special tabulations of data from the 1950 Census of Housing were prepared for the analysis below, to show the characteristics of open-country and community housing.

---

[10] Definitions are taken from the *1950 Census of Agriculture*, Vol. II, *General Reports, Statistics by Subject*, p. XXIX.

[11] See the report by the U. S. Bureau of the Census, "Intercensal Housing Surveys: Evaluation of their Importance, Description of Concepts and Definitions Involved in Producing Reliable Data," May 1957.

[12] Glenn H. Beyer, *Rural Housing in New York State*, Bulletin 893, Cornell University Agricultural Experiment Station, October 1952.

National sample of farm and nonfarm housing in rural areas

None of the information from the 1950 Census of Housing was tabulated in a way that would make possible an evaluation of the differences between nonfarm housing in open country and nonfarm housing in communities. In the tabulations all the nonfarm housing, except that in urban areas, was combined. Thus, the only way in which community and open-country housing could be compared was by a special tabulation. A sample of occupied dwelling units[13] that would be representative of open-country and community units in all parts of the country was therefore drawn.

Part of the reason for setting up the sample so that each type-of-farming region would be represented was to provide statistics for each region. The number of nonfarm dwelling units in open country in each region was too small to be significant, however, although the number of these units in the United States as a whole and in the regions combined was adequate. The tables below are derived from these tabulations.

Table A–1 demonstrates quite clearly the general thesis that the condition and equipment of nonfarm housing vary considerably. Urban housing, according to the data for 1950 carried in the regular census publications, was of significantly better quality, both as to condition and water supply, than the nonfarm housing in the open country. Rural community housing, which fell between the two extremes, was more like urban housing than like the nonfarm housing in the open country. The condition of farm housing was similar to that of rural community housing, but the percentages of farm units with and without running water were distributed in much the same way as the percentages of open-country nonfarm units. Because of the predominance of farm units in the open country and urban units in all communities, the composite percentages in each instance were very similar to those of the predominant group. The distributions of open-country and community units justifies completely the theory that these two groups should be classified separately.

In table A–2, which gives the distributions of dwelling units by toilet facilities and by family income, more pronounced differences are evident between all open-country and all community units. Again, the nonfarm units in the open country made a worse showing than any other type of units; and the urban units, by far the best.[14] The median income of families in urban dwelling units

---

[13] To assure a representative sample, 2 or 3 economic subregions (depending on the size of the region) were selected at random from each of the 12 type-of-farming regions. A random selection of 256 rural enumeration districts was made from these 35 subregions. Every fifth household within each enumeration district was used to make up the sample universe for which the data were tabulated.

[14] As indicated in the footnote to table A–2, the percentages in the urban column are actually those for nonfarm dwelling units inside metropolitan areas, which were estimated, according to an unpublished sample study of the 1950 Census of Housing, as being 90 percent urban. The rural-nonfarm dwelling units inside metropolitan areas were about equal in number to the urban dwelling units outside metropolitan areas. Further, it is assumed that the distribution by family income of rural-nonfarm families inside metropolitan areas was roughly similar to the distribution by family income of urban families outside metropolitan areas. Thus, the distribution in metropolitan areas of dwelling units by family income should be similar to that of dwelling units in all urban areas. Dwelling units in all urban areas were not tabulated by family income in the 1950 Census.

was nearly twice as large as that of families in nonfarm dwelling units in the open country. Both the income distribution and the median income of this last group were very much like those of the farm families.

TABLE **A-1.**—PERCENT DISTRIBUTION OF OCCUPIED DWELLING UNITS IN OPEN COUNTRY AND COMMUNITIES, BY CONDITION AND WATER SUPPLY: 1950

[100 percent equals the total number reporting each characteristic]

Condition and water supply	Open country			Communities		
	Total	Farm	Nonfarm	Total	Rural	Urban
CONDITION						
Total occupied units.............	100	100	100	100	100	100
Not dilapidated......................	85	86	75	89	87	90
Dilapidated.........................	15	14	25	11	13	10
WATER SUPPLY						
Total occupied units.............	100	100	100	100	100	100
Hot and cold running water[1]..........	34	34	30	66	51	70
Cold water only[1].....................	15	15	16	14	16	13
Piped water outside structure.........	2	2	1	3	5	2
No piped running water................	49	49	53	18	28	15

[1] Inside the structure but not necessarily in the dwelling unit.

Source: Special tabulation from the 1950 Census of Housing except for data on urban areas, which are from *1950 Census of Housing*, Vol. I, *General Characteristics*, Part 1, U. S. Summary, tables 7 and 8.

TABLE **A-2.**—PERCENT DISTRIBUTION OF OCCUPIED DWELLING UNITS IN OPEN COUNTRY AND COMMUNITIES, BY TOILET FACILITIES AND FAMILY INCOME: 1950

Subject	Open country			Communities		
	Total	Farm	Nonfarm	Total	Rural	Urban
TOILET FACILITIES						
Total occupied units....................	100	100	100	100	100	100
Flush toilet inside structure, exclusive use..	34	34	33	79	54	86
Flush toilet outside structure or shared....	(1)	(1)	...	5	2	6
Privy....................................	64	64	64	16	42	7
No toilet................................	2	2	3	1	2	1
FAMILY INCOME IN 1949						
Total occupied units....................	100	100	100	100	100	[2]100
Under $1,000.............................	32	31	35	15	23	13
$1,000 to $1,999.........................	22	23	20	12	20	11
$2,000 to $2,999.........................	19	19	20	19	22	18
$3,000 to $3,999.........................	11	11	13	20	16	21
$4,000 to $6,999.........................	12	12	11	25	16	27
$7,000 and over..........................	4	4	1	9	3	10
Median income....................dollars..	1,818	1,826	1,750	3,200	2,318	3,380

[1] Less than 0.5 percent.

[2] Since no distribution of all urban dwelling units by family income is available, the distribution of nonfarm dwelling units inside metropolitan areas was used as an approximate substitute.

Source: Special tabulation from 1950 Census of Housing except for data on urban areas, which are from *1950 Census of Housing*, Vol. I, *General Characteristics*, Part 1, U. S. Summary, table 8, and Vol. II, *Nonfarm Housing Characteristics*, Part 1, Chapter 1, United States, table C-7.

Farm and nonfarm dwelling units in the open country differed most in age. More farm units were built before 1920 and fewer after 1939. The largest proportions of new units were in rural communities. At first glance, this seems to contradict the general observation that most of the new construction occurred in and around urban centers. The most intensive new construction probably did take place on the outskirts of urban areas, but some of it understandably was within urbanized areas and therefore outside the scope of this special study. On the other hand, many of the new units around urban areas probably were included in this sample, either because the urban center had less than 50,000 inhabitants, and thus had no defined urbanized fringe, or because the units were just outside what the Bureau of the Census defined as the urban fringe for cities of 50,000 inhabitants or more. That the sample survey did not include a disproportionate number of such units is evident if the proportions in table A–3 are compared with the total rural-nonfarm proportion (28.4 percent) of units built 1940 or later.[15] As a matter of fact, the number of new units in the sample may have been slightly low, but this is not serious because the proportion of new farm units is also understated by comparison with the figures shown in Housing Volume I.

TABLE **A–3.**—PERCENT DISTRIBUTION OF OCCUPIED DWELLING UNITS IN OPEN COUNTRY AND COMMUNITIES, BY YEAR BUILT AND SELECTED TYPES OF EQUIPMENT: 1950

Subject	Open country			Communities		
	Total	Farm	Nonfarm	Total	Rural	Urban
YEAR BUILT						
Total occupied units..............	100	100	100	100	100	100
1940 or later........................	14	13	23	20	25	19
1930 to 1939........................	11	11	14	13	16	12
1920 to 1929........................	13	12	18	21	14	23
1919 or earlier......................	63	64	45	46	45	46
HEATING EQUIPMENT						
Total occupied units..............	100	100	100	100	100	100
Central heating......................	22	22	24	54	27	62
Noncentral heating....................	77	77	74	44	73	36
Not heated..........................	1	(¹)	2	2	1	2
REFRIGERATION EQUIPMENT						
Total occupied units..............	100	100	100	100	100	100
Electric, gas, or other mechanical....	68	69	56	83	74	86
Ice box.............................	9	9	15	10	11	10
Other or none.......................	23	22	29	7	15	4
KITCHEN SINK						
Total occupied units..............	100	100	100	100	100	100
Exclusive use........................	62	63	56	90	71	95
Shared or none......................	38	37	44	10	29	5

¹ Less than 0.5 percent.

Source: Special tabulation from the 1950 Census of Housing except for data on urban areas, which are from *1950 Census of Housing*, Vol. I, *General Characteristics*, Part 1, U. S. Summary, tables 6, 12, and 13.

---

[15] *1950 Census of Housing*, Vol. I, *General Characteristics*, Part 1, table 6, p. 3.

The proportions of dwelling units of all types with or without the facilities listed in table A–3 followed more closely the expected pattern. The nonfarm open-country group had the smallest proportions of units with central heating, mechanical refrigeration, and a kitchen sink. The proportions of farm units with these facilities were generally only slightly higher, and the proportions in rural communities were still higher.

In summary, the statistics drawn from this sample were in general accordance with the hypothesis that open-country dwelling units share similar characteristics whether they are located on farms or not, and that rural community housing is closer in character to urban housing than it is to nonfarm housing in the open country. This was especially true of modern equipment and facilities. Differences in family income suggest why relatively more dwelling units in some groups than in others possessed these conveniences, though these differences have little bearing on the proportions of newly built units.[16] Differences in condition, while correlated with income, were not pronounced.

Recommendations for new definitions and classifications

As indicated earlier in this appendix some of the definitions and residence classifications used by the Census of Population and the Census of Agriculture are not well adapted for use in the Census of Housing, or they result in unrealistic classifications of housing. The use of a farm sub-classification of housing located in open country is necessary if the characteristics of such housing are to be related to farming as a way of life. However, some consideration should be given to the definition of a farm. There is no reason for changing present census concepts unless they can definitely be improved. The criteria for determining what a farm is and who lives on a farm should have these qualities:

1. They should be of such a nature that they can easily distinguish between farming operations and other work.

2. They should be of such a type that they permit "measuring" size of farming operations. As little fluctuation as possible should exist.

3. They should be of such a type that data collected will have a high degree of reliability; this means that they should lend themselves to sound field survey application.

4. They should be sufficiently simple so that they can be utilized in all the Federal censuses without requiring a complete agriculture census. This would permit a higher degree of comparability between data in the Population and Housing Censuses, on the one hand, and the Agriculture Census, on the other, than has heretofore existed.

5. Whatever criterion is used for identifying land on which farming operations take place, additional criteria, other than opinion of the respondent, should be used to determine best what houses are "on that farm."

A criterion which seems to have the characteristics of the first five points is

---

[16] See p. 41 for an analysis of the effects of new construction.

the "amount of labor," or labor input[17] involved in the particular farming operation. This factor, it would seem, would serve as a good basis for establishing a new definition and, at the same time, for developing a definition which could be utilized in all censuses. Labor information of the general type that would be required has been obtained in Censuses of Agriculture in the past and could be obtained without too much difficulty in a Census of Housing.

An alternative criterion for identifying farm operations is the "value-of-product" approach now used in the Census of Agriculture both as a part of the definition of a farm and as a means of economic classification. This criterion has the advantage of identifying the low-production farm somewhat more specifically than can "amount of labor." It is, however, subject to fluctuations as a result of price changes. Furthermore, its use in housing surveys introduces more operational problems.

Present classifications of urban and rural population also have become outdated—or at least their deficiencies are more evident today than they were earlier. It therefore seems desirable to explore the possibility of establishing a classification that will reflect the real nature of our population and housing under today's, and possibly tomorrow's, conditions. This implies that we should not only look at the physical characteristics of dwelling units and the occupations or places of work of the occupants, but that we should also consider the important sociological factors which make the separation of farm and nonfarm population and housing groups desirable.

In setting up a new classification of urban and rural population, it is important that it should (a) be continuous with past housing statistics, (b) make possible the relation of housing and population statistics, and (c) for farm housing, make it possible to distinguish clearly between the number of farms and the number of farm dwelling units.

When these three requirements are added to the requirement that a new classification must show the distinctive characteristics of each of the population groups and the types of housing, the task of developing a new and better one becomes extremely difficult. One fact is obvious: it is unlikely that any single classification will serve all purposes.

In setting up a new classification, the individual elements that it will include must be analyzed. Only one group, the urban, is fairly clear cut; and even this group has some complexities, though they are not highly significant.

The real problems of the classification occur in the semiurban or nonurban groups, which consist of (a) the rural community and (b) the open country. In turn, open country consists of farm and nonfarm groups. There is evidence that the rural community group is sufficiently different from the others to warrant a separate classification.

The research undertaken for the Housing and Home Finance Agency[18]

---

[17] U. S. Bureau of the Census, "Intercensal Housing Surveys: Evaluation of their Importance, Description of Concepts and Definitions Involved in Producing Reliable Data," May 1957.

[18] See p. 124 of this appendix.

showed that farm and nonfarm housing in the open country did not differ much.   However, while the separate enumeration of the groups might constitute some problems, it seems highly desirable to retain the farm group as distinct in any new classification.   The retention of this group presupposes a uniform method of distinguishing between the farm and nonfarm house.   Only in this can there be agreement on the farm universe.   There are likely be both statistical and political reasons for making the farm group a separate one, and it follows from this that the open-country nonfarm group would also be separate.

In summary, then, a new classification might be set up as follows:

Urban housing.   All dwelling units in (*a*) all urban places and urbanized areas as defined by the Bureau of the Census in 1950 and (*b*) all dwelling units in the urban fringes of places having 10,000 to 50,000 inhabitants.

Rural community housing.   All dwelling units in incorporated or unincorporated places of more than 500 but less than 2,500 inhabitants and not a part of an urban area or an urbanized area as defined above.

Open-country housing.   All dwelling units in areas outside urban areas and rural communities.   This housing is of two types: (*a*) Farm housing and (*b*) open-country nonfarm housing.   The distinction between farm and nonfarm housing is based on a classification of the land with which the house is associated.   Furthermore, in the case of farm housing, some occupant such as an owner, renter, or laborer should have a part in the farm operation.

Unfortunately, even this classification would create some problems of comparability with all past statistics.[19]   Despite this limitation, this classification seems to describe the population and housing groups in modern America more effectively than the classification used up to now.

Migration trends and other data show that the urban population is continuing to grow at the expense of the rural population and that rural communities are likely to grow at the expense of open-country farms.   There seems also to be a tendency for some residents in the open country to transfer from the farm to the nonfarm category.   If these are the trends, then the type of classification described above would be likely to become more significant and more pertinent in the future.   Its value from this standpoint should be weighed against its disadvantage in breaking to some extent the continuity with past data and statistics.

---

[19] Continuity would be lost only in the sense that farm housing would be identified by a new method. At little extra cost both old and new methods could be used in the initial surveys or censuses, thus creating an overlap by which the effect of definitional changes could be measured.

A P P E N D I X   B

PROBLEMS OF RURAL CLASSIFICATION

Many attempts have been made to delineate broad areas of the United States in which some differentiation is clear in the social or economic aspects of farm life. The simplest of these classifications divides the States into regions and divisions such as those used by the Bureau of the Census. The four major regions—Northeast, North Central, South, and West—are usually considered to have some differences in cultural patterns. The nine geographic divisions are a convenient subdivision of the major regions into more workable units for statistical measurements, but most people would not consider them to be cultural units.

Probably the greatest disadvantage to using either regions or divisions as a basis for analysis is that they combine groups of States. Cultural or even physical differences do not necessarily follow State boundaries. In 1938, for instance, Howard Odum and Harry E. Moore used combinations of States as a basis for six "societal regions," [1] but they recognized the shortcomings of using State boundaries by suggesting that there was a 100-mile-wide band between areas that could not be allocated to the regions on either side of it. The use of any political boundary involves this problem of a shadowy area where peoples of unlike characteristics merge, but the use of smaller political areas than a State tends to reduce the width of this "no-man's-land."

Extensive use of the smaller areas has been made in at least three types of studies. In 1940 Mangus described 264 "rural cultural subregions" that could be combined in 34 "rural cultural regions." [2] In this work, each county was allocated to a subregion on the basis of type of farming. These counties were then shifted to other subregions if differences observed in various statistical indices were taken as measurements of cultural differences. Thus, the boundary lines of these areas were determined by a combination of sociological and economic criteria.

A second type of study, and the most extensive work done on rural regionalism, has been carried out by those whose interests are primarily in the economic aspects of farming as reflected by type of farming. Here again, at least in recent years, counties were taken as the basic units simply because statistics were available for determining whether there was a parallel between production figures and

---

[1] Howard W. Odum and Harry E. Moore, *American Regionalism*, Henry Holt and Co., New York, 1938.

[2] A. R. Mangus, *Rural Regions of the United States*, Works Projects Administration, 1940.

economic conditions. Defining regions by type of farming for a study of their economy does not preclude the possibility that such boundaries may also be adequate in differentiating between social groups. There is certainly a great deal of interaction between social and economic factors, particularly as they are related to housing.

Type-of-farming studies of the United States were initially done early in the twentieth century and were concerned only with broad regions; they did not, therefore, make use of small areas. After the 1930 Census of Agriculture, a monograph on types of farming was prepared from tabulations of farms classified as 12 major types.[3] The relationship of total gross income to the value of the principal product, or products, was the basis for the classification. Using these statistics by counties or townships, 514 major types of farming areas were delineated; these were later incorporated into 12 major regions. By 1950, through various revisions in this approach, the Bureau of Agricultural Economics had reduced the number of farming areas to 165 generalized types.[4]

A third type of study, making use of counties or other small areas, was a joint project of the Bureau of the Census and the Scripps Foundation for Research in Population Problems, with representatives of the Bureau of Agricultural Economics acting in an advisory capacity. The basic units used in this project were called State economic areas, and these were combined into 119 economic subregions.[5] The delimitations for both State economic areas and economic subregions were made by summarizing a comprehensive series of agricultural and nonagricultural indices and applying those factors to other sets of areas such as the generalized types described above. These earlier delimitations were used in combination with the indices in order to find a common denominator that would make it possible for the area delimitation to serve many purposes. Contiguity of counties and homogeneity of their characteristics (as indicated by the indices) were prime considerations in allocating the counties to a State economic area or the State economic areas to an economic subregion.

The State economic areas and the economic subregions are important new areal concepts in that they make it possible to analyze statistically areas that combine reasonably homogeneous counties. Since the 501 State economic areas are less unwieldy to analyze than 3,051 counties and do not have the heterogeneity of a State, they represent a useful unit for detailed analysis of relatively small areas. The 119 economic subregions help to bridge the gap between the State economic area and the country as a whole. In an analysis of national farm housing, however, one intermediate level is usually needed, since such an analysis is concerned with the characteristics of housing in general rather than with individual differences between small areas.

---

[3] *1930 Census of Agriculture, Types of Farming in the United States*, by F. F. Elliott.

[4] Bureau of Agricultural Economics, "Generalized Types of Farming in the United States," *U. S. Dept. Agr. Inf. Bul. No. 3*, 1950.

[5] For a complete description of the methods used, see U. S. Bureau of the Census, *State Economic Areas*, by Donald J. Bogue, 1951, and *Economic Subregions of the United States*, by Donald J. Bogue and Calvin L. Beale, 1953.

How this intermediate level was reached for the purposes of this monograph is described in Chapter 1, p. 7. The 12 type-of-farming regions so set up represent a compromise between the broad regions identified by the Bureau of Agricultural Economics and the 119 economic subregions and are based on combinations of the economic subregions. But it should be noted that the number and boundaries of these subregions do not tally consistently with the type-of-farming regions of the Bureau of Agricultural Economics. The number here is greater. For example, regions designated by the Bureau of Agricultural Economics as Northern and Southern Small Grains Regions and Northeastern and the Great Lakes Dairy Regions are split. In each of these pairs of areas there appears to be enough variation in the background of the people and in the climate, secondary crops, soil conditions, or topography to suggest that the characteristics of their housing may show some differences. Further, because the coastal farming areas along the Atlantic and Pacific consist of a wide variety of types of farms, they are considered as separate miscellaneous groups.

The Bureau of Agricultural Economics designated various types of grazing areas as subgroups of generalized farming. In this study, however, these subgroups are called the Year-Long and Seasonal Grazing Region and the Upland Grazing Region. For these two groups particularly, the economic subregions do not tally with the type-of-farming boundaries. Economic subregion 113, for example, is so large that it covers seasonal and year-long grazing areas as well as summer uplands and areas in which no farming is done.

The combination of economic subregions does not isolate some areas of specialty crops because these are generally much smaller than the economic subregions. Nor, generally, does the combination include small parts of crop areas that are a distance apart. The Tobacco and Northern Wheat Regions are the only instances in which an important exception is made in the attempt to use contiguous subregions. Even though there are some omissions of areas and overlapping of others, the regional divisions used here are believed to be representative enough of broad type-of-farming areas to point up the differences in housing arising from a variety of farm practices and traditions. In Chapter 3 farm housing characteristics on this regional basis are treated, while in Chapter 4 economic subregions selected as being representative of their type-of-farming regions are compared. The following listing identifies the counties in each of the 30 selected subregions:

Northeast Dairy Region

Economic Subregion 7
New York: Clinton, Essex, Franklin, Jefferson, Lewis, St. Lawrence.
Vermont: Addison, Chittenden, Franklin, Grand Isle, Orleans.
Economic Subregion 10
New York: Allegany, Broome, Cattaraugus, Chautauqua, Chemung, Chenango, Delaware, Otsego, Schoharie, Schuyler, Steuben, Tioga, Tompkins.
Pennsylvania: Bradford, Potter, Susquehanna, Tioga, Wayne, Wyoming.

Economic Subregion 27
Maryland: Allegany, Garrett.
Pennsylvania: Allegheny, Beaver, Cambria, Clarion, Clearfield, Fayette, Greene, Indiana, Jefferson, Somerset, Washington, Westmoreland.
West Virginia: Barbour, Harrison, Marion, Monongalia, Preston, Taylor.

GREAT LAKES DAIRY REGION

Economic Subregion 50
Michigan: Allegan, Benzie, Berrien, Grand Traverse, Kent, Leelanau, Manistee, Mason, Muskegon, Oceana, Ottawa, Van Buren.
Economic Subregion 66
Michigan: Alcona, Alger, Alpena, Antrim, Arenac, Baraga, Charlevoix, Cheboygan, Chippewa, Clare, Crawford, Delta, Dickinson, Emmet, Gladwin, Gogebic, Houghton, Iosco, Iron, Kalkaska, Keweenaw, Lake, Luce, Mackinac, Marquette, Mecosta, Menominee, Missaukee, Montmorency, Newaygo, Ogemaw, Ontonagon, Osceola, Oscoda, Otsego, Presque Isle, Roscommon, Schoolcraft, Wexford.
Minnesota: Aitkin, Beltrami, Carlton, Cass, Clearwater, Cook, Crow Wing, Hubbard, Itasca, Koochiching, Lake, Lake of the Woods, St. Louis.
Wisconsin: Ashland, Bayfield, Burnett, Douglas, Florence, Forest, Iron, Langlade, Lincoln, Oneida, Price, Rusk, Sawyer, Vilas, Washburn.

EAST AND GULF COAST MISCELLANEOUS REGION

Economic Subregion 21
North Carolina: Bertie, Chowan, Gates, Halifax, Hertford, Martin, Northampton, Perquimans, Washington.
Virginia: Hopewell (city), Greensville, Isle of Wight, Nansemond, Prince George, Southampton, Suffolk (city), Surry, Sussex.
Economic Subregion 39
Florida: Brevard, Broward, Charlotte, Citrus, Collier, Dade, DeSoto, Flagler, Glades, Hardee, Hendry, Hernando, Highlands, Hillsborough, Indian River, Lake, Lee, Manatee, Marion, Martin, Monroe, Okeechobee, Orange, Osceola, Palm Beach, Pasco, Pinellas, Polk, St. Lucie, Sarasota, Seminole, Sumter, Volusia.
Economic Subregion 58
Alabama: Baldwin, Escambia, Mobile.
Louisiana: East Baton Rouge, East Feliciana, Jefferson, Livingston, Orleans, Plaquemines, St. Bernard, St. Charles, St. Helena, St. Tammany, Tagipahoa, Washington, West Feliciana.
Mississippi: Forrest, George, Greene, Hancock, Harrison, Jackson, Lamar, Pearl River, Perry, Stone.

GENERAL AND SELF-SUFFICING REGION

Economic Subregion 31
Kentucky: Bell, Breathitt, Carter, Clay, Elliott, Estill, Floyd, Greenup, Harlan, Jackson, Johnson, Knott, Knox, Laurel, Lawrence, Lee, Leslie, Letcher, Lewis, Magoffin, Martin, McCreary, Menifee, Morgan, Owsley, Perry, Pike, Powell, Rowan, Whitley, Wolfe.
Tennessee: Bledsoe, Cumberland, Fentress, Grundy, Marion, Morgan, Scott, Sequatchie, Van Buren.
Virginia: Buchanan, Dickenson, Lee, Tazewell, Wise.
West Virginia: Boone, Fayette, Kanawha, Logan, McDowell, Mercer, Mingo, Raleigh, Wyoming.

Economic Subregion 72

Illinois: Bond, Clinton, Effingham, Fayette, Madison, Monroe, Randolph, St. Clair, Washington.

Missouri: Bollinger, Cape Girardeau, Cole, Franklin, Gasconade, Jefferson, Moniteau, Osage, Perry, St. Charles, St. Louis, Ste. Genevieve, Warren.

Economic Subregion 82

Arkansas: Benton, Washington.

Missouri: Barry, Jasper, Lawrence, McDonald, Newton.

Oklahoma: Adair, Cherokee, Delaware.

Tobacco Region

Economic Subregion 24

North Carolina: Edgecombe, Franklin, Greene, Harnett, Johnston, Lee, Lenoir, Nash, Pitt, Sampson, Wake, Warren, Wayne, Wilson.

Economic Subregion 53

Kentucky: Ballard, Barren, Calloway, Carlisle, Christian, Fulton, Graves, Hickman, Logan, Marshall, McCracken, Simpson, Todd, Trigg, Warren.

Tennessee: Cheatham, Montgomery, Robertson, Sumner.

Cotton Belt

Economic Subregion 35

Alabama: Russell.

Georgia: Bibb, Chattahoochee, Crawford, Glascock, Marion, Muscogee, Richmond, Taylor, Twiggs, Washington, Wilkinson.

Economic Subregion 35

South Carolina: Aiken, Chesterfield, Kershaw, Lexington, Richland.

Economic Subregion 43

Alabama: Calhoun, Cherokee, Etowah, Jefferson, St. Clair, Chelby, Talladega, Walker.

Georgia: Bartow, Catoosa, Chattooga, Dade, Floyd, Gordon, Murray, Polk, Whitfield.

Economic Subregion 97

Texas: Bell, Caldwell, Collin, Dallas, Delta, Ellis, Falls, Fannin, Fayette, Gonzales, Grayson, Guadalup, Hill, Hunt, Kaufman, Lamar, Lavaca, Limestone, McLennan, Milam, Navarro, Rockwall, Travis, Washington, Williamson.

Corn Belt

Economic Subregion 51

Illinois: Clark, Crawford, Edwards, Gallatin, Lawrence, Wabash, White.

Indiana: Clay, Daviess, Gibson, Greene, Knox, Morgan, Owen, Pike, Posey, Spencer, Sullivan, Vanderburgh, Vigo, Warrick.

Kentucky: Daviess, Henderson, McLean, Union, Webster.

Economic Subregion 86

Iowa: Boone, Calhoun, Clay, Dallas, Dickinson, Emmet, Franklin, Greene, Hamilton, Hancock, Hardin, Humboldt, Kossuth, Osceola, Palo Alto, Pocahontas, Polk, Story, Webster, Wright.

Minnesota: Cottonwood, Faribault, Jackson, Lincoln, Lyon, Martin, Murray, Nobles, Pipestone, Rock, Watonwan.

Economic Subregion 92

Nebraska: Antelope, Boone, Boyd, Buffalo, Colfax, Custer, Dawson, Greeley, Hall, Howard, Knox, Lincoln, Madison, Merrick, Nance, Pierce, Platte, Sherman, Stanton, Valley.

South Dakota: Aurora, Bon Homme, Brule, Buffalo, Charles Mix, Davison, Douglas, Gregory, Hanson, Hutchinson, Jerauld, McCook, Miner, Sanborn, Tripp.

Northern Wheat and Small Grains Region

Economic Subregion 90

North Dakota: Barnes, Benson, Bottineau, Burke, Burleigh, Cavalier, Divide, Eddy, Emmons, Foster, Griggs, Kidder, LaMoure, Logan, McHenry, McIntosh, McLean, Mountrail, Nelson, Pierce, Ramsey, Renville, Rolette, Sheridan, Steele, Stutsman, Towner, Ward, Wells, Williams.

Economic Subregion 110

Idaho: Benewah, Kootenai, Latah, Lewis, Nez Perce.

Oregon: Gilliam, Morrow, Sherman, Umatilla, Wasco.

Washington: Adams, Asotin, Columbia, Douglas, Franklin, Garfield, Grant, Lincoln, Spokane, Walla Walla, Whitman.

Southern Wheat and Small Grains Region

Economic Subregion 94

Kansas: Clay, Cloud, Dickinson, Harper, Harvey, Kingman, Marion, McPherson, Ottawa, Reno, Rice, Saline, Sedgwick, Sumner.

Oklahoma: Alfalfa, Blaine, Canadian, Garfield, Grant, Kay, Kingfisher, Major, Noble.

Year-Long and Seasonal Grazing Region

Economic Subregion 98

Texas: Aransas, Atascosa, Bee, Bexar, Brooks, De Witt, Dimmit, Duval, Frio, Goliad, Jim Hogg, Jim Wells, Karnes, Kenedy, Kleberg, LaSalle, Live Oak, Maverick, McMullen, Nueces, Refugio, San Patricio, Starr, Webb, Wilson, Zapata, Zavala.

Economic Subregion 102

Texas: Andrews, Bailey, Cochran, Crane, Crosby, Dawson, Ector, Gaines, Hockley, Howard, Lamb, Lubbock, Lynn, Martin, Midland, Terry, Winkler, Yoakum.

Economic Subregion 104

Montana: Carter, Custer, Garfield, Golden Valley, Musselshell, Petroleum, Powder River, Rosebud, Sweet Grass, Treasure, Wheatland.

Nebraska: Arthur, Blaine, Brown, Cherry, Dawes, Garden, Garfield, Grant, Holt, Hooker, Keya Paha, Logan, Loup, McPherson, Rock, Sheridan, Sioux, Thomas, Wheeler.

South Dakota: Armstrong, Bennett, Butte, Corson, Custer, Dewey, Fall River, Haakon, Harding, Jackson, Jones, Lawrence, Lyman, Meade, Mellette, Pennington, Perkins, Shannon, Stanley, Todd, Washabaugh, Ziebach.

Upland Summer Grazing Region

Economic Subregion 112

Idaho: Ada, Bannock, Bear Lake, Bingham, Bonneville, Cayon, Caribou, Cassia, Franklin, Fremont, Gem, Gooding, Jefferson, Jerome, Lincoln, Madison, Minidoka, Oneida, Owyhee, Payette, Power, Teton, Twin Falls, Washington, Yellowstone National Park (part).

Utah: Box Elder, Cache, Davis, Morgan, Rich, Salt Lake, Sanpete, Sevier, Summit, Utah, Wasatch, Weber.

West Coast Miscellaneous Region

Economic Subregion 115

California: Imperial, Los Angeles, Orange, Riverside, San Bernardino, San Diego, Santa Barbara, Ventura.

Economic Subregion 116

California: Butte, Colusa, Fresno, Glenn, Kern, Kings, Madera, Merced, Sacramento, San Joaquin, Stanislaus, Sutter, Tehama, Tulare, Yolo, Yuba.

Economic Subregion 119

Oregon: Benton, Clackamas, Hood River, Lane, Linn, Marion, Multnomah, Polk, Washington, Yamhill.

Washington: Clark, Cowlitz, King, Kitsap, Lewis, Pierce, Skamania, Thurston.

APPENDIX C

FARM FAMILY INCOME

Definitions and limitations of census procedure

In collecting information on total family income for the 1950 Census, enumerators used the following techniques. The head of the household was asked to report for the year 1949 the sum of the money received, less losses, from the following sources: wages or salary; net income (or loss) from the operation of a farm, ranch, business, or profession; net income (or loss) from rents or receipts from roomers or boarders; royalties, interest, dividends, and periodic income from estates and trust funds; pensions; veterans' payments, Armed Forces allotments for dependents, and other governmental payments or assistance; other income such as contributions for support from persons who are not members of the household, i.e., alimony; and periodic receipts for insurance policies or annuities. The income to be reported was that received before deductions for personal income taxes, social security, bond purchases, union dues, and the like. Receipts from the following sources were not to be included as income: money received from the sale of property—unless the recipient was engaged in the business of selling such property; the value of income "in kind," such as food produced and consumed in the home, or free living quarters; withdrawals of bank deposits; money borrowed; tax refunds; gifts; and lump-sum inheritances or insurance payments.

Family income was determined by asking the same questions about all related members of the family as a group, and adding that income to the income of the head of the household. Incomes of unrelated persons in the household were not included.

The figures in all field surveys of income are subject to errors of response and nonreporting. In most cases the schedule entries for income are based not on records but on memory, usually that of the housewife. The memory factor in data derived from field surveys of income probably produces underestimates, because the tendency is to forget minor or irregular sources of income. Other errors of reporting are due to misrepresentation or misunderstanding of the income questions.

Farmers typically receive an important part of their income in the form of goods produced and consumed on the farm rather than in money. Since the value of income "in kind" was not included as income, this factor should be taken into consideration in comparing the income of farm and nonfarm residents.

One of the factors which accounts for the higher incomes of urban families and individuals as compared with rural-farm families and individuals is the higher pay-and-price levels of the urban areas. Also, the paid employment of more than one family member is common in families living in urban and rural-nonfarm housing, whereas all members of the rural-farm family may contribute their services to the farm operation without pay and may not receive cash income from other sources.

A possible source of understatement in the figures on family income was the assumption that there was no other income in the family when only the head's income was reported. It is estimated that this editing assumption was made for about 5 percent of the families. This procedure was adopted in order to make maximum use of the information obtained. In the large majority of the fully-reported cases, the head's income constituted all or most of the total family income.

A P P E N D I X   D

ADDITIONAL DATA FOR CHAPTER 3

TABLE **D-1.**—ROOMS AND YEAR BUILT, BY TENURE, FOR ALL OCCUPIED AND
NONWHITE-OCCUPIED DWELLING UNITS: 1950

Year built and tenure	Total	1 and 2 rooms	3 and 4 rooms	5 and 6 rooms	7 rooms or more
ALL OCCUPIED UNITS					
Total..........................	5,659,600	301,700	1,721,400	2,059,500	1,458,000
Percent Distribution					
Total reporting.................	100	100	100	100	100
1945 or later...........................	10	23	13	10	3
1940 to 1944...........................	5	8	7	6	2
1930 to 1939...........................	15	23	20	15	7
1920 to 1929...........................	16	18	20	16	11
1919 or earlier.........................	54	29	40	53	77
Owner...........................	3,701,900	125,000	896,300	1,492,800	1,113,500
Percent Distribution					
Total reporting...................	100	100	100	100	100
1945 or later...........................	12	32	17	12	4
1940 to 1944...........................	6	9	9	7	2
1930 to 1939...........................	14	20	19	16	7
1920 to 1929...........................	15	13	17	16	12
1919 or earlier.........................	53	25	38	49	74
Renter and rent free..............	1,957,700	176,700	825,100	566,600	344,500
Percent Distribution					
Total reporting...................	100	100	100	100	100
1945 or later...........................	7	17	9	5	1
1940 to 1944...........................	4	7	5	3	1
1930 to 1939...........................	15	25	20	12	4
1920 to 1929...........................	19	21	23	17	9
1919 or earlier.........................	54	31	42	62	85
NONWHITE-OCCUPIED UNITS					
Total.........................	663,800	83,100	365,600	167,500	31,100
Percent Distribution					
Total reporting..................	100	100	100	100	100
1945 or later...........................	11	14	10	12	11
1940 to 1944...........................	6	6	6	7	6
1930 to 1939...........................	21	24	22	19	14
1920 to 1929...........................	24	24	26	20	17
1919 or earlier.........................	38	31	37	41	52
Owner...........................	219,500	19,900	89,900	83,500	19,600
Percent Distribution					
Total reporting...................	100	100	100	100	100
1945 or later...........................	19	28	17	20	16
1940 to 1944...........................	10	10	11	11	7
1930 to 1939...........................	21	23	22	21	17
1920 to 1929...........................	19	16	20	18	18
1919 or earlier.........................	31	23	30	30	42
Renter and rent free..............	444,400	63,200	275,700	84,000	11,500
Percent Distribution					
Total reporting...................	100	100	100	100	100
1945 or later...........................	7	10	7	5	4
1940 to 1944...........................	4	5	4	3	3
1930 to 1939...........................	21	25	22	17	8
1920 to 1929...........................	26	27	28	23	16
1919 or earlier.........................	42	33	39	52	70

Source: *1950 Census of Housing*, Vol. III, *Farm Housing Characteristics*, table E.

TABLE **D-2.**—CONDITION AND PLUMBING FACILITIES AND KITCHEN SINK, BY TENURE AND ROOMS: 1950

Condition and plumbing facilities and kitchen sink	Total occupied dwelling units	Percent distribution										
		Total	Owner			Renter			Rent free			Non-white-occupied units
			Total	1 to 4 rooms	5 or more	Total	1 to 4 rooms	5 or more	Total	1 to 4 rooms	5 or more	
Total................	5,659,600	...	...	...	...	...	...	...	...	...	...	...
CONDITION AND PLUMBING FACILITIES[1]												
Total reporting......	5,502,800	100	100	100	100	100	100	100	100	100	100	100
Not dilapidated..........	4,540,900	83	88	76	92	76	62	87	69	61	82	54
All facilities........	1,318,800	24	29	12	36	14	7	21	13	6	24	2
Some facilities.......	983,500	18	20	15	22	16	11	20	13	10	18	4
No facilities.........	2,238,500	41	39	50	34	46	45	46	43	45	40	48
Dilapidated..........	962,000	17	12	24	8	24	38	13	31	39	18	46
All or some facilities.	122,400	2	2	2	2	2	3	2	3	3	3	2
No facilities..........	839,600	15	10	22	6	22	35	11	28	37	16	45
KITCHEN SINK[2]												
Total reporting condition and plumbing.	5,502,800	100	100	100	100	100	100	100	100	100	100	100
With running water.......	2,424,700	44	51	29	60	32	20	43	29	18	45	7
No running water........	3,078,100	56	49	71	40	68	80	57	71	82	55	93
With kitchen sink......	750,500	14	14	12	15	16	8	22	9	6	14	3
No kitchen sink or not reporting sink.......	2,327,600	42	35	59	25	52	72	35	62	76	41	90

[1] Units with all plumbing facilities have all of the following facilities inside the structure: private flush toilet, private bath, and hot and cold running water. Units with no facilities have no private flush toilet, no private bath, and no running water inside the structure.

[2] Tabulation restricted to units with no running water inside structure.

Source: *1950 Census of Housing*, Vol. III, *Farm Housing Characteristics*, table F.

TABLE **D-3.**—TYPE OF COOKING AND HEATING FUEL, BY TENURE AND ROOMS: 1950

Cooking and heating fuel	Total occupied dwelling units	Percent distribution						
		Total	Owner		Renter		Rent free	
			1 to 4 rooms	5 rooms or more	1 to 4 rooms	5 rooms or more	1 to 4 rooms	5 rooms or more
COOKING FUEL								
Total...........................	5,659,600	100	100	100	100	100	100	100
Coal......................................	691,300	12	13	14	9	14	7	11
Wood......................................	2,172,600	38	47	30	55	28	60	39
Bottled gas...............................	1,008,300	18	14	20	11	27	9	20
Electricity...............................	871,400	15	10	22	5	15	4	14
Other, none, or not reported..........	915,800	16	16	14	20	16	19	15
HEATING FUEL								
Total reporting heating equipment.	5,452,800	100	100	100	100	100	100	100
Central heating........................	995,800	18	7	28	5	20	3	17
Coal...................................	590,600	11	3	16	2	13	1	10
Wood...................................	116,700	2	1	3	1	2	1	2
Liquid fuel............................	164,700	3	1	5	1	3	1	3
Other or not reported................	123,800	2	1	3	1	2	1	2
Noncentral heating.....................	4,457,000	82	93	72	95	80	97	83
Coal...................................	1,086,300	20	22	21	17	22	15	19
Wood...................................	2,099,500	39	49	28	58	28	63	40
Liquid fuel............................	682,600	13	11	12	11	21	10	14
Other or not reported................	588,500	11	12	11	9	10	9	10

Source: *1950 Census of Housing*, Vol. III, *Farm Housing Characteristics*, table G.

TABLE **D-4.**—PERSONS PER ROOM, BY TENURE AND ROOMS: 1950

Tenure and rooms	Percent of units reporting number of rooms by persons per room		Tenure and rooms	Percent of units reporting number of rooms by persons per room	
	1.00 or less	1.01 or more		1.00 or less	1.01 or more
ALL OCCUPIED UNITS			ALL OCCUPIED UNITS--Cont.		
Owner.....................	84	16	Rent free.................	62	38
1 to 4 rooms............	66	34	1 to 4 rooms............	51	49
5 rooms or more.........	91	9	5 rooms or more.........	78	22
Renter....................	71	29	NONWHITE-OCCUPIED UNITS		
1 to 4 rooms............	52	48	Total.....................	51	49
5 rooms or more.........	86	14	1 to 4 rooms............	47	53
			5 rooms or more.........	60	40

Source: *1950 Census of Housing*, Vol. III, *Farm Housing Characteristics*, table H.

TABLE **D-5.**—AGE OF HEAD OF HOUSEHOLD, BY TENURE AND ROOMS, FOR ALL OCCUPIED AND NONWHITE-OCCUPIED DWELLING UNITS: 1950

Tenure and rooms	Age of head of household			Tenure and rooms	Age of head of household		
	Under 45 years	45 to 64 years	65 and over		Under 45 years	45 to 64 years	65 and over
All occupied units............	2,469,700	2,282,200	907,700	Nonwhite-occupied units............	307,100	247,200	109,500
Percent Distribution				Percent Distribution			
Total reporting...	100	100	100	Total reporting...	100	100	100
Owner..................	51	75	81	Owner..................	22	39	51
1 to 4 rooms........	17	19	22	1 to 4 rooms........	12	18	27
5 rooms or more.....	34	56	59	5 rooms or more.....	9	21	24
Renter................	27	14	10	Renter................	29	24	19
1 to 4 rooms........	12	6	5	1 to 4 rooms........	23	17	15
5 rooms or more.....	15	8	4	5 rooms or more.....	6	7	4
Rent free.............	22	11	10	Rent free.............	49	37	30
1 to 4 rooms........	13	7	6	1 to 4 rooms........	40	28	25
5 rooms or more.....	8	5	3	5 rooms or more.....	9	9	5

Source: *1950 Census of Housing*, Vol. III, *Farm Housing Characteristics*, table J.

TABLE **D-6.**—YEAR BUILT, ELECTRIC LIGHTING, AND HEATING EQUIPMENT, BY CONDITION AND PLUMBING FACILITIES, FOR ALL OCCUPIED AND NONWHITE-OCCUPIED DWELLING UNITS: 1950

Condition and plumbing facilities[1]	All occupied units						Nonwhite-occupied units				
	Total	Built in 1940 or later		Percent with--			Total	Percent with--			
		Number	Percent of total	Electric lights	Heating equipment			Electric lights	Heating equipment		
					Central	Non-central, with flue			Central	Non-central, with flue	
Total..........	5,659,600	853,500	15	80	18	69	663,800	44	1	85	
Not dilapidated....	4,540,900	749,900	17	87	21	66	345,300	54	2	83	
All facilities...	1,318,900	236,500	18	99	49	39	12,000	99	23	51	
Some facilities..	983,300	137,700	14	95	20	66	23,100	80	4	76	
No facilities....	2,238,700	375,700	17	75	5	82	310,100	50	1	85	
Dilapidated........	961,000	86,600	9	53	3	83	297,900	32	1	85	
All or some facilities......	122,400	9,800	8	86	13	70	10,300	51	5	79	
No facilities....	838,600	76,800	9	48	1	85	287,600	31	1	86	

[1] See footnote 1, table D-2.

Source: *1950 Census of Housing*, Vol. III, *Farm Housing Characteristics*, table K.

TABLE **D-7.**—TYPE OF HOUSEHOLD, BY CONDITION AND PLUMBING FACILITIES, FOR ALL
OCCUPIED AND NONWHITE-OCCUPIED DWELLING UNITS: 1950

Condition and plumbing facilities[1]	Total	Husband-wife families, no non-relatives	Other family groups, no non-relatives	One-person households	Households with non-relatives
ALL OCCUPIED UNITS					
Total..........................	5,659,600	4,642,700	505,000	267,700	244,200
Percent Distribution					
Total reporting..................	100	100	100	100	100
Not dilapidated.....................	83	84	77	71	85
All facilities.....................	24	25	18	14	35
Some facilities....................	18	18	16	13	18
No facilities......................	41	41	43	44	32
Dilapidated.........................	17	16	23	29	15
NONWHITE-OCCUPIED UNITS					
Total..........................	663,800	516,000	83,600	35,500	28,600
Percent Distribution					
Total reporting..................	100	100	100	100	100
Not dilapidated.....................	54	55	49	45	56
All facilities.....................	2	2	2	2	4
Some facilities....................	4	4	3	3	5
No facilities......................	48	50	44	41	48
Dilapidated.........................	46	45	51	55	44

[1] See footnote 1, table D-2.

Source: *1950 Census of Housing*, Vol. III, *Farm Housing Characteristics*, table L.

TABLE **D-8.**—INCOME IN 1949, BY CONDITION AND PLUMBING FACILITIES, FOR ALL OCCUPIED
AND NONWHITE-OCCUPIED DWELLING UNITS: 1950

[Income of only primary families and individuals]

Condition and plumbing facilities[1]	Under $2,000	$2,000 to $3,999	$4,000 to $5,999	$6,000 and over	Median income (dollars)
ALL OCCUPIED UNITS					
Total..........................	3,132,300	1,478,400	469,200	313,500	...
Percent Distribution					
Total reporting..................	100	100	100	100	1,660
Not dilapidated:					
All or some facilities.............	28	54	69	79	2,540
No facilities......................	48	36	26	17	1,350
Dilapidated.........................	24	10	6	4	890
NONWHITE-OCCUPIED UNITS					
Total..........................	573,000	51,800	6,300	3,300	...
Percent Distribution					
Total reporting..................	100	100	100	100	740
Not dilapidated:					
All or some facilities.............	4	14	27	37	1,210
No facilities......................	48	52	46	38	760
Dilapidated.........................	48	35	27	25	690

[1] See footnote 1, table D-2.

Source: *1950 Census of Housing*, Vol. III, *Farm Housing Characteristics*, table M.

TABLE **D-9.**—ROOMS AND YEAR BUILT, BY TENURE, FOR TYPE-OF-FARMING REGIONS: 1950

Region, year built, and tenure	Total	1 and 2 rooms	3 and 4 rooms	5 and 6 rooms	7 rooms or more	Not re-ported
NORTHEAST DAIRY REGION						
All occupied dwelling units......	543,440	13,250	65,355	158,890	297,095	8,850
Owner.............................	424,000	5,525	36,130	121,415	254,550	6,380
Percent........................	100.0	100.0	100.0	100.0	100.0	100.0
1945 or later.........................	4.9	39.9	19.6	6.4	1.4	3.2
1940 to 1944.........................	2.5	6.1	7.0	4.0	1.1	1.6
1930 to 1939.........................	6.1	19.3	12.8	9.1	3.5	2.4
1920 to 1929.........................	6.7	8.0	9.3	8.9	5.4	4.0
1919 or earlier......................	78.2	24.4	49.5	70.4	87.7	57.7
Not reported........................	1.6	2.3	1.8	1.2	0.9	31.1
Renter............................	61,945	3,565	15,425	18,715	22,335	1,905
Percent........................	100.0	100.0	100.0	100.0	100.0	100.0
1945 or later.........................	3.9	15.5	7.3	3.0	0.8	...
1940 to 1944.........................	2.2	4.5	3.5	2.7	0.6	...
1930 to 1939.........................	5.5	17.3	8.2	5.2	2.4	3.1
1920 to 1929.........................	6.3	6.4	7.5	8.3	4.2	1.5
1919 or earlier......................	77.9	53.6	70.4	78.9	90.1	30.8
Not reported........................	4.2	2.7	3.1	1.9	1.9	64.6
Rent free.........................	57,495	4,160	13,800	18,760	20,210	565
Percent........................	100.0	100.0	100.0	100.0	100.0	100.0
1945 or later.........................	5.7	23.6	8.5	5.0	0.9	5.0
1940 to 1944.........................	2.5	4.5	4.0	3.1	0.5	5.0
1930 to 1939.........................	7.5	12.1	11.3	8.8	2.4	15.0
1920 to 1929.........................	7.6	7.6	10.8	8.9	4.4	...
1919 or earlier......................	74.3	49.0	62.4	72.0	90.1	65.0
Not reported........................	2.4	3.2	3.0	2.2	1.7	10.0
GREAT LAKES DAIRY REGION						
All occupied dwelling units......	447,355	15,240	69,015	146,205	208,790	8,105
Owner.............................	363,230	10,545	53,185	121,505	171,845	6,150
Percent........................	100.0	100.0	100.0	100.0	100.0	100.0
1945 or later.........................	7.1	31.1	17.8	7.1	2.3	9.2
1940 to 1944.........................	4.1	9.7	9.5	4.7	1.6	5.2
1930 to 1939.........................	10.0	19.7	17.3	12.5	5.3	6.6
1920 to 1929.........................	12.3	11.6	14.4	12.8	11.5	7.4
1919 or earlier......................	64.6	24.5	39.6	61.3	77.8	47.6
Not reported........................	1.9	3.4	1.4	1.6	1.5	24.0
Renter............................	56,165	2,110	9,455	16,960	25,985	1,655
Percent........................	100.0	100.0	100.0	100.0	100.0	100.0
1945 or later.........................	3.0	15.0	8.1	1.9	1.0	1.7
1940 to 1944.........................	1.7	6.3	2.7	2.9	0.2	...
1930 to 1939.........................	5.5	20.0	9.7	5.6	2.9	1.8
1920 to 1929.........................	10.5	20.0	15.4	10.6	8.4	3.5
1919 or earlier......................	76.1	33.7	60.9	77.7	86.3	42.1
Not reported........................	3.2	5.0	3.2	1.3	1.2	50.9
Rent free.........................	27,960	2,585	6,375	7,740	10,960	300
Percent........................	100.0	100.0	100.0	100.0	100.0	100.0
1945 or later.........................	6.9	20.7	13.9	5.5	0.7	...
1940 to 1944.........................	4.4	8.5	6.4	6.8	0.7	...
1930 to 1939.........................	10.1	28.3	10.4	11.9	4.5	10.0
1920 to 1929.........................	11.5	16.1	16.3	11.2	8.2	...
1919 or earlier......................	65.2	23.6	50.2	62.2	85.4	80.0
Not reported........................	1.9	2.8	2.8	2.4	0.5	10.0

TABLE **D–9.**—ROOMS AND YEAR BUILT, BY TENURE, FOR TYPE-OF-FARMING REGIONS: 1950—Cont.

Region, year built, and tenure	Total	1 and 2 rooms	3 and 4 rooms	5 and 6 rooms	7 rooms or more	Not re-ported
EAST AND GULF COAST MISCELLANEOUS REGION						
All occupied dwelling units......	273,490	20,235	88,620	110,105	48,485	6,045
Owner..........................	176,480	6,980	46,055	81,045	38,800	3,600
Percent........................	100.0	100.0	100.0	100.0	100.0	100.0
1945 or later..................	16.5	38.6	21.4	16.3	7.8	8.6
1940 to 1944...................	9.6	9.2	12.0	10.8	4.4	7.0
1930 to 1939...................	19.5	20.6	24.1	20.3	12.9	13.3
1920 to 1929...................	17.2	13.0	15.9	18.9	16.4	12.5
1919 or earlier................	34.8	13.3	24.0	32.1	57.3	33.6
Not reported...................	2.4	5.3	2.6	1.6	1.2	25.0
Renter.........................	36,295	2,765	15,670	11,915	4,500	1,445
Percent........................	100.0	100.0	100.0	100.0	100.0	100.0
1945 or later..................	8.2	11.5	9.7	7.9	3.2	4.8
1940 to 1944...................	4.6	11.5	5.1	4.2	0.6	1.6
1930 to 1939...................	17.6	28.9	20.0	15.4	9.1	14.2
1920 to 1929...................	23.1	17.3	26.7	26.1	11.1	6.4
1919 or earlier................	40.9	25.0	34.1	42.9	74.7	23.8
Not reported...................	5.6	5.8	4.4	3.5	1.3	49.2
Rent free......................	60,715	10,490	26,895	17,145	5,185	1,000
Percent........................	100.0	100.0	100.0	100.0	100.0	100.0
1945 or later..................	12.2	26.2	11.2	8.3	1.0	20.0
1940 to 1944...................	5.8	5.2	5.9	6.0	3.4	15.0
1930 to 1939...................	20.5	30.1	22.9	14.6	8.4	17.5
1920 to 1929...................	19.1	14.9	21.3	20.2	14.3	12.5
1919 or earlier................	40.4	20.8	36.7	49.2	71.4	32.5
Not reported...................	2.0	2.8	2.0	1.7	1.5	2.5
GENERAL AND SELF-SUFFICING REGION						
All occupied dwelling units......	881,955	46,885	306,340	342,210	168,845	17,675
Owner..........................	682,830	26,560	217,355	282,245	143,665	13,005
Percent........................	100.0	100.0	100.0	100.0	100.0	100.0
1945 or later..................	12.0	26.6	14.6	11.6	6.2	9.8
1940 to 1944...................	6.5	8.9	8.2	6.6	3.7	5.7
1930 to 1939...................	17.1	18.7	20.4	17.2	11.8	13.6
1920 to 1929...................	15.3	14.5	16.1	15.6	13.8	13.4
1919 or earlier................	47.3	29.6	39.3	47.5	63.1	38.4
Not reported...................	1.8	1.7	1.4	1.5	1.4	19.1
Renter.........................	123,705	10,565	54,300	38,870	16,360	3,610
Percent........................	100.0	100.0	100.0	100.0	100.0	100.0
1945 or later..................	7.0	18.0	8.5	4.7	1.3	2.2
1940 to 1944...................	4.2	6.8	5.1	3.4	0.6	6.7
1930 to 1939...................	15.5	21.6	20.7	11.0	5.9	10.4
1920 to 1929...................	16.0	17.2	18.2	16.3	8.7	9.6
1919 or earlier................	53.7	34.5	45.1	62.5	80.5	24.4
Not reported...................	3.6	1.9	2.4	2.1	3.0	46.7
Rent free......................	75,420	9,760	34,685	21,095	8,820	1,060
Percent........................	100.0	100.0	100.0	100.0	100.0	100.0
1945 or later..................	11.2	26.7	12.0	7.2	1.7	5.7
1940 to 1944...................	5.1	6.9	5.3	4.6	2.6	8.6
1930 to 1939...................	16.4	19.7	19.8	14.0	4.6	17.2
1920 to 1929...................	16.3	13.1	18.0	16.9	11.6	20.0
1919 or earlier................	49.2	32.5	42.9	55.5	78.6	37.1
Not reported...................	1.8	1.1	2.0	1.8	0.9	11.4

TABLE **D-9.**—ROOMS AND YEAR BUILT, BY TENURE, FOR TYPE-OF-FARMING REGIONS: 1950—Cont.

Region, year built, and tenure	Total	1 and 2 rooms	3 and 4 rooms	5 and 6 rooms	7 rooms or more	Not reported
TOBACCO REGION						
All occupied dwelling units......	238,465	9,040	85,280	94,815	44,020	5,310
Owner............................	131,015	3,205	34,175	57,080	33,625	2,930
Percent......................	100.0	100.0	100.0	100.0	100.0	100.0
1945 or later....................	10.5	23.3	13.9	10.2	6.6	6.6
1940 to 1944....................	5.1	5.0	6.7	4.9	4.1	2.9
1930 to 1939....................	14.9	13.3	16.2	15.5	12.6	16.2
1920 to 1929....................	16.9	18.4	15.2	17.8	16.9	16.2
1919 or earlier..................	50.8	37.5	46.6	50.5	58.2	35.2
Not reported....................	1.8	2.5	1.4	1.1	1.6	22.9
Renter...........................	48,170	2,315	22,415	16,920	4,955	1,565
Percent......................	100.0	100.0	100.0	100.0	100.0	100.0
1945 or later....................	6.7	15.9	8.2	5.1	1.8	5.4
1940 to 1944....................	4.5	6.4	5.4	4.3	1.8	...
1930 to 1939....................	12.8	11.7	14.9	11.6	10.6	3.6
1920 to 1929....................	20.3	27.7	19.7	21.5	16.6	16.4
1919 or earlier..................	52.2	38.3	49.8	54.7	66.3	34.6
Not reported....................	3.5	...	2.0	2.8	2.9	40.0
Rent free........................	59,280	3,520	28,690	20,815	5,440	815
Percent......................	100.0	100.0	100.0	100.0	100.0	100.0
1945 or later....................	7.3	11.2	8.5	5.8	3.9	6.9
1940 to 1944....................	4.0	6.0	4.7	3.0	2.5	10.3
1930 to 1939....................	13.1	18.7	14.6	12.2	5.9	6.9
1920 to 1929....................	20.0	17.1	21.8	20.2	11.3	17.3
1919 or earlier..................	53.7	47.0	48.7	56.8	73.5	48.3
Not reported....................	1.9	...	1.7	2.0	2.9	10.3
COTTON BELT						
All occupied dwelling units......	1,426,550	96,205	681,510	505,945	109,225	33,665
Owner............................	728,005	24,435	253,620	346,095	86,435	17,420
Percent......................	100.0	100.0	100.0	100.0	100.0	100.0
1945 or later....................	17.5	30.6	18.9	17.8	9.7	12.9
1940 to 1944....................	9.1	9.5	9.2	10.0	5.5	7.2
1930 to 1939....................	20.9	20.6	21.6	21.6	16.8	15.8
1920 to 1929....................	17.8	15.1	18.6	17.6	18.2	12.0
1919 or earlier..................	32.3	21.4	29.9	31.4	47.8	22.9
Not reported....................	2.4	2.8	1.8	1.6	2.0	29.2
Renter...........................	332,280	27,205	200,510	83,075	11,585	9,905
Percent......................	100.0	100.0	100.0	100.0	100.0	100.0
1945 or later....................	7.6	10.9	8.0	6.5	2.4	5.1
1940 to 1944....................	4.8	4.5	5.4	4.0	2.2	4.0
1930 to 1939....................	20.7	24.3	22.5	17.8	8.3	11.7
1920 to 1929....................	23.5	25.3	24.7	21.9	19.2	13.2
1919 or earlier..................	40.3	32.7	37.4	47.4	65.0	31.7
Not reported....................	3.1	2.3	2.0	2.4	2.9	34.3
Rent free........................	366,265	44,565	227,380	76,775	11,205	6,340
Percent......................	100.0	100.0	100.0	100.0	100.0	100.0
1945 or later....................	8.2	10.9	8.5	6.5	3.7	8.3
1940 to 1944....................	4.8	5.1	5.0	4.2	2.1	5.4
1930 to 1939....................	22.2	24.8	23.1	19.7	10.5	22.4
1920 to 1929....................	26.2	26.4	27.3	24.0	16.8	27.0
1919 or earlier..................	36.8	30.7	34.5	43.7	65.7	31.1
Not reported....................	1.8	2.1	1.6	1.9	1.2	5.8

TABLE **D–9.**—ROOMS AND YEAR BUILT, BY TENURE, FOR TYPE-OF-FARMING REGIONS: 1950—Cont.

Region, year built, and tenure	Total	1 and 2 rooms	3 and 4 rooms	5 and 6 rooms	7 rooms or more	Not re-ported
CORN BELT						
All occupied dwelling units......	954,360	18,155	131,355	361,200	425,080	18,570
Owner............................	594,965	9,980	79,095	231,260	263,210	11,420
Percent.......................	100.0	100.0	100.0	100.0	100.0	100.0
1945 or later....................	5.2	27.1	12.6	5.6	1.9	4.1
1940 to 1944.....................	2.5	9.4	5.9	2.5	1.2	1.5
1930 to 1939.....................	6.0	13.2	9.4	7.1	3.7	4.6
1920 to 1929.....................	10.3	5.4	9.8	11.0	9.9	11.2
1919 or earlier..................	74.3	40.3	60.7	72.5	82.2	55.5
Not reported.....................	1.7	4.6	1.6	1.3	1.1	23.1
Renter...........................	269,890	4,490	33,970	99,420	125,985	6,025
Percent.......................	100.0	100.0	100.0	100.0	100.0	100.0
1945 or later....................	2.0	12.8	6.0	1.8	0.6	1.0
1940 to 1944.....................	1.1	6.1	3.1	1.1	0.5	...
1930 to 1939.....................	3.8	10.1	7.4	4.5	2.2	1.9
1920 to 1929.....................	8.3	12.8	11.0	8.0	7.8	7.3
1919 or earlier..................	82.3	54.1	70.4	82.4	87.4	61.6
Not reported.....................	2.5	4.1	2.1	2.2	1.5	28.2
Rent free........................	89,505	3,685	18,290	30,520	35,885	1,125
Percent.......................	100.0	100.0	100.0	100.0	100.0	100.0
1945 or later....................	5.1	25.0	13.5	3.1	0.6	...
1940 to 1944.....................	2.2	5.9	6.2	1.8	0.2	...
1930 to 1939.....................	5.4	16.2	9.3	5.3	2.5	4.6
1920 to 1929.....................	7.5	14.0	9.9	7.7	5.5	7.0
1919 or earlier..................	78.4	35.3	59.6	81.3	89.9	79.1
Not reported.....................	1.4	3.6	1.5	0.8	1.3	9.3
NORTHERN WHEAT AND SMALL GRAINS REGION						
All occupied dwelling units......	125,685	7,090	27,515	46,770	41,985	2,325
Owner............................	92,685	4,675	19,990	34,890	31,430	1,700
Percent.......................	100.0	100.0	100.0	100.0	100.0	100.0
1945 or later....................	8.2	23.0	10.1	7.3	5.7	10.2
1940 to 1944.....................	3.4	6.2	4.3	4.0	1.8	2.6
1930 to 1939.....................	9.0	15.7	10.7	10.4	5.4	9.0
1920 to 1929.....................	16.2	13.0	14.7	17.7	16.6	3.8
1919 or earlier..................	61.2	41.0	58.4	59.7	68.9	37.2
Not reported.....................	2.0	1.1	1.8	0.9	1.6	37.2
Renter...........................	23,485	955	5,020	8,830	8,205	475
Percent.......................	100.0	100.0	100.0	100.0	100.0	100.0
1945 or later....................	2.6	11.4	4.4	2.4	1.0	...
1940 to 1944.....................	2.1	8.6	2.2	2.4	1.0	...
1930 to 1939.....................	5.5	22.8	7.6	4.5	3.5	...
1920 to 1929.....................	12.7	8.6	15.3	12.6	11.8	10.1
1919 or earlier..................	74.3	42.8	68.3	76.0	81.6	45.1
Not reported.....................	2.8	5.8	2.2	2.1	1.1	44.8
Rent free........................	9,515	1,460	2,505	3,050	2,350	150
Percent.......................	100.0	100.0	100.0	100.0	100.0	100.0
1945 or later....................	10.6	18.8	14.3	9.6	3.5	...
1940 to 1944.....................	2.0	1.9	1.2	1.9	2.3	11.3
1930 to 1939.....................	7.2	15.1	9.5	5.8	2.3	...
1920 to 1929.....................	17.9	22.7	23.8	13.5	14.0	22.0
1919 or earlier..................	60.9	41.5	48.8	67.3	77.9	55.3
Not reported.....................	1.4	...	2.4	1.9	...	11.4

TABLE **D-9.**—ROOMS AND YEAR BUILT, BY TENURE, FOR TYPE-OF-FARMING REGIONS: 1950—Cont.

Region, year built, and tenure	Total	1 and 2 rooms	3 and 4 rooms	5 and 6 rooms	7 rooms or more	Not re-ported
SOUTHERN WHEAT AND SMALL GRAINS REGION						
All occupied dwelling units......	104,190	3,865	26,330	44,660	26,830	2,505
Owner.............................	63,450	1,755	13,925	28,555	17,700	1,515
Percent........................	100.0	100.0	100.0	100.0	100.0	100.0
1945 or later.........................	10.5	37.1	12.8	10.0	7.1	10.7
1940 to 1944.........................	3.9	3.2	5.5	4.1	2.4	3.5
1930 to 1939.........................	10.1	9.7	12.7	11.3	6.9	1.8
1920 to 1929.........................	19.4	9.7	18.5	21.6	17.6	17.9
1919 or earlier......................	53.9	37.1	48.9	51.2	65.1	39.3
Not reported.........................	2.2	3.2	1.6	1.8	0.9	26.8
Renter..............................	30,575	890	8,325	12,875	7,665	820
Percent........................	100.0	100.0	100.0	100.0	100.0	100.0
1945 or later.........................	4.0	16.0	6.3	3.5	1.4	...
1940 to 1944.........................	1.8	8.0	2.2	1.6	1.1	...
1930 to 1939.........................	7.2	20.0	10.5	6.9	3.3	3.2
1920 to 1929.........................	15.9	24.0	19.3	16.6	10.5	12.9
1919 or earlier......................	68.4	32.0	59.5	69.0	82.6	54.9
Not reported.........................	2.7	...	2.2	2.4	1.1	29.0
Rent free..........................	10,165	1,220	4,080	3,230	1,465	170
Percent........................	100.0	100.0	100.0	100.0	100.0	100.0
1945 or later.........................	14.0	20.7	16.1	12.2	5.3	25.3
1940 to 1944.........................	5.2	8.6	5.8	4.3	3.5	...
1930 to 1939.........................	13.7	31.1	18.1	6.1	5.3	...
1920 to 1929.........................	21.8	12.0	25.8	23.5	17.5	...
1919 or earlier......................	42.9	22.4	33.6	50.4	68.4	49.4
Not reported.........................	2.4	5.2	0.6	3.5	...	25.3
YEAR-LONG AND SEASONAL GRAZING REGION						
All occupied dwelling units......	306,110	35,670	121,145	109,540	31,365	8,390
Owner.............................	184,170	14,250	63,640	77,100	24,160	5,020
Percent........................	100.0	100.0	100.0	100.0	100.0	100.0
1945 or later.........................	15.9	30.8	16.1	14.4	12.0	11.6
1940 to 1944.........................	8.0	9.4	8.2	8.4	5.9	3.9
1930 to 1939.........................	19.1	20.7	19.9	20.1	13.7	16.0
1920 to 1929.........................	20.6	16.0	20.9	21.2	21.0	20.5
1919 or earlier......................	33.4	20.0	32.1	34.3	45.4	17.1
Not reported.........................	3.0	3.1	2.8	1.6	2.0	30.9
Renter..............................	57,255	4,765	28,045	18,390	4,050	2,005
Percent........................	100.0	100.0	100.0	100.0	100.0	100.0
1945 or later.........................	6.8	11.5	8.4	4.4	3.5	4.2
1940 to 1944.........................	4.0	6.3	3.8	4.2	1.4	4.2
1930 to 1939.........................	18.1	23.6	21.3	14.5	9.0	9.9
1920 to 1929.........................	26.6	24.1	28.2	26.2	25.7	15.5
1919 or earlier......................	40.0	29.9	35.5	47.1	59.0	25.3
Not reported.........................	4.5	4.6	2.8	3.6	1.4	40.9
Rent free..........................	64,685	16,655	29,460	14,050	3,155	1,365
Percent........................	100.0	100.0	100.0	100.0	100.0	100.0
1945 or later.........................	13.3	20.2	12.4	8.4	7.1	13.0
1940 to 1944.........................	6.9	10.5	5.8	5.9	1.8	7.4
1930 to 1939.........................	23.4	28.2	23.8	18.6	15.2	24.1
1920 to 1929.........................	23.8	21.6	25.3	24.9	17.0	24.1
1919 or earlier......................	29.5	14.9	30.0	39.7	58.0	25.9
Not reported.........................	3.1	4.6	2.7	2.5	0.9	5.5

TABLE **D-9.**—ROOMS AND YEAR BUILT, BY TENURE, FOR TYPE-OF-FARMING REGIONS: 1950—Cont.

Region, year built, and tenure	Total	1 and 2 rooms	3 and 4 rooms	5 and 6 rooms	7 rooms or more	Not re-ported
UPLAND SUMMER GRAZING REGION						
All occupied dwelling units......	115,380	13,885	42,565	40,525	15,515	2,890
Owner.............................	87,020	8,335	30,495	32,850	13,200	2,140
Percent.....................	100.0	100.0	100.0	100.0	100.0	100.0
1945 or later.......................	15.5	26.2	17.1	14.0	8.7	15.8
1940 to 1944........................	8.1	12.1	8.8	7.5	6.9	1.3
1930 to 1939........................	16.5	24.0	17.5	15.8	11.8	13.2
1920 to 1929........................	18.1	12.8	20.5	18.6	16.0	10.5
1919 or earlier.....................	39.5	19.3	34.6	42.6	56.2	34.2
Not reported........................	2.3	5.6	1.5	1.5	0.4	25.0
Renter............................	13,415	1,685	5,855	4,135	1,195	545
Percent.....................	100.0	100.0	100.0	100.0	100.0	100.0
1945 or later.......................	8.5	25.8	8.3	5.4	...	...
1940 to 1944........................	4.4	3.0	5.5	4.7	...	4.9
1930 to 1939........................	15.2	25.8	17.9	11.4	4.8	4.9
1920 to 1929........................	21.9	15.1	24.8	20.1	26.9	15.1
1919 or earlier.....................	43.9	24.2	38.5	55.7	65.9	25.0
Not reported........................	6.1	6.1	5.0	2.7	2.4	50.1
Rent free........................	14,945	3,865	6,215	3,540	1,120	205
Percent.....................	100.0	100.0	100.0	100.0	100.0	100.0
1945 or later.......................	12.0	19.3	12.6	6.3	...	22.4
1940 to 1944........................	4.8	6.0	6.1	2.1	2.9	...
1930 to 1939........................	16.7	23.3	17.0	12.7	5.7	11.2
1920 to 1929........................	18.3	15.4	20.4	21.2	8.6	11.2
1919 or earlier.....................	43.3	25.3	40.0	55.6	82.8	55.2
Not reported........................	4.9	10.7	3.9	2.1	...	...
WEST COAST MISCELLANEOUS REGION						
All occupied dwelling units......	242,590	22,175	76,405	98,615	40,755	4,640
Owner.............................	174,025	8,710	48,665	78,795	34,830	3,025
Percent.....................	100.0	100.0	100.0	100.0	100.0	100.0
1945 or later.......................	17.8	49.8	24.6	14.3	8.8	10.6
1940 to 1944........................	7.9	10.1	9.9	8.2	3.8	4.4
1930 to 1939........................	22.0	19.9	24.1	23.0	17.7	16.0
1920 to 1929........................	20.0	9.5	17.9	22.5	20.1	17.7
1919 or earlier.....................	30.0	8.0	21.5	30.2	48.4	15.9
Not reported........................	2.3	2.7	2.0	1.8	1.2	35.4
Renter............................	30,595	3,675	12,535	10,115	3,165	1,105
Percent.....................	100.0	100.0	100.0	100.0	100.0	100.0
1945 or later.......................	13.6	22.4	18.2	9.5	0.9	5.9
1940 to 1944........................	6.6	11.2	8.6	4.7	0.9	2.0
1930 to 1939........................	19.1	24.6	23.2	15.0	13.0	9.8
1920 to 1929........................	21.2	14.2	22.1	24.0	24.1	2.0
1919 or earlier.....................	33.1	20.9	23.0	43.2	60.2	17.6
Not reported........................	6.4	6.7	4.9	3.6	0.9	62.7
Rent free........................	37,970	9,790	15,205	9,705	2,760	510
Percent.....................	100.0	100.0	100.0	100.0	100.0	100.0
1945 or later.......................	18.2	28.1	18.5	12.9	3.6	...
1940 to 1944........................	6.9	8.3	8.2	4.4	4.4	...
1930 to 1939........................	23.1	27.6	24.5	19.0	12.5	30.0
1920 to 1929........................	20.1	13.2	20.1	25.0	25.9	30.0
1919 or earlier.....................	27.0	15.4	23.4	36.8	52.7	30.0
Not reported........................	4.7	7.4	5.3	1.9	0.9	10.0

Source: Special tabulation from the 1950 Census of Housing.

TABLE D-10.—CONDITION AND PLUMBING FACILITIES, BY TENURE AND ROOMS, FOR TYPE-OF-FARMING REGIONS: 1950

Region and condition and plumbing facilities[1]	Total occupied dwelling units	Percent distribution								
		Owner			Renter			Rent free		
		Total	1 to 4 rooms	5 rooms or more	Total	1 to 4 rooms	5 rooms or more	Total	1 to 4 rooms	5 rooms or more
NORTHEAST DAIRY REGION										
Total...............	528,205	100.0	100.0	100.0	100.0	100.0	100.0	100.0	100.0	100.0
Not dilapidated...........	477,975	91.7	81.9	92.8	85.2	82.0	86.7	87.0	81.2	89.9
All facilities..........	239,375	48.0	24.4	50.6	33.3	27.8	36.0	37.9	24.7	44.0
Some facilities.........	133,590	25.0	26.8	24.8	27.4	30.6	25.8	25.1	27.4	24.3
No facilities...........	105,010	18.7	30.7	17.4	24.5	23.6	24.9	24.0	29.1	21.6
Kitchen sink..........	11,995	2.3	3.2	2.2	2.5	2.3	2.6	1.9	1.9	1.9
Dilapidated..............	50,230	8.3	18.1	7.2	14.8	18.0	13.3	13.0	18.8	10.1
All or some facilities...	18,565	3.4	3.9	3.3	4.4	4.7	4.3	3.7	3.8	3.6
No facilities..........	31,665	4.9	14.2	3.9	10.4	13.3	9.0	9.3	15.0	6.5
Kitchen sink..........	2,745	0.4	1.0	0.4	0.9	0.8	1.0	0.6	0.5	0.7
GREAT LAKES DAIRY REGION										
Total...............	435,650	100.0	100.0	100.0	100.0	100.0	100.0	100.0	100.0	100.0
Not dilapidated...........	398,550	92.1	82.4	94.2	88.6	80.5	90.7	89.0	81.5	92.6
All facilities..........	136,665	32.5	13.0	36.8	23.6	14.9	25.9	30.9	16.6	37.9
Some facilities.........	108,470	24.8	20.0	25.8	25.0	24.5	25.0	26.5	25.8	26.6
No facilities...........	153,415	34.8	49.4	31.6	40.0	41.1	39.8	31.6	39.1	28.1
Kitchen sink..........	17,665	4.0	3.9	4.0	5.0	3.2	9.3	3.5	3.2	3.6
Dilapidated..............	37,100	7.9	17.6	5.8	11.4	19.5	9.3	11.0	18.5	7.4
All or some facilities...	8,340	1.8	1.9	1.8	2.5	3.1	2.4	2.1	1.4	2.4
No facilities..........	28,760	6.1	15.7	4.0	8.9	16.4	6.9	8.9	17.1	5.0
Kitchen sink..........	1,905	0.4	0.7	0.3	0.7	0.7	0.7	0.4	0.4	0.4
EAST AND GULF COAST MISCELLANEOUS REGION										
Total...............	265,125	100.0	100.0	100.0	100.0	100.0	100.0	100.0	100.0	100.0
Not dilapidated...........	202,700	82.7	69.2	88.7	65.7	57.4	75.2	64.5	57.1	76.8
All facilities..........	55,580	27.2	11.9	34.0	11.4	6.4	17.3	8.4	3.9	15.9
Some facilities.........	49,865	21.5	17.0	23.5	15.0	11.8	18.7	13.1	10.6	17.6
No facilities...........	97,255	34.0	40.3	31.2	39.3	39.2	39.2	43.0	42.6	43.3
Kitchen sink..........	2,725	1.1	0.8	1.2	0.9	0.6	1.3	0.9	0.6	1.5
Dilapidated..............	62,425	17.3	30.8	11.3	34.3	42.6	24.8	35.5	42.9	23.2
All or some facilities...	7,500	2.8	3.2	2.6	3.4	2.7	4.1	2.8	2.7	3.0
No facilities...........	54,925	14.5	27.6	8.7	30.9	39.9	20.7	32.7	40.2	20.2
Kitchen sink..........	625	0.2	0.4	0.1	0.3	0.5	0.2	0.2	0.3	0.2
GENERAL AND SELF-SUFFICING REGION										
Total...............	858,035	100.0	100.0	100.0	100.0	100.0	100.0	100.0	100.0	100.0
Not dilapidated...........	687,410	83.3	71.5	90.0	69.5	59.8	80.7	68.3	61.0	79.2
All facilities..........	99,065	13.1	3.5	18.6	5.6	2.7	8.9	7.0	2.8	13.3
Some facilities.........	120,275	15.0	8.5	18.7	10.7	6.8	15.1	10.6	7.2	15.9
No facilities...........	468,070	55.2	59.5	52.7	53.2	50.3	56.7	50.7	51.0	50.0
Kitchen sink..........	21,575	2.7	1.8	3.1	2.2	1.3	3.2	1.7	1.2	2.6
Dilapidated..............	170,625	16.7	28.5	10.0	30.5	40.2	19.3	31.7	39.0	20.8
All or some facilities...	11,875	1.3	1.3	1.3	1.6	1.7	1.6	1.9	1.9	1.9
No facilities...........	158,750	15.4	27.2	8.7	28.9	38.5	17.7	29.8	37.1	18.9
Kitchen sink..........	2,620	0.3	0.3	2.5	0.5	0.4	0.6	0.4	0.4	0.4
TOBACCO REGION										
Total...............	232,270	100.0	100.0	100.0	100.0	100.0	100.0	100.0	100.0	100.0
Not dilapidated...........	184,745	86.7	75.8	91.1	71.0	65.7	77.0	70.7	66.6	75.7
All facilities..........	22,450	15.4	3.4	20.2	2.6	1.3	4.1	2.9	1.1	5.1
Some facilities.........	32,080	17.9	10.6	20.9	9.0	6.9	11.2	8.7	6.8	11.0
No facilities...........	130,215	53.4	61.8	50.0	59.4	57.5	61.7	59.1	58.7	59.6
Kitchen sink..........	4,310	2.2	1.8	2.4	1.6	1.1	2.0	1.3	1.0	1.6
Dilapidated..............	47,525	13.3	24.2	8.9	29.0	34.3	23.0	29.3	33.4	24.3
All or some facilities...	2,715	1.1	1.0	1.1	1.6	1.5	1.7	1.0	1.0	1.1
No facilities...........	44,810	12.2	23.2	7.8	27.4	32.8	21.3	28.3	32.4	23.2
Kitchen sink..........	590	0.2	0.2	0.2	0.3	0.3	0.3	0.3	0.3	0.2

[1] See footnote 1, table D-2.

TABLE **D-10.**—CONDITION AND PLUMBING FACILITIES, BY TENURE AND ROOMS, FOR TYPE-OF-FARMING REGIONS: 1950—Cont.

Region and condition and plumbing facilities[1]	Total occupied dwelling units	Percent distribution								
		Owner			Renter			Rent free		
		Total	1 to 4 rooms	5 rooms or more	Total	1 to 4 rooms	5 rooms or more	Total	1 to 4 rooms	5 rooms or more
COTTON BELT										
Total	1,385,375	100.0	100.0	100.0	100.0	100.0	100.0	100.0	100.0	100.0
Not dilapidated	949,465	80.5	69.0	87.9	56.5	51.6	68.3	55.7	52.2	66.3
All facilities	120,345	14.9	4.1	21.8	2.2	1.1	5.3	2.2	0.8	6.6
Some facilities	174,920	18.6	11.2	23.4	7.1	4.8	12.3	5.8	4.0	11.5
No facilities	654,200	47.0	53.7	42.7	47.2	45.7	50.7	47.7	47.4	48.2
Kitchen sink	14,355	1.4	1.1	1.6	0.8	0.6	1.2	0.5	0.4	0.9
Dilapidated	435,910	19.5	31.0	12.1	43.5	48.4	31.7	44.3	47.8	33.7
All or some facilities	26,640	2.0	1.8	2.1	2.0	1.9	2.3	1.7	1.5	2.5
No facilities	409,270	17.5	29.2	10.0	41.5	46.5	29.4	42.6	46.3	31.2
Kitchen sink	3,215	0.2	0.3	0.2	0.3	0.3	0.3	0.2	0.2	0.3
CORN BELT										
Total	929,895	100.0	100.0	100.0	100.0	100.0	100.0	100.0	100.0	100.0
Not dilapidated	875,080	94.7	87.0	96.1	93.4	84.7	94.8	92.4	85.1	94.8
All facilities	276,195	34.8	13.0	38.8	20.4	8.6	22.3	23.4	10.3	27.9
Some facilities	193,060	20.1	16.1	20.8	21.9	17.1	22.7	22.0	19.5	22.9
No facilities	405,825	39.8	57.9	36.5	51.1	59.0	49.8	47.0	55.3	44.0
Kitchen sink	39,785	3.7	3.7	3.7	5.4	3.6	5.6	4.9	4.5	5.0
Dilapidated	54,815	5.3	13.0	3.9	6.6	15.3	5.2	7.6	14.9	5.2
All or some facilities	9,450	1.0	1.2	1.0	1.0	1.2	1.0	1.1	1.1	1.1
No facilities	45,365	4.3	11.8	2.9	5.6	14.1	4.2	6.5	13.8	4.1
Kitchen sink	2,095	0.2	0.3	0.2	0.3	0.4	0.3	0.3	0.4	0.2
NORTHERN WHEAT AND SMALL GRAINS REGION										
Total	123,155	100.0	100.0	100.0	100.0	100.0	100.0	100.0	100.0	100.0
Not dilapidated	113,735	93.0	85.1	95.9	91.1	82.2	94.1	89.6	83.8	93.9
All facilities	28,490	24.5	10.4	29.6	15.4	7.5	18.0	28.9	15.9	38.0
Some facilities	19,830	16.3	12.5	17.8	15.0	10.7	16.5	16.5	15.1	17.7
No facilities	65,415	52.2	62.2	48.5	60.7	64.0	59.6	44.2	52.8	38.2
Kitchen sink	5,500	4.3	3.5	4.6	5.4	3.8	5.9	3.4	2.3	4.1
Dilapidated	9,420	7.0	14.9	4.1	8.9	17.8	5.9	10.4	16.2	6.1
All or some facilities	1,615	1.2	1.6	1.1	1.5	2.0	1.4	1.9	2.3	1.6
No facilities	7,805	5.8	13.3	3.0	7.4	15.8	4.5	8.5	13.9	4.5
Kitchen sink	370	0.3	0.6	0.2	0.2	0.3	0.2	0.3	0.4	0.2
SOUTHERN WHEAT AND SMALL GRAINS REGION										
Total	101,180	100.0	100.0	100.0	100.0	100.0	100.0	100.0	100.0	100.0
Not dilapidated	93,625	93.8	88.0	96.0	91.3	85.7	93.8	87.9	83.8	92.5
All facilities	38,395	45.1	24.3	52.2	24.6	15.2	28.8	33.1	23.4	44.2
Some facilities	22,440	20.7	22.1	20.3	24.4	22.0	25.5	24.6	25.8	23.1
No facilities	32,790	28.0	41.6	23.5	42.3	48.5	39.5	30.2	34.6	25.2
Kitchen sink	3,000	2.6	3.5	2.3	3.9	3.4	1.4	2.2	2.0	1.2
Dilapidated	7,555	6.2	12.0	4.0	8.7	14.3	6.2	12.1	16.2	7.5
All or some facilities	2,190	1.9	2.4	1.7	2.3	3.0	2.0	3.7	4.5	2.9
No facilities	5,365	4.3	9.6	2.3	6.4	11.3	4.2	8.4	11.7	4.6
Kitchen sink	235	0.3	0.3	0.2	0.3	0.5	0.3	0.2	0.2	0.1
YEAR-LONG AND SEASONAL GRAZING REGION										
Total	296,875	100.0	100.0	100.0	100.0	100.0	100.0	100.0	100.0	100.0
Not dilapidated	249,330	88.3	80.7	94.2	79.8	74.5	87.9	75.4	71.3	86.7
All facilities	90,505	37.9	19.5	52.2	19.9	13.3	29.5	18.6	11.7	37.1
Some facilities	71,895	24.2	23.4	25.0	25.6	23.2	29.2	23.1	21.4	27.9
No facilities	86,930	26.2	37.8	17.0	34.3	38.0	29.2	33.7	38.2	21.7
Kitchen sink	4,290	1.4	1.6	1.2	1.7	1.5	2.0	1.4	1.3	1.7
Dilapidated	47,545	11.7	19.3	5.8	20.2	25.5	12.1	24.6	28.7	13.3
All or some facilities	12,055	3.4	4.1	2.9	4.7	5.0	4.3	5.3	5.2	5.7
No facilities	35,490	8.3	15.2	2.9	15.5	20.5	7.8	19.3	23.5	7.6
Kitchen sink	785	0.3	0.3	0.2	0.3	0.3	0.3	0.3	0.3	0.1

[1] See footnote 1, table D-2.

TABLE **D–10.**—Condition and Plumbing Facilities, by Tenure and Rooms, for Type-of-Farming Regions: 1950—Cont.

Region and condition and plumbing facilities[1]	Total occupied dwell-ing units	Percent distribution								
		Owner			Renter			Rent free		
		Total	1 to 4 rooms	5 rooms or more	Total	1 to 4 rooms	5 rooms or more	Total	1 to 4 rooms	5 rooms or more
UPLAND SUMMER GRAZING REGION										
Total................	111,725	100.0	100.0	100.0	100.0	100.0	100.0	100.0	100.0	100.0
Not dilapidated............	99,085	90.2	84.7	94.8	84.2	81.3	88.2	83.5	80.9	89.4
All facilities..........	49,445	48.1	26.7	65.8	34.3	24.0	48.9	30.6	19.4	54.7
Some facilities.........	22,340	18.8	21.4	16.7	24.4	25.4	22.7	23.0	24.3	20.1
No facilities...........	27,300	23.3	36.6	12.3	25.5	31.9	16.6	29.9	37.2	14.6
Kitchen sink..........	1,285	1.1	1.4	0.9	1.5	1.6	1.3	0.9	1.1	0.4
Dilapidated................	12,640	9.8	15.3	5.2	15.8	18.7	11.8	16.5	19.1	10.6
All or some facilities...	3,975	3.2	3.6	2.9	5.1	4.4	6.0	4.3	3.8	5.2
No facilities...........	8,665	6.6	11.7	2.3	10.7	14.3	5.8	12.2	15.3	5.4
Kitchen sink...........	285	0.2	0.3	0.1	0.5	0.3	0.7	0.3	0.2	0.7
WEST COAST MISCELLANEOUS REGION										
Total................	235,315	100.0	100.0	100.0	100.0	100.0	100.0	100.0	100.0	100.0
Not dilapidated............	209,150	92.3	87.4	94.8	83.4	78.9	88.8	77.5	71.8	89.0
All facilities..........	162,325	74.2	55.6	83.6	61.2	49.7	75.0	50.8	37.7	76.8
Some facilities.........	34,730	13.6	22.1	9.3	17.5	22.3	11.8	18.2	22.0	10.9
No facilities...........	12,095	4.5	9.7	1.9	4.7	6.9	2.0	8.5	12.1	1.3
Kitchen sink..........	950	0.4	0.8	0.2	0.4	0.5	0.2	0.5	0.7	...
Dilapidated................	26,165	7.7	12.6	5.2	16.6	21.1	11.2	22.5	28.2	11.0
All or some facilities...	17,470	5.6	7.7	4.5	11.6	13.4	9.5	12.5	14.0	9.6
No facilities...........	8,695	2.1	4.9	0.7	5.0	7.7	1.7	10.0	14.2	1.4
Kitchen sink...........	515	0.2	0.3	0.1	0.3	0.4	0.1	0.4	0.5	0.1

[1] See footnote 1, table D–2.

Source: Special tabulation from the 1950 Census of Housing.

TABLE **D-11.**—TYPE OF COOKING AND HEATING FUEL, BY TENURE AND ROOMS,
FOR TYPE-OF-FARMING REGIONS: 1950

Region and cooking and heating fuel	Owner					Renter and rent free				
	Number of dwelling units	Percent distribution				Number of dwelling units	Percent distribution			
		1 and 2 rooms	3 and 4 rooms	5 and 6 rooms	7 rooms or more		1 and 2 rooms	3 and 4 rooms	5 and 6 rooms	7 rooms or more
NORTHEAST DAIRY REGION										
Cooking Fuel										
Total....................	424,000	100.0	100.0	100.0	100.0	119,440	100.0	100.0	100.0	100.0
Coal.........................	82,814	20.8	19.5	20.2	19.4	21,041	16.6	15.4	18.7	18.6
Wood.........................	106,292	29.0	22.2	21.2	27.5	31,638	27.4	22.9	28.5	27.7
Bottled gas..................	64,308	12.6	15.7	15.8	14.9	22,485	9.9	22.8	18.7	18.5
Electricity..................	95,927	13.4	20.8	25.2	22.1	18,395	9.0	14.7	15.5	17.4
Other, none or not reported...	74,656	24.3	21.8	17.6	16.1	25,885	37.1	24.2	18.5	17.7
Heating Fuel										
Total....................	424,000	100.0	100.0	100.0	100.0	119,440	100.0	100.0	100.0	100.0
Central heating..............	204,694	11.3	31.2	46.9	52.5	38,280	14.9	27.1	35.0	36.7
Coal.........................	132,083	8.9	21.1	31.6	33.0	24,672	9.3	16.6	22.3	24.4
Wood.........................	20,486	0.8	2.2	3.4	6.0	3,478	0.8	1.5	2.8	4.4
Liquid fuel..................	39,668	0.4	6.2	8.8	10.4	7,743	3.4	6.8	8.0	5.8
Other or not reported.......	12,457	1.2	1.7	3.1	3.1	2,387	1.3	2.2	1.9	2.1
Noncentral heating...........	212,095	84.7	66.6	51.7	46.4	76,599	74.4	70.7	62.0	61.3
Coal.........................	87,796	27.0	27.8	20.7	19.6	30,034	29.1	23.4	24.2	27.0
Wood.........................	79,618	33.9	20.5	19.5	18.0	26,385	24.2	21.9	22.2	22.4
Liquid fuel..................	29,064	17.3	12.6	7.2	5.7	14,210	13.6	18.7	10.3	8.6
Other or not reported.......	15,617	6.5	5.7	4.3	3.0	5,970	7.5	6.5	5.3	3.2
Not heated or heating equipment not reported...........	7,221	4.0	2.2	1.4	1.1	4,564	10.8	2.3	3.0	2.0
GREAT LAKES DAIRY REGION										
Cooking Fuel										
Total....................	363,230	100.0	100.0	100.0	100.0	84,125	100.0	100.0	100.0	100.0
Coal.........................	30,450	3.1	6.3	8.6	9.2	8,445	12.2	8.2	10.4	10.3
Wood.........................	130,548	60.8	45.5	35.0	32.2	21,153	32.0	24.7	26.3	24.5
Bottled gas..................	78,365	12.8	20.5	22.3	22.3	24,466	17.5	29.4	29.8	31.0
Electricity..................	93,280	9.2	19.4	26.3	28.6	19,612	13.4	22.4	23.4	25.2
Other, none or not reported...	30,594	14.1	8.3	7.8	7.7	10,450	24.9	15.2	10.1	9.0
Heating Fuel										
Total....................	363,230	100.0	100.0	100.0	100.0	84,125	100.0	100.0	100.0	100.0
Central heating..............	142,182	6.8	19.5	36.1	49.7	28,218	7.9	23.9	28.1	44.9
Coal.........................	82,803	2.8	10.2	20.8	29.5	17,560	2.1	14.1	17.8	28.7
Wood.........................	35,300	2.2	5.0	8.3	12.7	5,449	2.9	3.3	4.4	9.7
Liquid fuel..................	18,399	1.6	3.2	5.3	5.8	3,731	2.5	4.9	4.6	4.4
Other or not reported.......	5,680	0.2	1.1	1.8	1.6	1,478	0.4	1.6	1.3	2.1
Noncentral heating...........	213,892	91.0	78.8	61.9	49.1	52,854	83.9	73.8	69.5	53.1
Coal.........................	45,932	9.6	13.4	13.6	11.9	12,435	14.1	12.8	18.8	13.5
Wood.........................	100,355	60.1	43.1	27.3	21.4	17,225	34.9	25.8	20.8	16.9
Liquid fuel..................	58,825	17.0	19.2	18.4	13.8	20,278	28.7	31.5	25.8	20.2
Other or not reported.......	8,780	4.2	3.0	2.6	2.0	2,916	6.2	3.7	4.1	2.4
Not heated or heating equipment not reported...........	7,149	2.2	1.7	2.0	1.3	3,055	8.3	2.3	2.4	2.0
EAST AND GULF COAST MISCELLANEOUS REGION										
Cooking Fuel										
Total....................	176,480	100.0	100.0	100.0	100.0	97,010	100.0	100.0	100.0	100.0
Coal.........................	2,530	0.8	1.2	1.1	2.7	1,162	1.1	1.0	1.2	1.9
Wood.........................	69,276	39.2	47.8	38.1	31.7	49,979	44.7	54.2	51.0	53.5
Bottled gas..................	40,991	15.6	19.3	25.0	25.9	10,878	4.2	9.5	15.4	17.2
Electricity..................	24,162	6.5	8.1	13.1	23.2	4,459	2.6	3.1	6.5	9.6
Other, none or not reported...	39,523	38.0	23.6	22.7	16.4	30,534	47.4	32.3	25.9	17.8

TABLE **D-11.**—TYPE OF COOKING AND HEATING FUEL, BY TENURE AND ROOMS, FOR TYPE-OF-FARMING REGIONS: 1950—Cont.

Region and cooking and heating fuel	Owner					Renter and rent free				
	Number of dwelling units	Percent distribution				Number of dwelling units	Percent distribution			
		1 and 2 rooms	3 and 4 rooms	5 and 6 rooms	7 rooms or more		1 and 2 rooms	3 and 4 rooms	5 and 6 rooms	7 rooms or more
EAST AND GULF COAST MISCELLANEOUS REGION--Cont.										
Heating Fuel										
Total.....................	176,480	100.0	100.0	100.0	100.0	97,010	100.0	100.0	100.0	100.0
Central heating..............	14,734	2.3	3.7	7.4	16.8	3,570	2.1	2.2	4.9	9.6
Coal........................	5,021	0.3	1.2	2.6	5.9	1,118	0.3	0.4	1.7	4.1
Wood........................	1,030	1.0	0.6	0.4	0.7	564	0.5	0.5	0.5	1.7
Liquid fuel.................	6,085	0.3	0.9	2.8	8.3	1,030	0.5	0.6	1.3	3.1
Other or not reported......	2,598	0.7	1.1	1.6	1.8	858	0.7	0.7	1.4	0.7
Noncentral heating...........	152,728	87.9	90.8	88.5	79.0	84,399	71.9	91.1	90.1	86.1
Coal........................	8,752	2.3	3.0	4.1	9.7	3,262	1.4	2.5	4.3	6.9
Wood........................	86,502	56.7	57.1	49.1	38.9	57,319	45.6	63.8	61.9	50.6
Liquid fuel.................	22,343	16.4	10.2	12.6	15.5	11,965	15.9	12.0	10.7	16.0
Other or not reported......	35,131	12.5	20.5	22.8	14.9	11,853	9.0	12.9	13.2	12.7
Not heated or heating equipment not reported	9,015	9.8	5.5	4.1	4.1	9,042	26.0	6.8	5.1	4.3
GENERAL AND SELF-SUFFICING REGION										
Cooking Fuel										
Total.....................	682,830	100.0	100.0	100.0	100.0	199,125	100.0	100.0	100.0	100.0
Coal........................	151,244	17.9	22.9	22.5	21.4	40,167	18.2	21.5	20.0	19.8
Wood........................	317,889	65.6	55.9	43.5	35.4	100,976	62.6	57.0	44.4	36.3
Bottled gas.................	52,109	3.5	5.7	8.7	9.4	16,018	4.7	5.3	10.9	14.0
Electricity.................	78,367	2.9	5.7	12.9	19.5	13,710	2.5	4.8	8.9	12.9
Other, none or not reported...	83,226	10.2	9.8	12.4	14.3	28,264	11.9	11.4	15.8	16.9
Heating Fuel										
Total.....................	682,830	100.0	100.0	100.0	100.0	199,125	100.0	100.0	100.0	100.0
Central heating..............	63,604	1.8	3.4	10.1	18.6	9,478	2.3	2.7	5.5	12.9
Coal........................	43,614	0.7	2.1	6.9	13.2	6,708	1.4	1.8	3.9	9.7
Wood........................	5,211	0.5	0.5	0.8	1.2	994	0.5	0.4	0.4	1.0
Liquid fuel.................	6,116	0.2	0.3	1.0	1.9	616	0.3	0.1	0.3	0.9
Other or not reported......	8,663	0.4	0.5	1.4	2.3	1,160	0.1	0.3	0.9	1.3
Noncentral heating...........	600,203	94.5	93.9	87.7	79.2	181,833	93.1	94.1	92.4	84.0
Coal........................	247,376	24.4	36.0	38.1	35.9	66,999	29.6	33.4	35.8	36.1
Wood........................	286,855	64.0	50.8	39.2	30.4	96,864	57.5	53.5	45.3	34.5
Liquid fuel.................	21,467	2.4	2.6	3.2	4.0	6,916	2.3	2.6	4.5	5.3
Other or not reported......	44,505	3.7	4.5	7.2	8.8	11,056	3.7	4.5	6.8	8.1
Not heated or heating equipment not reported............	19,041	3.7	2.7	2.2	2.3	7,810	4.7	3.2	2.0	3.2
TOBACCO REGION										
Cooking Fuel										
Total.....................	131,015	100.0	100.0	100.0	100.0	107,450	100.0	100.0	100.0	100.0
Coal........................	17,334	12.3	14.9	12.2	13.3	11,860	12.0	10.0	10.3	18.6
Wood........................	64,747	60.7	56.0	50.3	40.6	67,659	58.0	67.4	62.0	50.5
Bottled gas.................	8,113	3.3	4.8	6.3	8.1	5,968	2.3	4.4	6.8	9.4
Electricity.................	23,905	5.7	10.3	19.2	26.7	5,200	4.3	3.6	5.8	8.1
Other, none or not reported...	16,907	18.0	14.0	11.9	11.2	16,752	23.3	14.5	15.0	13.5
Heating Fuel										
Total.....................	131,015	100.0	100.0	100.0	100.0	107,450	100.0	100.0	100.0	100.0
Central heating..............	8,196	3.2	2.6	5.3	12.0	1,851	1.1	1.4	1.9	3.2
Coal........................	4,447	1.9	1.0	2.6	7.4	783	0.7	0.3	0.7	2.6
Wood........................	728	0.6	0.5	0.5	0.7	399	...	0.4	0.5	0.2
Liquid fuel.................	1,683	...	0.7	1.3	2.2	424	...	0.3	0.5	0.5
Other or not reported......	1,338	0.6	0.4	1.0	1.7	245	0.4	0.3	0.2	...
Noncentral heating...........	117,261	93.6	93.1	90.9	85.3	100,594	95.0	94.9	93.5	93.2
Coal........................	43,345	35.0	34.8	32.6	32.9	28,675	26.2	25.3	26.7	35.5
Wood........................	58,731	50.3	51.1	45.8	36.9	64,884	58.3	63.0	61.0	50.4
Liquid fuel.................	9,761	4.5	4.4	8.2	9.8	4,793	7.2	4.5	4.1	5.0
Other or not reported......	5,424	3.8	2.8	4.3	5.7	2,242	3.3	2.1	1.8	2.3
Not heated or heating equipment not reported............	5,545	3.2	4.4	3.8	2.7	4,992	4.0	3.7	4.5	3.5

TABLE **D-11.**—TYPE OF COOKING AND HEATING FUEL, BY TENURE AND ROOMS,
FOR TYPE-OF-FARMING REGIONS: 1950—Cont.

Region and cooking and heating fuel	Owner					Renter and rent free				
	Number of dwelling units	Percent distribution				Number of dwelling units	Percent distribution			
		1 and 2 rooms	3 and 4 rooms	5 and 6 rooms	7 rooms or more		1 and 2 rooms	3 and 4 rooms	5 and 6 rooms	7 rooms or more
COTTON BELT										
Cooking Fuel										
Total.....................	728,005	100.0	100.0	100.0	100.0	698,545	100.0	100.0	100.0	100.0
Coal......................	22,529	2.8	3.2	3.2	2.5	22,955	4.1	3.3	2.9	2.8
Wood......................	383,241	71.6	62.5	47.8	40.1	512,631	79.6	76.3	66.6	59.9
Bottled gas...............	101,447	5.9	10.5	16.6	16.3	27,794	1.8	2.9	7.1	9.2
Electricity...............	91,362	2.2	6.4	15.1	24.7	17,933	0.9	1.8	4.4	9.0
Other, none or not reported...	129,406	17.5	17.4	17.3	16.4	117,146	13.6	15.6	19.0	19.1
Heating Fuel										
Total.....................	728,005	100.0	100.0	100.0	100.0	698,545	100.0	100.0	100.0	100.0
Central heating..............	21,054	0.7	1.7	3.0	6.7	7,059	1.0	0.8	1.3	2.6
Coal......................	3,221	...	0.3	0.4	1.1	1,033	0.2	0.1	0.1	0.5
Wood......................	3,381	0.3	0.5	0.4	0.6	2,969	0.6	0.4	0.4	0.2
Liquid fuel...............	3,741	...	0.1	0.5	1.9	548	...	...	0.1	0.5
Other or not reported.......	10,711	0.4	0.8	1.7	3.1	2,508	0.2	0.3	0.6	1.4
Noncentral heating...........	667,752	92.9	93.5	92.8	89.0	658,159	94.5	95.1	94.0	93.0
Coal......................	84,502	8.7	10.2	12.3	13.9	62,726	8.4	9.0	9.4	9.2
Wood......................	405,473	69.5	65.3	52.3	43.8	525,121	79.2	77.7	69.7	62.7
Liquid fuel...............	47,556	5.7	5.5	6.9	8.4	31,823	3.7	4.1	5.7	8.3
Other or not reported.......	130,221	9.0	12.5	21.3	22.9	38,489	3.1	4.2	9.1	12.9
Not heated or heating equipment not reported...........	39,125	6.4	4.8	4.2	4.3	33,251	4.5	4.0	4.7	4.3
CORN BELT										
Cooking Fuel										
Total.....................	594,965	100.0	100.0	100.0	100.0	359,395	100.0	100.0	100.0	100.0
Coal......................	107,900	16.1	20.3	18.6	17.2	65,590	18.3	18.2	19.1	17.7
Wood......................	90,350	28.3	20.6	14.8	13.5	46,973	17.9	17.2	12.7	11.9
Bottled gas...............	171,639	21.5	25.5	29.9	29.6	130,378	22.1	32.8	37.5	37.8
Electricity...............	147,453	9.5	16.1	23.7	29.3	65,033	9.1	11.6	16.2	22.5
Other, none or not reported...	77,555	24.5	17.5	13.0	10.4	51,369	32.6	20.3	14.4	10.1
Heating Fuel										
Total.....................	594,965	100.0	100.0	100.0	100.0	359,395	100.0	100.0	100.0	100.0
Central heating..............	217,609	6.7	15.8	31.4	49.0	91,077	9.3	12.0	18.5	36.4
Coal......................	147,424	3.6	9.9	20.8	33.9	65,665	4.5	7.3	12.8	27.2
Wood......................	17,104	1.3	1.2	2.2	4.1	8,162	1.3	1.3	1.4	3.4
Liquid fuel...............	34,161	0.7	2.6	5.3	7.3	11,395	1.4	2.4	2.9	3.8
Other or not reported.......	18,920	1.1	2.2	3.1	3.7	5,855	2.1	1.1	1.4	2.0
Noncentral heating...........	364,295	89.8	82.3	66.8	49.6	258,516	82.0	85.7	79.4	61.7
Coal......................	154,958	35.6	37.1	28.6	20.4	95,457	26.5	35.4	28.8	22.1
Wood......................	70,301	29.3	22.2	12.6	7.6	38,734	21.7	17.2	11.2	7.9
Liquid fuel...............	107,642	18.5	17.2	19.8	17.1	103,963	27.0	27.2	32.9	26.9
Other or not reported.......	31,394	6.4	5.8	5.8	4.5	20,362	6.7	5.9	6.5	4.8
Not heated or heating equipment not reported...........	13,040	3.5	1.9	1.8	1.4	9,773	8.7	2.3	2.1	1.9
NORTHERN WHEAT AND SMALL GRAINS REGION										
Cooking Fuel										
Total.....................	92,685	100.0	100.0	100.0	100.0	33,000	100.0	100.0	100.0	100.0
Coal......................	24,192	24.4	29.6	25.8	24.2	9,066	39.8	26.2	27.0	27.5
Wood......................	14,157	34.9	21.4	15.3	8.7	3,708	27.1	17.7	8.9	5.5
Bottled gas...............	28,563	16.3	25.3	31.6	36.3	10,559	5.5	30.3	36.8	37.4
Electricity...............	16,666	5.8	14.4	18.1	22.6	5,332	3.1	12.0	16.6	22.1
Other, none or not reported...	9,106	18.6	9.3	9.2	8.3	4,334	24.6	13.9	10.6	10.7

TABLE D-11.—Type of Cooking and Heating Fuel, by Tenure and Rooms, for Type-of-Farming Regions: 1950—Cont.

Region and cooking and heating fuel	Owner					Renter and rent free				
	Number of dwelling units	Percent distribution				Number of dwelling units	Percent distribution			
		1 and 2 rooms	3 and 4 rooms	5 and 6 rooms	7 rooms or more		1 and 2 rooms	3 and 4 rooms	5 and 6 rooms	7 rooms or more
NORTHERN WHEAT AND SMALL GRAINS REGION--Cont.										
Heating Fuel										
Total.....................	92,685	100.0	100.0	100.0	100.0	33,000	100.0	100.0	100.0	100.0
Central heating...............	31,791	6.0	17.4	34.0	50.4	8,615	5.5	16.9	23.5	41.0
Coal.......................	22,141	3.2	10.8	23.1	36.6	6,467	4.6	11.5	17.8	31.4
Wood.......................	1,475	0.9	1.4	1.5	2.0	248	...	1.1	0.4	1.2
Liquid fuel.................	5,951	1.4	4.1	6.7	8.6	1,315	...	2.9	4.0	5.8
Other or not reported.......	2,224	0.4	1.1	2.7	3.2	585	1.0	1.3	1.4	2.6
Noncentral heating............	59,591	92.2	81.0	64.9	48.8	23,659	90.0	81.9	75.6	58.0
Coal.......................	24,243	43.1	37.0	25.1	17.8	9,066	29.4	37.3	26.8	21.7
Wood.......................	9,485	26.6	14.5	9.7	5.8	2,667	33.8	11.2	6.2	2.6
Liquid fuel.................	21,616	18.4	25.1	24.6	21.6	9,982	20.3	26.7	36.3	28.8
Other or not reported.......	4,247	4.1	4.4	5.5	3.6	1,944	6.5	6.7	6.3	5.0
Not heated or heating equipment not reported...........	1,299	1.8	1.6	1.1	0.8	721	4.5	1.3	0.9	1.0
SOUTHERN WHEAT AND SMALL GRAINS REGION										
Cooking Fuel										
Total.....................	63,450	100.0	100.0	100.0	100.0	40,740	100.0	100.0	100.0	100.0
Coal.......................	3,977	10.8	10.9	4.1	5.6	2,105	10.8	6.5	4.5	3.4
Wood.......................	3,636	18.9	7.0	4.4	5.2	1,515	1.3	6.3	2.8	2.8
Bottled gas..................	29,901	25.7	42.3	51.8	47.1	19,851	29.6	48.0	50.7	51.2
Electricity.................	7,897	2.7	9.0	12.1	17.4	3,531	5.6	4.3	10.9	11.9
Other, none or not reported...	18,037	41.9	30.8	27.6	24.7	13,739	52.6	34.8	31.0	30.6
Heating Fuel										
Total.....................	63,450	100.0	100.0	100.0	100.0	40,740	100.0	100.0	100.0	100.0
Central heating...............	15,434	2.4	11.7	24.6	36.1	5,346	1.6	7.2	14.4	22.0
Coal.......................	3,354	...	2.5	5.4	7.8	992	...	1.2	1.6	6.3
Wood.......................	626	2.4	0.5	0.7	1.6	233	...	0.4	0.5	1.2
Liquid fuel.................	2,616	...	1.8	4.3	6.1	1,074	...	1.6	2.9	3.8
Other or not reported.......	8,838	...	6.9	14.2	20.6	3,047	1.6	4.0	9.4	10.7
Noncentral heating............	46,529	91.7	86.3	74.1	61.9	34,318	96.0	90.4	84.0	76.5
Coal.......................	7,483	23.8	16.8	10.2	9.9	5,373	18.7	14.4	14.4	8.9
Wood.......................	4,771	22.6	10.7	6.8	4.8	3,342	10.9	10.9	5.8	8.3
Liquid fuel.................	13,382	26.2	25.1	20.9	17.5	10,759	25.5	29.2	25.4	25.5
Other or not reported.......	20,893	19.1	33.7	36.2	29.7	14,844	40.9	35.8	38.4	33.8
Not heated or heating equipment not reported...........	1,475	5.9	2.0	1.3	2.0	1,070	2.4	2.4	1.5	1.4
YEAR-LONG AND SEASONAL GRAZING REGION										
Cooking Fuel										
Total.....................	184,170	100.0	100.0	100.0	100.0	121,940	100.0	100.0	100.0	100.0
Coal.......................	18,007	10.9	9.7	9.4	11.2	9,806	7.4	7.0	9.5	13.6
Wood.......................	37,237	47.9	24.8	13.3	13.7	24,556	33.1	21.1	11.6	12.6
Bottled gas..................	68,484	18.8	36.1	42.0	38.4	40,426	17.5	33.3	42.3	42.4
Electricity.................	21,438	4.6	8.0	13.7	20.1	7,517	2.7	4.6	9.2	15.5
Other, none or not reported...	38,989	17.9	21.4	21.6	16.7	39,630	39.3	34.0	27.4	15.9
Heating Fuel										
Total.....................	184,170	100.0	100.0	100.0	100.0	121,940	100.0	100.0	100.0	100.0
Central heating...............	16,677	1.3	4.5	10.5	21.8	4,710	1.0	2.4	5.8	15.1
Coal.......................	5,587	0.4	1.4	3.6	7.1	1,662	0.3	0.7	1.9	7.7
Wood.......................	981	0.3	0.5	0.5	1.1	187	0.2	...	0.4	0.2
Liquid fuel.................	2,772	...	0.6	1.6	4.7	667	0.1	0.4	0.8	1.9
Other or not reported.......	7,337	0.6	2.0	4.7	8.9	2,194	0.5	1.3	2.7	5.3
Noncentral heating............	157,911	88.2	90.1	86.0	75.4	109,230	86.8	92.4	90.2	83.1
Coal.......................	19,626	12.5	11.7	9.6	10.4	11,718	9.8	9.6	9.0	13.0
Wood.......................	43,404	49.2	27.0	18.7	15.1	30,345	38.2	25.6	18.0	12.9
Liquid fuel.................	30,582	10.6	17.5	17.1	16.9	26,702	18.7	21.9	23.8	24.6
Other or not reported.......	64,299	16.0	34.0	40.7	32.9	40,465	20.1	35.3	39.4	32.6
Not heated or heating equipment not reported...........	9,563	10.4	5.3	3.5	2.9	7,984	12.2	5.1	4.0	1.8

TABLE **D-11.**—TYPE OF COOKING AND HEATING FUEL, BY TENURE AND ROOMS, FOR TYPE-OF-FARMING REGIONS: 1950—Cont.

	Owner					Renter and rent free				
Region and cooking and heating fuel	Number of dwelling units	Percent distribution				Number of dwelling units	Percent distribution			
		1 and 2 rooms	3 and 4 rooms	5 and 6 rooms	7 rooms or more		1 and 2 rooms	3 and 4 rooms	5 and 6 rooms	7 rooms or more
UPLAND SUMMER GRAZING REGION										
Cooking Fuel										
Total.....................	87,020	100.0	100.0	100.0	100.0	28,360	100.0	100.0	100.0	100.0
Coal......................	26,179	24.6	31.5	31.6	27.1	10,360	37.4	40.8	30.3	34.9
Wood......................	25,045	57.6	33.5	20.1	23.4	7,850	40.8	25.4	22.6	29.0
Bottled gas...............	3,540	3.2	4.1	4.3	4.0	1,052	1.5	4.5	4.1	4.8
Electricity...............	27,101	8.7	26.6	38.1	39.5	6,794	10.4	23.2	36.1	26.5
Other, none or not reported...	5,149	5.9	4.2	5.9	6.0	2,303	9.8	6.1	6.9	4.7
Heating Fuel										
Total.....................	87,020	100.0	100.0	100.0	100.0	28,360	100.0	100.0	100.0	100.0
Central heating...........	16,351	2.2	9.3	24.2	38.5	2,142	1.3	4.6	14.1	16.6
Coal....................	9,092	1.0	4.6	13.7	22.2	1,194	1.3	2.2	8.1	9.0
Wood....................	1,398	0.3	0.9	2.2	2.9	193	...	0.2	1.7	0.7
Liquid fuel.............	4,212	0.2	2.7	5.9	10.0	463	...	1.0	2.8	5.3
Other or not reported...	1,649	0.7	1.1	2.4	3.4	292	...	1.2	1.4	1.6
Noncentral heating...........	66,765	80.8	87.3	74.5	59.8	24,737	91.0	92.5	82.6	80.8
Coal....................	26,412	28.6	33.8	30.9	24.4	10,154	41.5	36.7	33.0	34.1
Wood....................	20,438	42.1	29.4	16.8	15.8	7,176	38.6	24.3	20.2	18.2
Liquid fuel.............	15,483	7.4	19.3	20.4	15.5	6,072	7.1	26.0	25.2	23.0
Other or not reported...	4,432	2.7	4.8	6.4	4.1	1,335	3.8	5.5	4.3	5.5
Not heated or heating equipment not reported............	3,896	17.0	3.4	1.3	1.7	1,484	7.7	2.9	3.2	2.5
WEST COAST MISCELLANEOUS REGION										
Cooking Fuel										
Total.....................	174,025	100.0	100.0	100.0	100.0	68,565	100.0	100.0	100.0	100.0
Coal......................	1,815	0.9	1.0	1.1	1.0	444	1.0	0.5	0.8	0.4
Wood......................	42,933	37.7	28.7	21.1	24.3	12,962	30.7	17.2	14.0	18.5
Bottled gas...............	32,722	26.7	21.5	19.7	11.7	22,207	25.1	36.7	34.8	24.8
Electricity...............	63,482	15.7	29.8	39.2	46.2	13,830	7.5	18.4	27.5	35.4
Other, none or not reported...	33,060	19.0	19.0	18.9	16.8	19,120	35.8	27.2	22.9	20.8
Heating Fuel										
Total.....................	174,025	100.0	100.0	100.0	100.0	68,565	100.0	100.0	100.0	100.0
Central heating...........	32,365	4.7	11.3	21.1	26.9	6,590	2.7	8.7	13.0	18.4
Coal....................	1,275	2.0	0.3	0.8	0.8	303	0.5	0.3	0.4	0.8
Wood....................	5,486	0.7	1.5	3.4	5.3	446	0.2	0.3	1.0	1.9
Liquid fuel.............	8,262	...	2.6	5.3	7.8	1,192	0.6	1.1	2.1	5.9
Other or not reported...	17,342	2.0	6.9	11.6	13.0	4,649	1.4	7.0	9.4	9.8
Noncentral heating...........	137,287	89.8	86.8	77.0	71.4	57,780	84.9	87.4	84.6	79.5
Coal....................	1,698	1.0	1.2	1.0	0.7	598	0.6	1.0	0.7	1.5
Wood....................	54,872	43.2	37.1	28.4	28.8	17,045	35.9	22.4	20.9	28.8
Liquid fuel.............	38,204	17.4	22.1	22.0	23.5	14,810	17.7	21.7	23.4	27.3
Other or not reported...	42,513	28.2	26.4	25.6	18.4	25,327	30.6	42.3	39.5	21.9
Not heated or heating equipment not reported............	4,361	5.5	1.9	1.9	1.7	4,196	12.4	3.8	2.5	2.2

Source: Special tabulation from the 1950 Census of Housing.

TABLE D-12.—PERSONS PER ROOM, BY TENURE AND ROOMS, FOR TYPE-OF-FARMING REGIONS: 1950

Region, tenure, and rooms	Percent of units reporting number of rooms by persons per room			Region, tenure, and rooms	Percent of units reporting number of rooms by persons per room		
	Total	1.00 or less	1.01 or more		Total	1.00 or less	1.01 or more
NORTHEAST DAIRY REGION				**GENERAL AND SELF-SUFFICING REGION**			
Owner				*Owner*			
1 and 2 rooms..............	100.0	54.7	45.3				
3 and 4 rooms..............	100.0	76.3	23.7	1 and 2 rooms.............	100.0	40.5	59.5
5 and 6 rooms..............	100.0	89.4	10.6	3 and 4 rooms.............	100.0	62.9	37.1
7 rooms or more..........	100.0	96.8	3.2	5 and 6 rooms.............	100.0	84.0	16.0
				7 rooms or more...........	100.0	95.2	4.8
Renter				*Renter*			
1 and 2 rooms..............	100.0	49.2	50.8				
3 and 4 rooms..............	100.0	73.1	26.9	1 and 2 rooms.............	100.0	29.4	70.6
5 and 6 rooms..............	100.0	82.3	17.7	3 and 4 rooms.............	100.0	52.6	47.4
7 rooms or more..........	100.0	93.5	6.5	5 and 6 rooms.............	100.0	77.0	23.0
				7 rooms or more...........	100.0	92.9	7.1
Rent Free				*Rent Free*			
1 and 2 rooms..............	100.0	57.6	42.4				
3 and 4 rooms..............	100.0	72.1	27.9	1 and 2 rooms.............	100.0	39.7	60.3
5 and 6 rooms..............	100.0	82.6	17.4	3 and 4 rooms.............	100.0	56.1	43.9
7 rooms or more..........	100.0	94.9	5.1	5 and 6 rooms.............	100.0	76.9	23.1
				7 rooms or more...........	100.0	92.2	7.8
GREAT LAKES DAIRY REGION				**TOBACCO REGION**			
Owner				*Owner*			
1 and 2 rooms..............	100.0	55.9	44.1				
3 and 4 rooms..............	100.0	73.8	26.2	1 and 2 rooms.............	100.0	49.6	50.4
5 and 6 rooms..............	100.0	88.1	11.9	3 and 4 rooms.............	100.0	66.9	33.1
7 rooms or more..........	100.0	95.9	4.1	5 and 6 rooms.............	100.0	84.4	15.6
				7 rooms or more...........	100.0	92.3	7.7
Renter				*Renter*			
1 and 2 rooms..............	100.0	46.7	53.3				
3 and 4 rooms..............	100.0	69.5	30.5	1 and 2 rooms.............	100.0	39.3	60.7
5 and 6 rooms..............	100.0	84.3	15.7	3 and 4 rooms.............	100.0	50.2	49.8
7 rooms or more..........	100.0	96.2	3.8	5 and 6 rooms.............	100.0	66.3	33.7
				7 rooms or more...........	100.0	87.3	12.7
Rent Free				*Rent Free*			
1 and 2 rooms..............	100.0	59.4	40.6				
3 and 4 rooms..............	100.0	78.0	22.0	1 and 2 rooms.............	100.0	45.7	54.3
5 and 6 rooms..............	100.0	87.8	12.2	3 and 4 rooms.............	100.0	49.3	50.7
7 rooms or more..........	100.0	96.9	3.1	5 and 6 rooms.............	100.0	61.1	38.9
				7 rooms or more...........	100.0	84.0	16.0
EAST AND GULF COAST MISCELLANEOUS REGION				**COTTON BELT**			
Owner				*Owner*			
1 and 2 rooms..............	100.0	43.2	56.8	1 and 2 rooms.............	100.0	46.1	53.9
3 and 4 rooms..............	100.0	65.6	34.4	3 and 4 rooms.............	100.0	66.2	33.8
5 and 6 rooms..............	100.0	83.3	16.7	5 and 6 rooms.............	100.0	83.8	16.2
7 rooms or more..........	100.0	94.0	6.0	7 rooms or more...........	100.0	93.5	6.5
Renter				*Renter*			
1 and 2 rooms..............	100.0	40.0	60.0	1 and 2 rooms.............	100.0	39.1	60.9
3 and 4 rooms..............	100.0	51.2	48.8	3 and 4 rooms.............	100.0	47.4	52.6
5 and 6 rooms..............	100.0	70.0	30.0	5 and 6 rooms.............	100.0	64.2	35.8
7 rooms or more..........	100.0	88.9	11.1	7 rooms or more...........	100.0	80.5	19.5
Rent Free				*Rent Free*			
1 and 2 rooms..............	100.0	37.6	62.4	1 and 2 rooms.............	100.0	49.1	50.9
3 and 4 rooms..............	100.0	49.7	50.3	3 and 4 rooms.............	100.0	48.3	51.7
5 and 6 rooms..............	100.0	66.5	33.5	5 and 6 rooms.............	100.0	57.8	42.2
7 rooms or more..........	100.0	86.7	13.3	7 rooms or more...........	100.0	74.7	25.3

TABLE **D-12.**—Persons Per Room, by Tenure and Rooms, for Type-of-Farming Regions: 1950—Cont.

Region, tenure, and rooms	Percent of units reporting number of rooms by persons per room			Region, tenure, and rooms	Percent of units reporting number of rooms by persons per room		
	Total	1.00 or less	1.01 or more		Total	1.00 or less	1.01 or more
CORN BELT				YEAR-LONG AND SEASONAL GRAZING REGION			
Owner				Owner			
1 and 2 rooms.............	100.0	55.2	44.8				
3 and 4 rooms.............	100.0	80.3	19.7	1 and 2 rooms.............	100.0	37.3	62.7
5 and 6 rooms.............	100.0	92.4	7.6	3 and 4 rooms.............	100.0	72.6	27.4
7 rooms or more...........	100.0	97.6	2.4	5 and 6 rooms.............	100.0	89.7	10.3
				7 rooms or more...........	100.0	96.4	3.6
Renter							
				Renter			
1 and 2 rooms.............	100.0	46.3	53.7				
3 and 4 rooms.............	100.0	71.4	28.6	1 and 2 rooms.............	100.0	37.4	62.6
5 and 6 rooms.............	100.0	90.0	10.0	3 and 4 rooms.............	100.0	60.9	39.1
7 rooms or more...........	100.0	97.6	2.4	5 and 6 rooms.............	100.0	84.1	15.9
				7 rooms or more...........	100.0	96.2	3.8
Rent Free							
				Rent Free			
1 and 2 rooms.............	100.0	50.5	49.5				
3 and 4 rooms.............	100.0	72.1	27.9	1 and 2 rooms.............	100.0	36.1	63.9
5 and 6 rooms.............	100.0	88.8	11.2	3 and 4 rooms.............	100.0	48.7	51.3
7 rooms or more...........	100.0	97.5	2.5	5 and 6 rooms.............	100.0	70.2	29.8
				7 rooms or more...........	100.0	83.4	16.6
NORTHERN WHEAT AND SMALL GRAINS REGION				UPLAND SUMMER GRAZING REGION			
Owner				Owner			
1 and 2 rooms.............	100.0	51.8	48.2				
3 and 4 rooms.............	100.0	69.3	30.7	1 and 2 rooms.............	100.0	33.8	66.2
5 and 6 rooms.............	100.0	85.1	14.9	3 and 4 rooms.............	100.0	65.4	34.6
7 rooms or more...........	100.0	93.9	6.1	5 and 6 rooms.............	100.0	84.6	15.4
				7 rooms or more...........	100.0	94.8	5.2
Renter							
				Renter			
1 and 2 rooms.............	100.0	47.1	52.9				
3 and 4 rooms.............	100.0	64.6	35.4	1 and 2 rooms.............	100.0	44.2	55.8
5 and 6 rooms.............	100.0	84.2	15.8	3 and 4 rooms.............	100.0	58.6	41.4
7 rooms or more...........	100.0	96.2	3.8	5 and 6 rooms.............	100.0	81.6	18.4
				7 rooms or more...........	100.0	95.0	5.0
Rent Free							
				Rent Free			
1 and 2 rooms.............	100.0	48.6	51.4				
3 and 4 rooms.............	100.0	72.1	27.9	1 and 2 rooms.............	100.0	45.4	54.6
5 and 6 rooms.............	100.0	88.2	11.8	3 and 4 rooms.............	100.0	63.5	36.5
7 rooms or more...........	100.0	95.7	4.3	5 and 6 rooms.............	100.0	82.2	17.8
				7 rooms or more...........	100.0	97.8	2.2
SOUTHERN WHEAT AND SMALL GRAINS REGION				WEST COAST MISCELLANEOUS REGION			
Owner				Owner			
1 and 2 rooms.............	100.0	56.1	43.9	1 and 2 rooms.............	100.0	52.9	47.1
3 and 4 rooms.............	100.0	77.4	22.6	3 and 4 rooms.............	100.0	80.7	19.3
5 and 6 rooms.............	100.0	91.7	8.3	5 and 6 rooms.............	100.0	91.9	8.1
7 rooms or more...........	100.0	96.7	3.3	7 rooms or more...........	100.0	97.2	2.8
Renter				Renter			
1 and 2 rooms.............	100.0	46.6	53.4	1 and 2 rooms.............	100.0	50.3	49.7
3 and 4 rooms.............	100.0	70.9	29.1	3 and 4 rooms.............	100.0	67.1	32.9
5 and 6 rooms.............	100.0	89.2	10.8	5 and 6 rooms.............	100.0	84.7	15.3
7 rooms or more...........	100.0	97.7	2.3	7 rooms or more...........	100.0	95.6	4.4
Rent Free				Rent Free			
1 and 2 rooms.............	100.0	49.2	50.8	1 and 2 rooms.............	100.0	50.3	49.7
3 and 4 rooms.............	100.0	65.6	34.4	3 and 4 rooms.............	100.0	66.6	33.4
5 and 6 rooms.............	100.0	87.6	12.4	5 and 6 rooms.............	100.0	85.1	14.9
7 rooms or more...........	100.0	97.6	2.4	7 rooms or more...........	100.0	95.5	4.5

Source: Special tabulation from the 1950 Census of Housing.

TABLE D-13.—Age of Head of Household, by Tenure and Rooms, for Type-of-Farming Regions: 1950

Region, tenure, and rooms	Age of head of household			Region, tenure, and rooms	Age of head of household		
	Under 45 years	45 to 64 years	65 and over		Under 45 years	45 to 64 years	65 and over
NORTHEAST DAIRY REGION				**TOBACCO REGION**			
All occupied dwelling units..........	210,990	228,200	104,250	All occupied dwelling units..........	111,650	89,955	36,860
Percent Distribution				Percent Distribution			
Total reporting.....	100.0	100.0	100.0	Total reporting.....	100.0	100.0	100.0
Owner..................	64.6	86.3	87.5	Owner..................	38.3	65.4	79.7
1 to 4 rooms.........	7.9	7.3	8.5	1 to 4 rooms.........	14.2	16.3	21.0
5 rooms or more......	56.7	79.0	79.0	5 rooms or more......	24.1	49.1	58.7
Renter.................	18.4	7.1	5.8	Renter.................	27.0	15.7	9.3
1 to 4 rooms.........	6.4	1.6	2.1	1 to 4 rooms.........	15.4	6.9	5.2
5 rooms or more......	12.0	5.5	3.7	5 rooms or more......	11.6	8.8	4.1
Rent free..............	17.0	6.6	6.7	Rent free..............	34.7	18.9	11.0
1 to 4 rooms.........	5.5	1.8	2.5	1 to 4 rooms.........	20.7	8.2	6.5
5 rooms or more......	11.5	4.8	4.2	5 rooms or more......	14.0	10.7	4.5
GREAT LAKES DAIRY REGION				**COTTON BELT**			
All occupied dwelling units..........	183,795	191,195	72,365	All occupied dwelling units..........	656,960	550,055	219,535
Percent Distribution				Percent Distribution			
Total reporting.....	100.0	100.0	100.0	Total reporting.....	100.0	100.0	100.0
Owner..................	69.3	89.5	90.0	Owner..................	39.9	58.2	66.4
1 to 4 rooms.........	13.8	14.0	17.7	1 to 4 rooms.........	18.0	20.3	25.2
5 rooms or more......	55.5	75.5	72.3	5 rooms or more......	21.9	37.9	41.2
Renter.................	20.8	7.2	5.1	Renter.................	28.2	20.2	15.3
1 to 4 rooms.........	4.3	1.4	1.8	1 to 4 rooms.........	20.6	13.3	11.1
5 rooms or more......	16.5	5.8	3.3	5 rooms or more......	7.6	6.9	4.2
Rent free..............	9.9	3.3	4.9	Rent free..............	31.9	21.6	18.3
1 to 4 rooms.........	2.9	1.0	2.6	1 to 4 rooms.........	24.7	15.4	14.4
5 rooms or more......	7.0	2.3	2.3	5 rooms or more......	7.2	6.2	3.9
EAST AND GULF COAST MISCELLANEOUS REGION				**CORN BELT**			
All occupied dwelling units..........	119,815	110,185	43,490	All occupied dwelling units..........	424,365	386,590	143,405
Percent Distribution				Percent Distribution			
Total reporting.....	100.0	100.0	100.0	Total reporting.....	100.0	100.0	100.0
Owner..................	51.4	72.9	80.3	Owner..................	42.8	75.2	85.5
1 to 4 rooms.........	19.1	19.4	23.0	1 to 4 rooms.........	7.6	10.1	13.7
5 rooms or more......	32.3	53.5	57.3	5 rooms or more......	35.2	65.1	71.8
Renter.................	17.4	10.4	7.6	Renter.................	43.0	18.9	9.6
1 to 4 rooms.........	9.7	4.9	4.1	1 to 4 rooms.........	6.2	2.4	2.5
5 rooms or more......	7.7	5.5	3.5	5 rooms or more......	36.8	16.5	7.1
Rent free..............	31.2	16.7	12.1	Rent free..............	14.2	5.9	4.9
1 to 4 rooms.........	20.2	9.6	8.0	1 to 4 rooms.........	3.6	1.2	1.9
5 rooms or more......	11.0	7.1	4.1	5 rooms or more......	10.6	4.7	3.0
GENERAL AND SELF-SUFFICING REGION				**NORTHERN WHEAT AND SMALL GRAINS REGION**			
All occupied dwelling units..........	355,810	361,550	164,595	All occupied dwelling units..........	60,690	49,845	15,150
Percent Distribution				Percent Distribution			
Total reporting.....	100.0	100.0	100.0	Total reporting.....	100.0	100.0	100.0
Owner..................	65.9	84.4	87.3	Owner..................	61.2	84.8	87.6
1 to 4 rooms.........	28.2	27.3	30.2	1 to 4 rooms.........	18.4	19.8	26.9
5 rooms or more......	37.7	57.1	57.1	5 rooms or more......	42.8	65.0	60.7
Renter.................	21.1	10.0	7.0	Renter.................	28.0	10.9	6.5
1 to 4 rooms.........	11.7	4.9	4.2	1 to 4 rooms.........	7.2	2.7	2.3
5 rooms or more......	9.4	5.1	2.8	5 rooms or more......	20.8	8.2	4.2
Rent free..............	13.0	5.6	5.7	Rent free..............	10.8	4.3	5.9
1 to 4 rooms.........	8.0	3.0	3.6	1 to 4 rooms.........	4.2	1.8	4.1
5 rooms or more......	5.0	2.6	2.1	5 rooms or more......	6.6	2.5	1.8

TABLE **D-13.**—AGE OF HEAD OF HOUSEHOLD, BY TENURE AND ROOMS, FOR TYPE-OF-FARMING REGIONS: 1950—Cont.

Region, tenure, and rooms	Age of head of household			Region, tenure, and rooms	Age of head of household		
	Under 45 years	45 to 64 years	65 and over		Under 45 years	45 to 64 years	65 and over
SOUTHERN WHEAT AND SMALL GRAINS REGION				UPLAND SUMMER GRAZING REGION			
All occupied dwelling units..........	49,490	41,115	13,585	All occupied dwelling units..........	53,695	46,635	15,050
Percent Distribution				Percent Distribution			
Total reporting.....	100.0	100.0	100.0	Total reporting.....	100.0	100.0	100.0
Owner...................	43.4	74.0	85.1	Owner...................	64.1	85.1	86.0
1 to 4 rooms..........	12.8	16.9	20.8	1 to 4 rooms..........	32.1	35.7	39.3
5 rooms or more.......	30.6	57.1	64.3	5 rooms or more.......	32.0	49.4	46.7
Renter..................	42.0	20.2	10.3	Renter..................	16.9	7.0	5.8
1 to 4 rooms..........	13.1	5.7	4.4	1 to 4 rooms..........	9.9	3.9	4.0
5 rooms or more.......	28.9	14.5	5.9	5 rooms or more.......	7.0	3.1	1.8
Rent free..............	14.6	5.8	4.6	Rent free..............	19.0	7.9	8.2
1 to 4 rooms..........	7.8	2.8	2.8	1 to 4 rooms..........	12.9	5.4	5.9
5 rooms or more.......	6.8	3.0	1.8	5 rooms or more.......	6.1	2.5	2.3
YEAR-LONG AND SEASONAL GRAZING REGION				WEST COAST MISCELLANEOUS REGION			
All occupied dwelling units..........	142,405	121,580	42,125	All occupied dwelling units..........	99,985	105,310	37,295
Percent Distribution				Percent Distribution			
Total reporting.....	100.0	100.0	100.0	Total reporting.....	100.0	100.0	100.0
Owner...................	44.8	71.1	80.7	Owner...................	58.1	81.0	83.1
1 to 4 rooms..........	21.9	28.6	33.6	1 to 4 rooms..........	21.7	25.4	26.8
5 rooms or more.......	22.9	42.5	47.1	5 rooms or more.......	36.4	55.6	56.3
Renter..................	25.6	13.9	8.2	Renter..................	18.8	8.2	7.1
1 to 4 rooms..........	15.2	7.9	5.8	1 to 4 rooms..........	10.3	4.4	4.6
5 rooms or more.......	10.4	6.0	2.4	5 rooms or more.......	8.5	3.8	2.5
Rent free..............	29.6	15.0	11.1	Rent free..............	23.1	10.8	9.8
1 to 4 rooms..........	21.8	10.5	8.5	1 to 4 rooms..........	15.2	7.2	6.9
5 rooms or more.......	7.8	4.5	2.6	5 rooms or more.......	7.9	3.6	2.9

Source: Special tabulation from the 1950 Census of Housing.

TABLE **D-14.**—YEAR BUILT, ELECTRIC LIGHTING, AND HEATING EQUIPMENT, BY CONDITION
AND PLUMBING FACILITIES, FOR TYPE-OF-FARMING REGIONS: 1950

Region and condition and plumbing facilities	All occupied dwelling units	Built in 1940 or later		Percent with--		
		Number	Per-cent of total	Elec-tric lights	Heating equipment	
					Central	Non-central, with flue
NORTHEAST DAIRY REGION						
Total..	543,426	40,453	7.4	92.1	44.7	47.9
Not dilapidated..............................	477,986	36,487	7.6	94.9	48.6	45.2
With private toilet & bath, & hot running water.....	239,403	20,897	8.7	99.4	72.1	24.0
With private toilet and bath, and only cold water...	16,487	1,151	7.0	97.7	47.1	46.1
With run'g water & priv. toilet, lack'g priv. bath..	16,488	1,429	8.7	96.0	42.2	50.5
With run'g water & priv. bath, lack'g priv. toilet..	12,789	984	7.7	93.4	40.3	49.6
With run'g water, lack'g both priv. toilet & bath...	87,865	4,026	4.6	96.0	29.7	63.1
No running water................................	104,954	8,000	7.6	83.4	13.0	76.9
Dilapidated..................................	50,206	2,976	5.9	71.2	14.1	74.6
With private toilet & bath, & hot running water.....	5,405	213	3.9	98.5	51.5	42.6
With running water, lacking private toilet or bath..	13,149	496	3.8	88.5	20.7	68.2
No running water................................	31,652	2,267	7.2	59.4	5.0	82.7
Condition or plumbing facilities not reported........	15,234	990	6.5	73.2	24.2	45.3
GREAT LAKES DAIRY REGION						
Total..	447,333	46,973	10.5	90.8	38.2	51.6
Not dilapidated..............................	398,533	42,991	10.8	93.1	41.1	49.7
With private toilet & bath, & hot running water.....	136,658	17,948	13.1	99.0	73.5	22.4
With private toilet and bath, and only cold water...	14,280	1,363	9.5	99.3	52.0	42.4
With run'g water & priv. toilet, lack'g priv. bath..	14,688	1,782	12.1	98.0	51.8	41.0
With run'g water & priv. bath, lack'g priv. toilet..	13,474	1,185	8.8	95.1	42.3	48.8
With run'g water, lack'g both priv. toilet & bath...	66,023	4,764	7.2	97.5	30.4	58.9
No running water................................	153,410	15,949	10.4	84.8	14.8	71.6
Dilapidated..................................	37,097	3,086	8.3	72.2	10.8	74.7
With private toilet & bath, & hot running water.....	1,945	102	5.2	100.0	54.7	35.1
With running water, lacking private toilet or bath..	6,395	606	9.5	93.8	22.5	68.8
No running water................................	28,757	2,378	8.3	65.6	5.3	78.7
Condition or plumbing facilities not reported........	11,703	896	7.7	69.2	25.6	45.2
EAST AND GULF COAST MISCELLANEOUS REGION						
Total..	273,476	61,392	22.4	74.3	6.7	65.6
Not dilapidated..............................	202,685	51,507	25.4	84.2	8.4	63.3
With private toilet & bath, & hot running water.....	55,573	14,370	25.9	99.2	23.4	42.8
With private toilet and bath, and only cold water...	12,275	3,609	29.4	96.7	6.7	42.7
With run'g water & priv. toilet, lack'g priv. bath..	3,775	998	26.4	94.5	12.1	58.2
With run'g water & priv. bath, lack'g priv. toilet..	9,049	1,935	21.4	90.2	4.0	56.1
With run'g water, lack'g both priv. toilet & bath...	24,763	6,026	24.3	97.0	4.6	67.0
No running water................................	97,250	24,569	25.3	69.8	1.2	77.7
Dilapidated..................................	62,427	8,388	13.4	44.6	1.3	74.7
With private toilet & bath, & hot running water.....	1,210	190	15.7	92.7	11.9	47.4
With running water, lacking private toilet or bath..	6,290	551	8.8	78.0	4.3	62.8
No running water................................	54,927	7,647	13.9	39.7	0.7	76.6
Condition or plumbing facilities not reported........	8,364	1,497	17.9	54.7	5.1	54.1
GENERAL AND SELF-SUFFICING REGION						
Total..	881,896	153,420	17.4	72.3	8.2	79.9
Not dilapidated..............................	687,371	132,470	19.3	79.1	10.0	79.1
With private toilet & bath, & hot running water.....	99,058	22,089	22.3	98.5	41.5	48.3
With private toilet and bath, and only cold water...	8,944	1,718	19.2	97.4	29.4	65.1
With run'g water & priv. toilet, lack'g priv. bath..	10,914	2,419	22.2	93.8	26.8	60.4
With run'g water & priv. bath, lack'g priv. toilet..	25,235	4,489	17.8	83.4	13.6	73.7
With run'g water, lack'g both priv. toilet & bath...	75,133	11,877	15.8	95.6	9.4	81.0
No running water................................	468,087	89,878	19.2	71.4	2.5	86.3
Dilapidated..................................	170,612	17,530	10.3	47.2	1.3	85.5
With private toilet & bath, & hot running water.....	1,685	190	11.3	89.1	37.3	49.3
With running water, lacking private toilet or bath..	10,189	939	9.2	78.4	5.0	80.7
No running water................................	158,738	16,401	10.3	44.8	0.7	86.2
Condition or plumbing facilities not reported........	23,913	3,420	14.3	55.9	7.1	61.7

TABLE **D-14.**—YEAR BUILT, ELECTRIC LIGHTING, AND HEATING EQUIPMENT, BY CONDITION
AND PLUMBING FACILITIES, FOR TYPE-OF-FARMING REGIONS: 1950—Cont.

Region and condition and plumbing facilities	All occupied dwelling units	Built in 1940 or later		Percent with--		
		Number	Per-cent of total	Elec-tric lights	Heating equipment	
					Central	Non-central, with flue
TOBACCO REGION						
Total...	238,447	32,868	13.8	77.4	4.2	83.8
Not dilapidated...............................	184,732	30,216	16.4	84.4	5.0	83.3
With private toilet & bath, & hot running water.....	22,448	4,632	20.6	98.5	28.2	62.5
With private toilet and bath, and only cold water...	1,800	277	15.4	98.8	8.4	84.5
With run'g water & priv. toilet, lack'g priv. bath..	2,631	389	14.8	93.6	15.7	71.9
With run'g water & priv. bath, lack'g priv. toilet..	5,540	941	17.0	91.9	8.6	77.2
With run'g water, lack'g both priv. toilet & bath...	22,109	3,222	14.6	98.3	2.1	88.9
No running water....................................	130,204	20,755	15.9	78.9	1.0	86.4
Dilapidated...................................	47,521	2,141	4.5	53.9	1.1	88.8
With private toilet & bath, & hot running water.....	390	56	14.4	93.8	21.0	63.1
With running water, lacking private toilet or bath..	2,325	81	3.5	84.9	4.0	89.0
No running water....................................	44,806	2,004	4.5	51.9	0.8	89.0
Condition or plumbing facilities not reported........	6,194	511	8.2	49.6	3.0	60.5
COTTON BELT						
Total...	1,426,482	282,675	19.8	67.8	1.9	76.1
Not dilapidated...............................	949,398	238,178	25.1	78.3	2.4	73.9
With private toilet & bath, & hot running water.....	120,344	36,005	29.9	98.9	10.6	47.8
With private toilet and bath, and only cold water...	19,148	5,285	27.6	97.5	4.0	58.6
With run'g water & priv. toilet, lack'g priv. bath..	15,068	4,122	27.4	95.2	8.2	60.9
With run'g water & priv. bath, lack'g priv. toilet..	39,340	9,575	24.3	87.4	2.7	67.2
With run'g water, lack'g both priv. toilet & bath...	101,220	23,061	22.8	97.0	1.7	70.9
No running water....................................	654,278	160,130	24.5	70.1	0.8	80.4
Dilapidated...................................	435,915	39,341	9.0	46.7	0.9	82.8
With private toilet & bath, & hot running water.....	3,225	415	12.9	92.9	10.8	54.4
With running water, lacking private toilet or bath..	23,419	1,975	8.4	73.8	2.6	76.1
No running water....................................	409,271	36,951	9.0	44.7	0.7	83.4
Condition or plumbing facilities not reported........	41,169	5,156	12.5	50.1	1.9	56.2
CORN BELT						
Total...	954,390	60,686	6.4	87.9	32.3	60.8
Not dilapidated...............................	875,113	57,228	6.5	90.2	34.1	59.8
With private toilet & bath, & hot running water.....	276,195	27,936	10.1	98.7	70.6	26.2
With private toilet and bath, and only cold water...	21,718	1,996	9.2	95.2	51.1	43.6
With run'g water & priv. toilet, lack'g priv. bath..	20,938	1,956	9.3	95.8	48.2	46.1
With run'g water & priv. bath, lack'g priv. toilet..	44,939	1,965	4.4	90.9	30.6	62.9
With run'g water, lack'g both priv. toilet & bath...	105,438	4,598	4.4	95.2	24.5	69.7
No running water....................................	405,885	18,777	4.6	82.4	10.5	81.3
Dilapidated...................................	54,814	2,248	4.1	62.1	8.1	83.0
With private toilet & bath, & hot running water.....	2,684	58	2.2	97.2	56.7	39.4
With running water, lacking private toilet or bath..	6,764	317	4.7	85.4	19.4	71.8
No running water....................................	45,366	1,873	4.1	56.6	3.5	87.3
Condition or plumbing facilities not reported........	24,463	1,210	4.9	66.7	22.2	48.0
NORTHERN WHEAT AND SMALL GRAINS REGION						
Total...	125,688	13,161	10.5	76.6	32.2	59.3
Not dilapidated...............................	113,738	12,594	11.1	79.8	34.4	57.8
With private toilet & bath, & hot running water.....	28,490	4,979	17.5	97.7	55.1	40.7
With private toilet and bath, and only cold water...	1,175	95	8.1	85.1	59.3	35.6
With run'g water & priv. toilet, lack'g priv. bath..	1,710	265	15.5	95.4	58.3	36.4
With run'g water & priv. bath, lack'g priv. toilet..	5,535	346	6.3	86.6	41.6	54.9
With run'g water, lack'g both priv. toilet & bath...	11,410	1,070	9.4	91.0	31.7	61.3
No running water....................................	65,418	5,839	8.9	69.1	24.1	65.7
Dilapidated...................................	8,435	281	3.3	46.0	8.6	79.8
With private toilet & bath, & hot running water.....	465	...	...	100.0	23.4	70.1
With running water, lacking private toilet or bath..	1,150	55	4.8	89.1	11.1	83.3
No running water....................................	6,820	226	3.3	35.0	7.1	79.8
Condition or plumbing facilities not reported........	3,515	286	8.1	44.7	16.7	60.5

TABLE **D-14.**—YEAR BUILT, ELECTRIC LIGHTING, AND HEATING EQUIPMENT, BY CONDITION AND PLUMBING FACILITIES, FOR TYPE-OF-FARMING REGIONS: 1950—Cont.

Region and condition and plumbing facilities	All occupied dwelling units	Built in 1940 or later		Percent with--		
		Number	Per-cent of total	Elec-tric lights	Heating equipment	
					Central	Non-central, with flue
SOUTHERN WHEAT AND SMALL GRAINS REGION						
Total...	104,184	13,160	12.6	83.8	19.6	66.1
Not dilapidated...............................	93,619	12,526	13.4	86.0	21.2	65.3
With private toilet & bath, & hot running water.....	38,390	'8,079	21.0	96.8	38.0	45.7
With private toilet and bath, and only cold water...	2,170	139	6.4	83.5	30.0	61.8
With run'g water & priv. toilet, lack'g priv. bath..	1,365	154	11.3	96.6	26.2	61.5
With run'g water & priv. bath, lack'g priv. toilet..	7,890	472	6.0	85.0	15.8	73.4
With run'g water, lack'g both priv. toilet & bath...	11,015	1,088	9.9	87.2	9.1	74.5
No running water..................................	32,789	2,594	7.9	72.9	6.2	83.4
Dilapidated...................................	7,555	317	4.2	63.9	4.8	79.8
With private toilet & bath, & hot running water.....	575	108	18.8	96.3	28.0	60.0
With running water, lacking private toilet or bath..	1,615	79	4.9	85.5	8.1	73.3
No running water..................................	5,365	130	2.4	53.9	1.3	83.8
Condition or plumbing facilities not reported........	3,010	317	10.5	64.7	5.7	56.8
YEAR-LONG AND SEASONAL GRAZING REGION						
Total...	306,113	63,689	20.8	79.7	7.1	56.5
Not dilapidated...............................	249,331	57,909	23.2	85.2	8.2	55.0
With private toilet & bath, & hot running water.....	90,506	27,850	30.8	96.9	16.9	41.6
With private toilet and bath, and only cold water...	11,865	2,308	19.5	95.1	5.0	49.5
With run'g water & priv. toilet, lack'g priv. bath..	3,710	868	23.4	94.9	9.3	49.7
With run'g water & priv. bath, lack'g priv. toilet..	16,867	2,802	16.6	87.7	4.4	53.0
With run'g water, lack'g both priv. toilet & bath...	39,448	6,996	17.7	89.9	3.5	60.7
No running water..................................	86,935	17,085	19.7	68.6	2.5	67.8
Dilapidated...................................	47,546	4,622	9.7	55.6	1.4	66.8
With private toilet & bath, & hot running water.....	2,160	240	11.1	90.6	3.4	36.8
With running water, lacking private toilet or bath..	9,896	836	8.4	77.7	3.0	60.9
No running water..................................	35,490	3,546	10.0	47.3	0.8	70.3
Condition or plumbing facilities not reported........	9,236	1,158	12.5	55.9	5.3	43.8
UPLAND SUMMER GRAZING REGION						
Total...	115,383	24,879	21.6	85.8	16.2	72.4
Not dilapidated...............................	99,092	23,010	23.2	89.2	18.3	72.0
With private toilet & bath, & hot running water.....	49,448	12,054	24.4	98.6	33.2	62.0
With private toilet and bath, and only cold water...	625	139	22.2	100.0	8.3	83.4
With run'g water & priv. toilet, lack'g priv. bath..	1,355	296	21.8	98.2	16.7	72.3
With run'g water & priv. bath, lack'g priv. toilet..	4,166	784	18.8	90.0	8.3	81.2
With run'g water, lack'g both priv. toilet & bath...	16,196	2,925	18.1	96.1	4.6	87.1
No running water..................................	27,302	6,812	25.0	67.3	1.3	79.3
Dilapidated...................................	12,640	1,521	12.0	65.9	2.4	81.9
With private toilet & bath, & hot running water.....	1,015	51	5.0	94.1	16.7	76.0
With running water, lacking private toilet or bath..	2,960	114	3.9	86.2	2.2	88.9
No running water..................................	8,665	1,356	15.6	55.6	0.8	80.2
Condition or plumbing facilities not reported........	3,651	348	9.5	61.2	6.6	51.5
WEST COAST MISCELLANEOUS REGION						
Total...	242,599	60,508	24.9	95.1	16.1	65.1
Not dilapidated...............................	209,159	55,247	26.4	97.1	18.0	64.9
With private toilet & bath, & hot running water.....	162,332	40,251	24.8	98.9	22.1	61.6
With private toilet and bath, and only cold water...	4,220	944	22.4	96.8	4.5	70.7
With run'g water & priv. toilet, lack'g priv. bath..	2,256	828	36.7	98.9	17.6	64.7
With run'g water & priv. bath, lack'g priv. toilet..	9,780	2,491	25.5	94.0	4.0	78.9
With run'g water, lack'g both priv. toilet & bath...	18,476	5,607	30.3	95.4	4.0	77.4
No running water..................................	12,095	5,126	42.4	78.7	0.5	75.7
Dilapidated...................................	26,165	4,183	16.0	87.8	3.2	71.7
With private toilet & bath, & hot running water.....	6,746	672	10.0	97.8	8.6	71.9
With running water, lacking private toilet or bath..	10,724	1,536	14.3	93.1	1.6	71.7
No running water..................................	8,695	1,975	22.7	73.6	0.8	71.4
Condition or plumbing facilities not reported........	7,275	1,078	14.8	64.4	7.1	49.4

Source: Special tabulation from the 1950 Census of Housing.

TABLE **D-15.**—TYPE OF HOUSEHOLD, BY CONDITION AND PLUMBING FACILITIES, FOR
TYPE-OF-FARMING REGIONS: 1950

Region and condition and plumbing facilities[1]	Total	Husband-wife families, no non-relatives	Other family groups, no non-relatives	One-person households	Households with non-relatives
NORTHEAST DAIRY REGION					
All occupied dwelling units....	543,440	417,735	51,140	27,575	46,990
Percent Distribution					
Total reporting...............	100.0	100.0	100.0	100.0	100.0
Not dilapidated......................	90.5	91.6	87.5	78.3	90.7
All facilities....................	45.3	46.8	36.9	25.3	52.7
Some facilities..................	25.3	26.0	25.7	20.6	21.6
No facilities....................	19.9	18.9	24.9	32.3	16.3
Dilapidated..........................	9.5	8.4	12.5	21.7	9.3
GREAT LAKES DAIRY REGION					
All occupied dwelling units....	447,355	354,410	41,515	24,495	26,935
Percent Distribution					
Total reporting...............	100.0	100.0	100.0	100.0	100.0
Not dilapidated......................	91.5	92.9	88.3	75.5	92.7
All facilities....................	31.4	32.9	22.6	11.6	41.9
Some facilities..................	24.9	25.9	23.0	15.3	23.2
No facilities....................	35.2	34.0	42.7	48.6	27.6
Dilapidated..........................	8.5	7.1	11.7	24.5	7.3
EAST AND GULF COAST MISCELLANEOUS REGION					
All occupied dwelling units....	273,490	220,715	27,435	13,445	11,895
Percent Distribution					
Total reporting...............	100.0	100.0	100.0	100.0	100.0
Not dilapidated......................	76.5	78.1	69.3	65.3	74.1
All facilities....................	21.0	21.9	15.5	14.8	23.6
Some facilities..................	18.8	19.7	15.5	13.0	15.9
No facilities....................	36.7	36.5	38.3	37.5	34.6
Dilapidated..........................	23.5	21.9	30.7	34.7	25.9
GENERAL AND SELF-SUFFICING REGION					
All occupied dwelling units....	881,955	725,740	89,745	39,635	26,835
Percent Distribution					
Total reporting...............	100.0	100.0	100.0	100.0	100.0
Not dilapidated......................	80.1	81.4	74.2	68.7	82.3
All facilities....................	11.5	11.9	8.6	6.2	19.1
Some facilities..................	14.0	14.5	11.7	8.9	15.8
No facilities....................	54.6	55.0	53.9	53.6	47.4
Dilapidated..........................	19.9	18.6	25.8	31.3	17.7
TOBACCO REGION					
All occupied dwelling units....	238,465	199,685	22,770	7,260	8,750
Percent Distribution					
Total reporting...............	100.0	100.0	100.0	100.0	100.0
Not dilapidated......................	79.5	80.7	74.1	66.3	78.3
All facilities....................	9.7	9.7	9.0	7.7	13.2
Some facilities..................	13.8	14.1	12.7	8.0	14.0
No facilities....................	56.1	56.9	52.3	50.7	51.1
Dilapidated..........................	20.5	19.3	25.9	33.7	21.7

[1] See footnote 1, table D-2.

TABLE **D-15.**—TYPE OF HOUSEHOLD, BY CONDITION AND PLUMBING FACILITIES, FOR
TYPE-OF-FARMING REGIONS: 1950—Cont.

Region and condition and plumbing facilities[1]	Total	Husband-wife families, no non-relatives	Other family groups, no non-relatives	One-person households	Households with non-relatives
COTTON BELT					
All occupied dwelling units....	1,426,550	1,195,500	138,575	54,605	37,870
Percent Distribution					
Total reporting................	100.0	100.0	100.0	100.0	100.0
Not dilapidated....................	68.5	69.9	61.8	57.5	65.6
All facilities..................	8.7	9.0	6.8	5.7	9.8
Some facilities................	12.6	13.1	10.3	8.3	10.8
No facilities..................	47.2	47.8	44.7	43.6	45.0
Dilapidated........................	31.5	30.1	38.2	42.5	34.4
CORN BELT					
All occupied dwelling units....	954,360	802,800	68,660	41,940	40,960
Percent Distribution					
Total reporting................	100.0	100.0	100.0	100.0	100.0
Not dilapidated....................	94.1	94.9	91.4	82.1	95.4
All facilities..................	29.7	30.6	23.4	14.0	39.4
Some facilities................	20.8	21.4	18.1	13.3	20.8
No facilities..................	43.6	43.0	49.9	54.8	35.2
Dilapidated........................	5.9	5.1	8.6	17.9	4.6
NORTHERN WHEAT AND SMALL GRAINS REGION					
All occupied dwelling units....	125,685	96,660	11,145	7,860	10,020
Percent Distribution					
Total reporting................	100.0	100.0	100.0	100.0	100.0
Not dilapidated....................	93.1	94.3	90.8	79.5	94.6
All facilities..................	23.3	24.1	14.9	7.7	36.3
Some facilities................	16.2	16.7	14.6	11.1	16.9
No facilities..................	53.5	53.4	61.4	60.7	41.4
Dilapidated........................	6.9	5.7	9.2	20.5	5.4
SOUTHERN WHEAT AND SMALL GRAINS REGION					
All occupied dwelling units....	104,190	88,790	6,855	5,070	3,475
Percent Distribution					
Total reporting................	100.0	100.0	100.0	100.0	100.0
Not dilapidated....................	92.5	93.4	89.8	80.0	93.9
All facilities..................	37.9	39.3	27.4	16.9	54.1
Some facilities................	22.2	22.7	20.9	18.5	17.6
No facilities..................	32.4	31.4	41.5	44.6	22.2
Dilapidated........................	7.5	6.6	10.2	20.0	6.1
YEAR-LONG AND SEASONAL GRAZING REGION					
All occupied dwelling units....	306,110	253,315	21,485	18,660	12,650
Percent Distribution					
Total reporting................	100.0	100.0	100.0	100.0	100.0
Not dilapidated....................	84.0	85.3	78.4	71.0	85.1
All facilities..................	30.5	31.6	22.9	16.4	40.6
Some facilities................	24.2	25.2	22.5	17.8	17.3
No facilities..................	29.3	28.5	32.9	36.8	27.1
Dilapidated........................	16.0	14.7	21.6	29.0	14.9

[1] See footnote 1, table D-2.

TABLE **D-15.**—TYPE OF HOUSEHOLD, BY CONDITION AND PLUMBING FACILITIES, FOR
TYPE-OF-FARMING REGIONS: 1950—Cont.

Region and condition and plumbing facilities[1]	Total	Husband-wife families, no non-relatives	Other family groups, no non-relatives	One-person households	Households with non-relatives
UPLAND SUMMER GRAZING REGION					
All occupied dwelling units....	115,380	94,545	8,085	7,280	5,470
Percent Distribution					
Total reporting................	100.0	100.0	100.0	100.0	100.0
Not dilapidated......................	88.7	90.1	83.0	74.7	90.1
All facilities....................	44.3	46.8	32.8	19.3	48.7
Some facilities...................	20.0	20.7	16.5	16.6	18.2
No facilities.....................	24.4	22.6	33.7	38.8	23.3
Dilapidated..........................	11.3	9.9	17.0	25.3	9.9
WEST COAST MISCELLANEOUS REGION					
All occupied dwelling units....	242,590	192,805	17,560	19,835	12,390
Percent Distribution					
Total reporting................	100.0	100.0	100.0	100.0	100.0
Not dilapidated......................	88.9	90.5	85.6	77.3	86.2
All facilities....................	69.0	72.3	63.4	41.9	66.7
Some facilities...................	14.8	14.2	16.5	19.5	14.2
No facilities.....................	5.1	4.0	5.7	15.8	5.3
Dilapidated..........................	11.1	9.5	14.4	22.7	13.8

[1] See footnote 1, table D-2.

Source: Special tabulation from the 1950 Census of Housing.

TABLE **D-16.**—INCOME IN 1949, BY CONDITION AND PLUMBING FACILITIES,
FOR TYPE-OF-FARMING REGIONS: 1950

[Income of only primary families and individuals]

Region and condition and plumbing facilities	Under $2,000	$2,000 to $3,999	$4,000 to $5,999	$6,000 and over	Not re-ported	Median income (dollars)
NORTHEAST DAIRY REGION						
All occupied dwelling units...................	220,780	179,145	61,980	45,135	36,400	2,365
Percent Distribution						
Total reporting..............................	100.0	100.0	100.0	100.0	100.0	2,374
Not dilapidated....................................	86.6	92.0	94.9	96.6	91.8	2,470
With private toilet & bath, & hot running water...	33.9	46.8	58.9	71.6	51.2	2,935
With private toilet & bath, & only cold water.....	3.0	3.4	3.1	2.5	3.3	2,435
With running water and private toilet, lacking private bath....................................	3.2	3.4	2.9	2.3	3.2	2,323
With running water and private bath, lacking private toilet....................................	2.4	2.6	2.4	2.0	2.2	2,366
With run'g water, lack'g both priv. toilet & bath.	17.6	17.7	15.1	11.3	14.8	2,242
No running water.................................	26.5	18.1	12.5	6.9	17.1	1,743
Dilapidated.......................................	13.4	8.0	5.1	3.4	8.2	1,646
With private toilet & bath, & hot running water...	1.0	1.0	1.2	1.1	1.2	2,480
With running water, lacking priv. toilet or bath..	3.0	2.6	1.6	1.0	2.0	1,907
No running water.................................	9.4	4.4	2.3	1.3	5.0	1,484
GREAT LAKES DAIRY REGION						
All occupied dwelling units...................	201,515	146,830	49,815	27,610	21,585	2,155
Percent Distribution						
Total reporting..............................	100.0	100.0	100.0	100.0	100.0	2,152
Not dilapidated....................................	88.3	93.4	95.8	96.8	91.2	2,242
With private toilet & bath, & hot running water...	21.5	34.0	45.6	59.7	36.8	2,917
With private toilet & bath, & only cold water.....	3.0	3.5	3.8	2.8	3.9	2,349
With running water and private toilet, lacking private bath....................................	3.0	3.8	3.6	3.0	3.2	2,360
With running water and private bath, lacking private toilet....................................	2.9	3.2	3.7	3.0	3.1	2,322
With run'g water, lack'g both priv. toilet & bath.	14.6	16.9	15.0	11.5	13.8	2,242
No running water.................................	43.3	32.0	24.1	16.8	30.4	1,726
Dilapidated.......................................	11.7	6.6	4.2	3.2	8.8	1,538
With private toilet & bath, & hot running water...	0.3	0.5	0.6	0.6	0.6	2,667
With running water, lacking priv. toilet or bath..	1.6	1.6	1.1	0.9	1.6	2,002
No running water.................................	9.8	4.5	2.5	1.7	6.6	1,424
EAST AND GULF COAST MISCELLANEOUS REGION						
All occupied dwelling units...................	168,510	59,365	17,535	11,680	16,400	1,526
Percent Distribution						
Total reporting..............................	100.0	100.0	100.0	100.0	100.0	1,528
Not dilapidated....................................	69.8	86.4	91.9	95.0	78.5	1,671
With private toilet & bath, & hot running water...	11.0	29.4	50.9	67.3	27.3	2,904
With private toilet & bath, & only cold water.....	3.4	7.3	7.6	4.8	4.2	2,121
With running water and private toilet, lacking private bath....................................	1.0	2.2	2.3	2.0	1.2	2,151
With running water and private bath, lacking private toilet....................................	3.2	4.1	3.8	3.1	3.6	1,651
With run'g water, lack'g both priv. toilet & bath.	8.1	12.6	10.7	8.8	9.3	1,768
No running water.................................	43.1	30.8	16.6	9.0	32.9	1,308
Dilapidated.......................................	30.2	13.6	8.1	5.0	21.5	1,199
With private toilet & bath, & hot running water...	0.3	0.6	0.9	1.2	0.6	2,424
With running water, lacking priv. toilet or bath..	2.4	2.8	1.7	1.1	2.3	1,520
No running water.................................	27.5	10.2	5.5	2.7	18.6	1,160

TABLE **D-16.**—INCOME IN 1949, BY CONDITION AND PLUMBING FACILITIES, FOR TYPE-OF-FARMING REGIONS: 1950—Cont.

[Income of only primary families and individuals]

Region and condition and plumbing facilities	Under $2,000	$2,000 to $3,999	$4,000 to $5,999	$6,000 and over	Not re- ported	Median income (dol- lars)
GENERAL AND SELF-SUFFICING REGION						
All occupied dwelling units..................	570,675	201,740	45,330	21,405	42,805	1,470
Percent Distribution						
Total reporting.............................	100.0	100.0	100.0	100.0	100.0	1,471
Not dilapidated.............................	75.6	88.0	92.8	94.5	82.5	1,557
With private toilet & bath, & hot running water...	6.3	17.0	32.0	48.2	15.4	2,673
With private toilet & bath, & only cold water.....	0.8	1.4	2.1	1.8	1.2	1,938
With running water and private toilet, lacking private bath...................................	1.0	1.8	2.3	2.7	1.4	1,929
With running water and private bath, lacking private toilet..............................	2.6	3.6	3.7	4.0	3.3	1,673
With run'g water, lack'g both priv. toilet & bath.	7.0	12.2	13.7	11.1	9.1	1,830
No running water.................................	57.9	52.0	39.0	26.7	52.1	1,389
Dilapidated...	24.4	12.0	7.2	5.5	17.5	1,206
With private toilet & bath, & hot running water...	0.2	0.2	0.4	0.7	0.2	1,958
With running water, lacking priv. toilet or bath..	1.2	1.2	1.0	0.8	1.0	1,438
No running water.................................	23.0	10.6	5.8	4.0	16.3	1,189
TOBACCO REGION						
All occupied dwelling units..................	147,290	57,875	13,165	6,480	13,655	1,526
Percent Distribution						
Total reporting.............................	100.0	100.0	100.0	100.0	100.0	1,526
Not dilapidated.............................	74.7	87.2	92.3	93.7	80.5	1,624
With private toilet & bath, & hot running water...	4.8	13.3	26.8	46.9	12.9	2,934
With private toilet & bath, & only cold water.....	0.6	1.0	1.4	1.3	1.3	2,009
With running water and private toilet, lacking private bath...................................	0.8	1.4	2.0	2.6	1.5	2,025
With running water and private bath, lacking private toilet..............................	2.0	3.0	3.7	2.9	2.6	1,804
With run'g water, lack'g both priv. toilet & bath.	7.3	13.4	15.7	13.0	9.7	2,001
No running water.................................	59.2	55.1	42.7	27.0	52.5	1,450
Dilapidated...	25.3	12.8	7.7	6.3	19.5	1,237
With private toilet & bath, & hot running water...	0.1	0.3	0.2	0.6	0.3	2,517
With running water, lacking priv. toilet or bath..	1.0	1.0	0.9	0.7	1.0	1,512
No running water.................................	24.2	11.5	6.6	5.0	18.2	1,220
COTTON BELT						
All occupied dwelling units..................	1,058,255	227,545	48,380	25,375	66,995	1,285
Percent Distribution						
Total reporting.............................	100.0	100.0	100.0	100.0	100.0	1,285
Not dilapidated.............................	64.0	82.1	89.6	91.9	70.4	1,375
With private toilet & bath, & hot running water...	4.4	17.4	34.2	51.8	11.2	2,564
With private toilet & bath, & only cold water.....	1.0	2.6	3.5	2.9	1.6	1,810
With running water and private toilet, lacking private bath...................................	0.8	1.9	3.1	3.2	1.2	1,814
With running water and private bath, lacking private toilet..............................	2.4	4.2	5.1	4.4	3.0	1,519
With run'g water, lack'g both priv. toilet & bath.	5.7	12.7	14.2	10.2	7.7	1,634
No running water.................................	49.7	43.3	29.5	19.4	45.7	1,224
Dilapidated...	36.0	17.9	10.4	8.1	29.6	1,125
With private toilet & bath, & hot running water...	0.1	0.5	0.8	0.9	0.3	2,324
With running water, lacking priv. toilet or bath..	1.7	1.9	1.7	1.2	1.8	1,303
No running water.................................	34.2	15.5	7.9	6.0	27.5	1,112

TABLE **D-16.**—INCOME IN 1949, BY CONDITION AND PLUMBING FACILITIES,
FOR TYPE-OF-FARMING REGIONS: 1950—Cont.

[Income of only primary families and individuals]

Region and condition and plumbing facilities	Under $2,000	$2,000 to $3,999	$4,000 to $5,999	$6,000 and over	Not re- ported	Median income (dol- lars)
CORN BELT						
All occupied dwelling units..................	369,410	328,700	125,085	81,480	49,685	2,524
Percent Distribution						
Total reporting.............................	100.0	100.0	100.0	100.0	100.0	2,508
Not dilapidated.............................	91.2	95.4	97.0	97.7	94.1	2,570
With private toilet & bath, & hot running water...	19.0	30.3	42.7	53.7	32.9	3,273
With private toilet & bath, & only cold water.....	2.2	2.5	2.6	2.2	2.1	2,645
With running water and private toilet, lacking private bath..................................	2.0	2.4	2.5	2.5	2.2	2,723
With running water and private bath, lacking private toilet.................................	4.5	5.1	5.1	5.0	4.4	2,637
With run'g water, lack'g both priv. toilet & bath.	10.1	12.7	12.1	10.4	11.4	2,671
No running water.................................	53.4	42.4	32.0	23.8	40.9	2,156
Dilapidated....................................	8.8	4.6	3.0	2.3	6.0	1,637
With private toilet & bath, & hot running water...	0.2	0.3	0.3	0.3	0.4	2,810
With running water, lacking priv. toilet or bath..	0.8	0.7	0.6	0.6	0.7	2,250
No running water.................................	7.8	3.6	2.1	1.4	4.8	1,539
NORTHERN WHEAT AND SMALL GRAINS REGION						
All occupied dwelling units..................	47,870	37,975	16,540	16,995	6,305	2,622
Percent Distribution						
Total reporting.............................	100.0	100.0	100.0	100.0	100.0	2,623
Not dilapidated.............................	89.7	94.4	96.1	97.1	92.0	2,722
With private toilet & bath, & hot running water...	12.7	21.6	30.7	48.0	27.2	3,880
With private toilet & bath, & only cold water.....	0.9	1.0	1.0	0.9	1.2	2,804
With running water and private toilet, lacking private bath..................................	1.1	1.5	1.7	1.7	1.2	3,080
With running water and private bath, lacking private toilet.................................	4.0	4.5	5.4	5.5	4.3	2,941
With run'g water, lack'g both priv. toilet & bath.	8.6	9.9	10.3	9.4	8.9	2,796
No running water.................................	62.4	55.9	47.0	31.6	49.2	2,449
Dilapidated....................................	10.3	5.6	3.9	2.9	8.0	1,670
With private toilet & bath, & hot running water...	0.2	0.4	0.3	0.7	0.4	2,474
With running water, lacking priv. toilet or bath..	1.1	1.0	0.8	0.3	1.2	2,116
No running water.................................	9.0	4.1	2.8	1.8	6.3	1,554
SOUTHERN WHEAT AND SMALL GRAINS REGION						
All occupied dwelling units..................	41,630	30,645	13,325	13,695	4,895	2,523
Percent Distribution						
Total reporting.............................	100.0	100.0	100.0	100.0	100.0	2,531
Not dilapidated.............................	89.1	93.6	95.7	96.9	94.0	2,622
With private toilet & bath, & hot running water...	24.8	37.2	49.9	65.0	45.5	3,465
With private toilet & bath, & only cold water.....	2.0	2.4	2.2	1.8	1.9	2,540
With running water and private toilet, lacking private bath..................................	1.4	1.4	1.4	1.0	1.8	2,440
With running water and private bath, lacking private toilet.................................	8.4	8.3	7.7	5.4	6.4	2,334
With run'g water, lack'g both priv. toilet & bath.	11.0	12.3	10.4	8.5	9.7	2,468
No running water.................................	41.5	32.0	24.1	15.2	28.7	1,879
Dilapidated....................................	10.9	6.4	4.3	3.1	6.0	1,653
With private toilet & bath, & hot running water...	0.6	0.5	0.5	0.8	0.9	2,607
With running water, lacking priv. toilet or bath..	2.0	1.6	1.1	0.9	1.3	1,885
No running water.................................	8.3	4.3	2.7	1.4	3.8	1,547

TABLE **D-16.**—INCOME IN 1949, BY CONDITION AND PLUMBING FACILITIES,
FOR TYPE-OF-FARMING REGIONS: 1950—Cont.

[Income of only primary families and individuals]

Region and condition and plumbing facilities	Under $2,000	$2,000 to $3,999	$4,000 to $5,999	$6,000 and over	Not re- ported	Median income (dol- lars)
YEAR-LONG AND SEASONAL GRAZING REGION						
All occupied dwelling units..................	138,550	87,845	31,995	30,550	17,170	2,135
Percent Distribution						
Total reporting.............................	100.0	100.0	100.0	100.0	100.0	2,147
Not dilapidated.............................	77.1	87.8	92.7	94.7	84.1	2,385
With private toilet & bath, & hot running water...	17.9	32.3	47.5	59.8	37.5	3,316
With private toilet & bath, & only cold water.....	4.0	4.4	3.8	3.1	3.4	2,145
With running water and private toilet, lacking private bath..................................	1.1	1.4	1.5	1.6	1.0	2,489
With running water and private bath, lacking private toilet................................	5.6	6.2	5.5	5.4	5.3	2,211
With run'g water, lack'g both priv. toilet & bath.	13.0	15.4	13.1	9.9	11.3	2,216
No running water................................	35.5	28.1	21.3	14.9	25.6	1,737
Dilapidated.................................	22.9	12.2	7.3	5.3	15.9	1,467
With private toilet & bath, & hot running water...	0.6	0.9	0.7	0.9	1.1	2,694
With running water, lacking priv. toilet or bath..	4.0	3.3	2.1	1.6	3.2	1,746
No running water................................	18.3	8.0	4.5	2.8	11.6	1,368
UPLAND SUMMER GRAZING REGION						
All occupied dwelling units..................	49,585	37,280	12,635	8,300	7,580	2,231
Percent Distribution						
Total reporting.............................	100.0	100.0	100.0	100.0	100.0	2,247
Not dilapidated.............................	84.4	90.7	95.1	95.4	88.7	2,367
With private toilet & bath, & hot running water...	32.5	47.8	62.3	70.0	44.5	2,877
With private toilet & bath, & only cold water.....	0.6	0.6	0.5	0.3	0.3	2,302
With running water and private toilet, lacking private bath..................................	1.1	1.2	1.6	1.8	1.0	2,616
With running water and private bath, lacking private toilet................................	3.6	4.0	3.7	4.0	3.3	2,382
With run'g water, lack'g both priv. toilet & bath.	13.8	17.4	13.1	9.3	12.4	2,328
No running water................................	32.8	19.7	13.9	10.0	27.2	1,615
Dilapidated.................................	15.6	9.3	4.9	4.6	11.3	1,583
With private toilet & bath, & hot running water...	0.8	0.9	0.9	1.2	1.3	2,477
With running water, lacking priv. toilet or bath..	2.9	3.0	1.7	0.9	2.6	1,975
No running water................................	11.9	5.4	2.3	2.5	7.4	1,431
WEST COAST MISCELLANEOUS REGION						
All occupied dwelling units..................	86,360	83,425	33,365	24,755	14,685	2,661
Percent Distribution						
Total reporting.............................	100.0	100.0	100.0	100.0	100.0	2,670
Not dilapidated.............................	83.6	90.1	93.9	95.9	89.3	2,781
With private toilet & bath, & hot running water...	57.1	70.4	80.6	88.5	71.0	3,000
With private toilet & bath, & only cold water.....	2.2	2.1	1.2	0.6	1.4	2,249
With running water and private toilet, lacking private bath..................................	1.2	1.0	0.7	0.5	0.9	2,213
With running water and private bath, lacking private toilet................................	4.6	4.3	3.7	2.8	3.5	2,425
With run'g water, lack'g both priv. toilet & bath.	10.1	8.1	5.8	2.4	7.2	2,103
No running water................................	8.4	4.2	1.9	1.1	5.3	1,605
Dilapidated.................................	16.4	9.9	6.1	4.1	10.7	1,802
With private toilet & bath, & hot running water...	3.1	3.1	2.5	2.2	2.9	2,509
With running water, lacking priv. toilet or bath..	6.4	4.5	2.4	1.3	4.2	1,889
No running water................................	6.9	2.3	1.2	0.6	3.6	1,417

Source: Special tabulation from the 1950 Census of Housing.

APPENDIX E

ADDITIONAL DATA FOR CHAPTER 4

Source of Tables in Appendix E

1950 Census of Housing, Vol. III, *Farm Housing Characteristics*, subregion tables 1 and 2; compilations of county data from *1950 Census of Housing*, Vol. I, *General Characteristics*, Parts 2 to 6, tables 32 and 33, and from *1940 Census of Housing*, Vol. II, *General Characteristics*, Parts 2 to 5, tables 22 and 23.

TABLE E-1.—NORTHEAST DAIRY REGION—CHARACTERISTICS OF DWELLING UNITS IN SELECTED ECONOMIC SUBREGIONS: 1950 AND 1940

Characteristic	Subregion 7		Subregion 10		Subregion 27	
	1950	1940	1950	1940	1950	1940
ALL DWELLING UNITS						
Number..................................	29,918	33,510	63,756	73,622	56,001	67,725
Percent by year built................	100.0	100.0	100.0	100.0	100.0	100.0
1920 or later.............................	15.3	9.0	14.4	10.6	28.6	22.4
1919 or earlier...........................	84.7	91.0	85.6	89.4	71.4	77.6
Percent by number of rooms...........	100.0	100.0	100.0	100.0	100.0	100.0
1 to 3 rooms.............................	6.3	4.0	5.0	4.1	10.0	11.7
4 rooms..................................	6.6	4.9	5.9	4.7	13.8	13.5
5 rooms..................................	8.8	7.6	9.0	7.7	15.2	14.6
6 rooms or more..........................	78.3	83.5	80.1	83.5	61.0	60.2
Median number of rooms...................	7.1	7.8	7.0	7.8	6.0	6.0
Percent by condition[1]................	100.0	100.0	100.0	100.0	100.0	100.0
Not dilapidated...........................	87.2	69.3	88.1	65.6	84.9	65.0
Dilapidated...............................	12.8	30.7	11.9	34.4	15.1	35.0
Percent by plumbing facilities.......	100.0	100.0	100.0	100.0	100.0	100.0
With running water........................	68.5	37.4	78.4	46.3	63.6	31.9
Without running water.....................	31.5	62.6	21.6	53.7	36.4	68.1
Percent by toilet facilities.........	100.0	100.0	100.0	100.0	100.0	100.0
With private flush toilet.................	49.0	24.5	55.9	27.6	35.0	17.9
Without private flush toilet..............	51.0	75.5	44.1	72.4	65.0	82.1
Percent by bathing facilities........	100.0	100.0	100.0	100.0	100.0	100.0
With private bathtub or shower...........	45.2	21.7	54.5	26.4	35.3	17.4
Without private bathtub or shower........	54.8	78.3	45.5	73.6	64.7	82.6
Percent by electric lighting.........	100.0	100.0	100.0	100.0	100.0	100.0
With electric lights......................	89.8	54.6	92.6	56.3	88.3	48.5
Without electric lights...................	10.2	45.4	7.4	43.7	11.7	51.5
ALL OCCUPIED UNITS						
Number..................................	25,365	30,252	53,435	65,707	52,910	65,528
Percent by heating equipment.........	100.0	100.0	100.0	100.0	100.0	100.0
Steam or hot water........................	4.8	2.8	8.7	4.8	8.9	6.7
Warm air furnace..........................	26.6	18.7	29.8	18.8	33.6	19.7
Heating stove, other or none.............	68.6	78.5	61.5	76.4	57.5	73.6
Percent by cooking fuel...............	100.0	100.0	100.0	100.0	100.0	100.0
Coal or coke..............................	5.8	3.0	17.7	12.5	44.0	63.5
Wood.....................................	52.5	87.7	34.8	73.0	3.2	5.5
Utility and bottled gas...................	15.4	0.5	26.3	6.9	34.0	26.1
Electricity...............................	10.8	1.3	15.9	2.7	15.7	1.9
Liquid fuel...............................	14.8	7.4	4.8	4.8	2.3	2.9
Other or none.............................	0.7	0.1	0.5	0.1	0.8	0.1
Percent by tenure.....................	100.0	100.0	100.0	100.0	100.0	100.0
Owner....................................	78.9	75.3	82.9	77.3	78.5	72.1
Renter and rent free......................	21.1	24.7	17.1	22.7	21.5	27.9
Percent by number of persons.........	100.0	100.0	100.0	100.0	100.0	100.0
1 person.................................	4.7	5.1	5.3	6.7	5.2	5.2
2 persons................................	21.4	19.1	24.7	22.7	21.2	17.3
3 persons................................	19.9	20.1	20.1	21.2	20.2	18.5
4 persons................................	17.6	17.3	18.0	17.4	17.5	17.0
5 persons................................	13.5	13.2	14.1	12.6	13.0	13.6
6 persons or more.........................	22.9	25.2	17.8	19.3	22.9	28.4
Median number of persons.................	3.7	3.8	3.5	3.5	3.7	4.0
Percent by persons per room..........	100.0	100.0	100.0	100.0	100.0	100.0
1.00 or less..............................	92.0	91.1	93.7	93.9	82.4	77.6
1.01 or more..............................	8.0	8.9	6.3	6.1	17.6	22.4
RENTER- AND RENT-FREE- OCCUPIED UNITS						
Number..................................	5,350	7,468	9,160	14,916	11,365	18,253
Percent by persons per room..........	100.0	100.0	100.0	100.0	100.0	100.0
1.00 or less..............................	85.3	85.8	87.1	88.9	72.2	66.5
1.01 or more..............................	14.7	14.2	12.9	11.1	27.8	33.5

[1] The 1950 and 1940 data on condition are not entirely comparable; see glossary for explanation of differences.

Source: See page 173.

TABLE **E-2**.—Great Lakes Dairy Region—Characteristics of Dwelling Units in
Selected Economic Subregions: 1950 and 1940

Characteristic	Subregion 50		Subregion 66		Subregion 88	
	1950	1940	1950	1940	1950	1940
ALL DWELLING UNITS						
Number..................	42,262	47,090	87,661	109,499	37,862	41,900
Percent by year built.................	100.0	100.0	100.0	100.0	100.0	100.0
1920 or later..........................	35.3	24.8	53.1	46.1	35.7	29.1
1919 or earlier........................	64.7	75.2	46.9	53.9	64.3	70.9
Percent by number of rooms...........	100.0	100.0	100.0	100.0	100.0	100.0
1 to 3 rooms..........................	11.5	10.5	20.1	30.5	13.3	20.6
4 rooms...............................	11.9	10.4	18.3	18.4	14.1	15.2
5 rooms...............................	15.8	15.3	17.9	15.2	16.9	15.4
6 rooms or more.......................	60.8	63.8	43.7	35.9	55.7	48.8
Median number of rooms................	6.1	6.2	5.1	4.6	5.8	5.4
Percent by condition[1]................	100.0	100.0	100.0	100.0	100.0	100.0
Not dilapidated.......................	89.5	73.6	83.9	63.9	88.1	69.9
Dilapidated...........................	10.5	26.4	16.1	36.1	11.9	30.1
Percent by plumbing facilities.......	100.0	100.0	100.0	100.0	100.0	100.0
With running water....................	77.4	40.2	42.7	11.5	31.0	6.1
Without running water.................	22.6	59.8	57.3	88.5	69.0	93.9
Percent by toilet facilities.........	100.0	100.0	100.0	100.0	100.0	100.0
With private flush toilet.............	54.0	23.7	21.1	4.7	14.7	3.3
Without private flush toilet..........	46.0	76.3	78.9	95.3	85.3	96.7
Percent by bathing facilities........	100.0	100.0	100.0	100.0	100.0	100.0
With private bathtub or shower........	50.4	22.4	20.2	4.6	15.6	3.4
Without private bathtub or shower.....	49.6	77.6	79.8	95.4	84.4	96.6
Percent by electric lighting.........	100.0	100.0	100.0	100.0	100.0	100.0
With electric lights..................	95.0	70.9	80.4	29.0	72.6	17.6
Without electric lights...............	5.0	29.1	19.6	71.0	27.4	82.4
ALL OCCUPIED UNITS						
Number..................	35,405	42,284	73,345	99,137	34,525	39,456
Percent by heating equipment.........	100.0	100.0	100.0	100.0	100.0	100.0
Steam or hot water....................	4.1	2.5	1.0	0.7	1.6	1.3
Warm air furnace......................	42.0	28.3	21.2	10.0	20.5	11.0
Heating stove, other or none.........	53.9	69.2	77.8	89.3	77.9	87.7
Percent by cooking fuel..............	100.0	100.0	100.0	100.0	100.0	100.0
Coal or coke..........................	10.7	18.5	5.0	1.8	7.4	1.6
Wood..................................	15.3	42.7	63.4	93.5	52.6	94.6
Utility and bottled gas...............	23.6	4.6	16.9	0.8	25.4	0.8
Electricity...........................	42.7	15.1	11.0	1.2	8.8	0.3
Liquid fuel...........................	6.7	18.9	3.2	2.6	5.4	2.5
Other or none.........................	1.0	0.2	0.5	0.1	0.4	0.2
Percent by tenure....................	100.0	100.0	100.0	100.0	100.0	100.0
Owner.................................	83.9	77.6	90.2	81.6	86.4	68.0
Renter and rent free..................	16.1	22.4	9.8	18.4	13.6	32.0
Percent by number of persons.........	100.0	100.0	100.0	100.0	100.0	100.0
1 person..............................	7.4	7.6	7.6	9.7	6.1	6.2
2 persons.............................	27.0	24.2	24.0	19.2	21.2	16.4
3 persons.............................	20.4	20.3	18.7	18.4	19.8	19.5
4 persons.............................	16.7	16.9	17.5	16.7	18.6	18.6
5 persons.............................	12.8	12.5	12.7	12.9	14.3	14.7
6 persons or more.....................	15.7	18.5	19.5	23.1	20.0	24.6
Median number of persons..............	3.3	3.4	3.5	3.7	3.7	3.9
Percent by persons per room..........	100.0	100.0	100.0	100.0	100.0	100.0
1.00 or less..........................	89.6	87.9	81.1	71.1	84.1	75.4
1.01 or more..........................	10.4	12.1	18.9	28.9	15.9	24.6
RENTER- AND RENT-FREE-OCCUPIED UNITS						
Number..................	5,715	9,456	7,165	18,245	4,695	12,612
Percent by persons per room..........	100.0	100.0	100.0	100.0	100.0	100.0
1.00 or less..........................	82.3	81.5	74.9	65.3	82.8	70.0
1.01 or more..........................	17.7	18.5	25.1	34.7	17.2	30.0

[1] The 1950 and 1940 data on condition are not entirely comparable; see glossary for explanation of differences.
Source: See page 173.

TABLE **E-3.**—East and Gulf Coast Miscellaneous Region—Characteristics of Dwelling Units in Selected Economic Subregions: 1950 and 1940

Characteristic	Subregion 21		Subregion 39		Subregion 58	
	1950	1940	1950	1940	1950	1940
ALL DWELLING UNITS						
Number..................	32,604	39,212	29,265	35,064	39,905	45,508
Percent by year built...............	100.0	100.0	100.0	100.0	100.0	100.0
1920 or later..........................	43.9	29.7	84.1	72.8	78.5	57.8
1919 or earlier.........................	56.1	70.3	15.9	27.2	21.5	42.2
Percent by number of rooms.........	100.0	100.0	100.0	100.0	100.0	100.0
1 to 3 rooms...........................	16.7	26.9	28.0	35.7	22.6	36.0
4 rooms................................	24.3	23.9	21.6	19.3	26.6	26.4
5 rooms................................	17.8	15.2	21.7	18.5	23.1	17.5
6 rooms or more........................	41.2	34.0	28.7	26.5	27.7	20.1
Median number of rooms.............	5.0	4.5	4.5	4.2	4.5	4.0
Percent by condition[1].............	100.0	100.0	100.0	100.0	100.0	100.0
Not dilapidated.........................	72.1	58.5	81.3	73.9	71.3	71.8
Dilapidated............................	27.9	41.5	18.7	26.1	28.7	28.2
Percent by plumbing facilities.......	100.0	100.0	100.0	100.0	100.0	100.0
With running water.....................	22.3	3.6	71.2	32.0	48.2	11.2
Without running water..................	77.7	96.4	28.8	68.0	51.8	88.8
Percent by toilet facilities.........	100.0	100.0	100.0	100.0	100.0	100.0
With private flush toilet..............	10.4	2.7	52.6	25.8	25.6	7.6
Without private flush toilet..........	89.6	97.3	47.4	74.2	74.4	92.4
Percent by bathing facilities.......	100.0	100.0	100.0	100.0	100.0	100.0
With private bathtub or shower.........	11.7	2.7	54.7	25.8	28.7	8.2
Without private bathtub or shower......	88.3	97.3	45.3	74.2	71.3	91.8
Percent by electric lighting.........	100.0	100.0	100.0	100.0	100.0	100.0
With electric lights...................	65.0	11.2	84.3	37.2	77.1	19.0
Without electric lights................	35.0	88.8	15.7	62.8	22.9	81.0
ALL OCCUPIED UNITS						
Number................................	29,887	37,360	24,435	32,114	37,165	43,049
Percent by heating equipment.........	100.0	100.0	100.0	100.0	100.0	100.0
Steam or hot water.....................	0.7	0.3	0.7	0.3	0.8	0.1
Warm air furnace.......................	0.9	0.2	2.4	1.0	2.0	0.3
Heating stove, other or none..........	98.4	99.5	96.9	98.7	97.2	99.6
Percent by cooking fuel...............	100.0	100.0	100.0	100.0	100.0	100.0
Coal or coke...........................	0.7	0.2	0.1	...	0.2	0.1
Wood..................................	76.7	97.3	12.3	42.5	43.9	91.8
Utility and bottled gas................	5.8	...	24.0	3.3	39.1	1.5
Electricity............................	7.9	0.5	26.7	7.1	4.7	1.1
Liquid fuel............................	7.7	1.8	31.4	46.0	10.4	5.3
Other or none..........................	1.2	0.2	5.5	1.1	1.7	0.2
Percent by tenure.....................	100.0	100.0	100.0	100.0	100.0	100.0
Owner.................................	45.4	37.5	68.5	56.3	76.8	59.1
Renter and rent free...................	54.6	62.5	31.5	43.7	23.2	40.9
Percent by number of persons.........	100.0	100.0	100.0	100.0	100.0	100.0
1 person...............................	3.0	3.6	8.1	10.4	4.1	5.0
2 persons..............................	14.3	12.5	30.5	25.4	21.2	17.6
3 persons..............................	16.9	16.2	20.0	19.0	19.0	17.9
4 persons..............................	15.6	15.9	16.1	15.8	17.2	16.6
5 persons..............................	14.0	13.7	10.9	11.5	12.9	13.4
6 persons or more......................	36.1	38.1	14.4	17.9	25.6	29.5
Median number of persons..............	4.5	4.6	3.1	3.2	3.8	4.1
Percent by persons per room.........	100.0	100.0	100.0	100.0	100.0	100.0
1.00 or less...........................	62.5	55.8	79.0	69.5	67.9	57.4
1.01 or more...........................	37.5	44.2	21.0	30.5	32.1	42.6
RENTER- AND RENT-FREE- OCCUPIED UNITS						
Number................................	16,445	23,348	7,700	14,046	8,605	17,623
Percent by persons per room..........	100.0	100.0	100.0	100.0	100.0	100.0
1.00 or less...........................	49.5	45.3	64.1	56.2	51.9	47.7
1.01 or more...........................	50.5	54.7	35.9	43.8	48.1	52.3

[1] The 1950 and 1940 data on condition are not entirely comparable; see glossary for explanation of differences.

Source: See page 173.

TABLE **E-4.**—GENERAL AND SELF-SUFFICING REGION—CHARACTERISTICS OF DWELLING UNITS IN SELECTED ECONOMIC SUBREGIONS: 1950 AND 1940

Characteristic	Subregion 31		Subregion 72		Subregion 82	
	1950	1940	1950	1940	1950	1940
ALL DWELLING UNITS						
Number..................................	110,201	129,260	49,069	55,894	35,591	40,570
Percent by year built................	100.0	100.0	100.0	100.0	100.0	100.0
1920 or later...........................	71.2	56.4	32.5	24.0	56.8	42.7
1919 or earlier.........................	28.8	43.6	67.5	76.0	43.2	57.3
Percent by number of rooms...........	100.0	100.0	100.0	100.0	100.0	100.0
1 to 3 rooms............................	22.8	39.0	15.1	19.5	25.2	39.6
4 rooms..................................	29.9	26.7	20.5	20.6	28.3	23.7
5 rooms..................................	20.2	15.2	21.0	19.8	21.5	15.4
6 rooms or more.........................	27.1	19.1	43.4	40.1	25.0	21.3
Median number of rooms..................	4.4	3.9	5.2	5.0	4.4	3.9
Percent by condition[1].................	100.0	100.0	100.0	100.0	100.0	100.0
Not dilapidated.........................	72.7	56.9	86.9	66.0	81.0	52.0
Dilapidated.............................	27.3	43.1	13.1	34.0	19.0	48.0
Percent by plumbing facilities.......	100.0	100.0	100.0	100.0	100.0	100.0
With running water.....................	17.6	4.3	27.8	9.7	33.7	7.6
Without running water..................	82.4	95.7	72.2	90.3	66.3	92.4
Percent by toilet facilities.........	100.0	100.0	100.0	100.0	100.0	100.0
With private flush toilet..............	7.4	2.3	21.2	7.2	18.9	4.5
Without private flush toilet...........	92.6	97.7	78.8	92.8	81.1	95.5
Percent by bathing facilities........	100.0	100.0	100.0	100.0	100.0	100.0
With private bathtub or shower..........	9.4	2.3	23.8	7.3	20.7	4.9
Without private bathtub or shower.......	90.6	97.7	76.2	92.7	79.3	95.1
Percent by electric lighting.........	100.0	100.0	100.0	100.0	100.0	100.0
With electric lights...................	65.8	14.1	76.6	25.6	73.4	15.0
Without electric lights................	34.2	85.9	23.4	74.4	26.6	85.0
ALL OCCUPIED UNITS						
Number..................................	103,904	125,077	42,750	52,346	33,773	38,530
Percent by heating equipment.........	100.0	100.0	100.0	100.0	100.0	100.0
Steam or hot water......................	1.0	0.5	3.3	1.9	0.5	0.2
Warm air furnace........................	2.3	0.6	19.1	8.9	3.5	1.2
Heating stove, other or none...........	96.7	98.9	77.6	89.2	96.0	98.6
Percent by cooking fuel..............	100.0	100.0	100.0	100.0	100.0	100.0
Coal or coke............................	58.4	40.9	14.2	18.8	2.2	0.9
Wood....................................	29.4	55.6	36.8	68.3	51.6	89.8
Utility and bottled gas.................	6.8	3.1	25.3	1.7	20.4	0.9
Electricity.............................	4.5	0.2	17.2	3.2	7.8	0.5
Liquid fuel.............................	0.7	0.2	5.3	7.8	16.2	7.8
Other or none...........................	0.2	...	1.2	0.2	1.8	0.1
Percent by tenure....................	100.0	100.0	100.0	100.0	100.0	100.0
Owner...................................	78.1	65.1	74.6	64.7	79.3	58.3
Renter and rent free...................	21.9	34.9	25.4	35.3	20.7	41.7
Percent by number of persons.........	100.0	100.0	100.0	100.0	100.0	100.0
1 person................................	3.0	2.0	4.9	5.2	5.8	5.0
2 persons...............................	15.8	11.9	27.5	21.0	30.6	23.0
3 persons...............................	17.0	15.2	21.2	21.0	20.0	20.7
4 persons...............................	16.6	15.6	18.8	18.5	17.1	17.6
5 persons...............................	13.1	14.2	11.6	13.4	10.7	12.8
6 persons or more.......................	34.5	41.1	16.0	20.9	15.8	20.9
Median number of persons................	4.4	4.9	3.3	3.7	3.2	3.6
Percent by persons per room..........	100.0	100.0	100.0	100.0	100.0	100.0
1.00 or less............................	58.5	43.7	84.0	76.9	75.2	62.5
1.01 or more............................	41.5	56.3	16.0	23.1	24.8	37.5
RENTER- AND RENT-FREE- OCCUPIED UNITS						
Number..................................	22,765	43,663	10,875	18,461	6,975	16,072
Percent by persons per room..........	100.0	100.0	100.0	100.0	100.0	100.0
1.00 or less............................	46.9	32.6	78.6	70.8	64.5	52.0
1.01 or more............................	53.1	67.4	21.4	29.2	35.5	48.0

[1] The 1950 and 1940 data on condition are not entirely comparable; see glossary for explanation of differences.

Source: See page 173.

TABLE **E-5.**—TOBACCO REGION—CHARACTERISTICS OF DWELLING UNITS IN SELECTED
ECONOMIC SUBREGIONS: 1950 AND 1940

Characteristic	Subregion 24		Subregion 53	
	1950	1940	1950	1940
ALL DWELLING UNITS				
Number.....................................	71,297	78,154	50,699	59,715
Percent by year built..................	100.0	100.0	100.0	100.0
1920 or later............................	50.4	35.6	45.3	30.5
1919 or earlier..........................	49.6	64.4	54.7	69.5
Percent by number of rooms............	100.0	100.0	100.0	100.0
1 to 3 rooms............................	16.1	27.1	23.9	39.3
4 rooms.................................	28.2	27.5	27.6	24.0
5 rooms.................................	21.8	18.6	19.4	15.0
6 rooms or more........................	33.9	26.8	29.1	21.7
Median number of rooms.................	4.8	4.3	4.5	3.9
Percent by condition[1].................	100.0	100.0	100.0	100.0
Not dilapidated..........................	75.0	54.9	79.8	58.0
Dilapidated..............................	25.0	45.1	20.2	42.0
Percent by plumbing facilities........	100.0	100.0	100.0	100.0
With running water......................	26.3	3.9	22.8	4.1
Without running water...................	73.7	96.1	77.2	95.9
Percent by toilet facilities...........	100.0	100.0	100.0	100.0
With private flush toilet................	10.2	2.5	11.3	2.8
Without private flush toilet............	89.8	97.5	88.7	97.2
Percent by bathing facilities..........	100.0	100.0	100.0	100.0
With private bathtub or shower..........	11.6	2.5	13.4	2.9
Without private bathtub or shower.......	88.4	97.5	86.6	97.1
Percent by electric lighting...........	100.0	100.0	100.0	100.0
With electric lights....................	82.7	20.6	70.1	16.3
Without electric lights.................	17.3	79.4	29.9	83.7
ALL OCCUPIED UNITS				
Number.....................................	65,205	74,954	47,342	56,569
Percent by heating equipment...........	100.0	100.0	100.0	100.0
Steam or hot water......................	0.5	0.2	0.8	0.3
Warm air furnace........................	1.4	0.7	3.9	1.0
Heating stove, other or none...........	98.1	99.1	95.3	98.7
Percent by cooking fuel................	100.0	100.0	100.0	100.0
Coal or coke............................	1.7	0.3	20.6	9.2
Wood....................................	60.0	94.6	41.1	85.6
Utility and bottled gas.................	6.2	0.1	6.8	0.9
Electricity.............................	12.9	0.7	19.4	0.7
Liquid fuel.............................	17.0	4.0	10.1	3.4
Other or none...........................	2.2	0.3	2.0	0.2
Percent by tenure.......................	100.0	100.0	100.0	100.0
Owner...................................	37.2	33.6	68.7	54.5
Renter and rent free....................	62.8	66.4	31.3	45.5
Percent by number of persons...........	100.0	100.0	100.0	100.0
1 person................................	1.9	2.8	3.3	3.6
2 persons...............................	14.2	11.9	26.4	21.3
3 persons...............................	16.9	16.3	22.8	22.6
4 persons...............................	18.0	17.1	18.6	18.5
5 persons...............................	14.6	14.6	12.0	13.2
6 persons or more.......................	34.4	37.3	16.9	20.8
Median number of persons................	4.4	4.6	3.4	3.6
Percent by persons per room............	100.0	100.0	100.0	100.0
1.00 or less............................	62.3	54.3	64.4	75.9
1.01 or more............................	37.7	45.7	35.6	24.1
RENTER- AND RENT-FREE- **OCCUPIED UNITS**				
Number.....................................	40,960	49,784	14,795	25,766
Percent by persons per room............	100.0	100.0	100.0	100.0
1.00 or less............................	52.4	46.9	62.4	52.6
1.01 or more............................	47.6	53.1	37.6	47.4

[1] The 1950 and 1940 data on condition are not entirely comparable; see glossary for explanation of differences.

Source: See page 173.

TABLE E-6.—COTTON BELT—CHARACTERISTICS OF DWELLING UNITS IN SELECTED ECONOMIC SUBREGIONS: 1950 AND 1940

Characteristic	Subregion 35		Subregion 43		Subregion 97	
	1950	1940	1950	1940	1950	1940
ALL DWELLING UNITS						
Number....................	30,889	43,973	41,216	52,645	89,208	133,938
Percent by year built..............	100.0	100.0	100.0	100.0	100.0	100.0
1920 or later.........................	48.7	32.0	61.8	43.0	50.7	35.0
1919 or earlier........................	51.3	68.0	38.2	57.0	49.3	65.0
Percent by number of rooms...........	100.0	100.0	100.0	100.0	100.0	100.0
1 to 3 rooms..........................	26.6	41.7	18.0	33.8	24.2	36.5
4 rooms...............................	29.1	27.5	33.4	32.2	29.8	28.4
5 rooms...............................	19.5	14.1	24.0	18.0	24.5	18.4
6 rooms or more.......................	24.8	16.7	24.6	16.0	21.5	16.7
Median number of rooms................	4.3	3.8	4.5	4.0	4.4	4.0
Percent by condition[1]...............	100.0	100.0	100.0	100.0	100.0	100.0
Not dilapidated.......................	61.9	60.0	73.0	59.3	73.8	67.3
Dilapidated...........................	38.1	40.0	27.0	40.7	26.2	32.7
Percent by plumbing facilities.......	100.0	100.0	100.0	100.0	100.0	100.0
With running water....................	29.7	7.0	27.1	5.5	43.1	15.5
Without running water.................	70.3	93.0	72.9	94.5	56.9	84.5
Percent by toilet facilities.........	100.0	100.0	100.0	100.0	100.0	100.0
With private flush toilet.............	15.2	4.4	12.0	3.5	17.5	4.7
Without private flush toilet..........	84.8	95.6	88.0	96.5	82.5	95.3
Percent by bathing facilities........	100.0	100.0	100.0	100.0	100.0	100.0
With private bathtub or shower........	15.9	4.5	13.7	3.5	26.1	8.8
Without private bathtub or shower.....	84.1	95.5	86.3	96.5	73.9	91.2
Percent by electric lighting.........	100.0	100.0	100.0	100.0	100.0	100.0
With electric lights..................	66.1	14.3	84.8	27.6	74.3	20.4
Without electric lights...............	33.9	85.7	15.2	72.4	25.7	79.6
ALL OCCUPIED UNITS						
Number....................	26,485	39,872	38,800	49,892	75,420	120,890
Percent by heating equipment.........	100.0	100.0	100.0	100.0	100.0	100.0
Steam or hot water....................	0.3	0.1	0.2	0.2	1.4	0.1
Warm air furnace......................	1.5	0.2	2.6	0.5	1.4	0.3
Heating stove, other or none.........	98.2	99.7	97.2	99.3	97.2	99.6
Percent by cooking fuel..............	100.0	100.0	100.0	100.0	100.0	100.0
Coal or coke..........................	0.8	0.2	10.4	5.8	0.8	0.2
Wood..................................	78.0	96.6	62.3	90.9	22.5	57.1
Utility and bottled gas...............	3.1	0.1	3.9	0.1	31.9	3.7
Electricity...........................	11.2	1.3	17.5	1.9	5.9	0.7
Liquid fuel...........................	5.7	1.7	5.1	1.2	34.2	38.1
Other or none.........................	1.2	0.1	0.8	0.1	4.7	0.2
Percent by tenure.....................	100.0	100.0	100.0	100.0	100.0	100.0
Owner.................................	49.6	33.0	64.6	44.1	51.9	33.1
Renter and rent free.................	50.4	67.0	35.4	55.9	48.1	66.9
Percent by number of persons.........	100.0	100.0	100.0	100.0	100.0	100.0
1 person..............................	3.8	4.4	2.4	2.4	4.9	4.3
2 persons.............................	17.7	16.7	19.6	19.6	29.2	21.0
3 persons.............................	16.9	17.1	18.9	18.9	22.1	21.5
4 persons.............................	16.4	15.9	17.5	17.5	17.3	18.3
5 persons.............................	13.4	12.9	13.8	13.8	10.8	12.8
6 persons or more.....................	31.8	33.0	27.8	27.8	15.7	22.1
Median number of persons..............	4.2	4.2	4.0	4.2	3.2	3.7
Percent by persons per room..........	100.0	100.0	100.0	100.0	100.0	100.0
1.00 or less..........................	59.7	52.1	65.2	52.9	77.6	64.0
1.01 or more..........................	40.3	47.9	34.8	47.1	22.4	36.0
RENTER- AND RENT-FREE- OCCUPIED UNITS						
Number....................	13,350	26,700	13,730	27,903	36,270	80,899
Percent by persons per room..........	100.0	100.0	100.0	100.0	100.0	100.0
1.00 or less..........................	45.8	43.7	50.0	43.1	67.3	56.1
1.01 or more..........................	54.2	56.3	50.0	56.9	32.7	43.9

[1] The 1950 and 1940 data on condition are not entirely comparable; see glossary for explanation of differences.
Source: See page 173.

TABLE **E-7**.—CORN BELT—CHARACTERISTICS OF DWELLING UNITS IN SELECTED ECONOMIC SUBREGIONS: 1950 AND 1940

Characteristic	Subregion 51		Subregion 86		Subregion 92	
	1950	1940	1950	1940	1950	1940
ALL DWELLING UNITS						
Number..................................	51,431	62,104	66,078	69,284	49,444	57,794
Percent by year built................	100.0	100.0	100.0	100.0	100.0	100.0
1920 or later...........................	30.5	23.6	24.9	18.4	22.1	17.0
1919 or earlier.........................	69.5	76.4	75.1	81.6	77.9	83.0
Percent by number of rooms...........	100.0	100.0	100.0	100.0	100.0	100.0
1 to 3 rooms.............................	13.8	21.5	5.3	6.4	6.2	9.3
4 rooms..................................	25.6	24.5	6.6	6.3	13.1	14.8
5 rooms..................................	24.2	20.8	13.1	13.3	18.5	18.4
6 rooms or more.........................	36.4	33.2	75.0	74.0	62.2	57.5
Median number of rooms..................	4.9	4.7	6.7	6.7	6.1	5.9
Percent by condition[1].................	100.0	100.0	100.0	100.0	100.0	100.0
Not dilapidated.........................	87.9	70.1	95.8	78.1	91.6	66.9
Dilapidated.............................	12.1	29.9	4.2	21.9	8.4	33.1
Percent by plumbing facilities.......	100.0	100.0	100.0	100.0	100.0	100.0
With running water......................	38.1	7.3	53.9	17.6	48.9	19.0
Without running water...................	61.9	92.7	46.1	82.4	51.1	81.0
Percent by toilet facilities.........	100.0	100.0	100.0	100.0	100.0	100.0
With private flush toilet..............	20.9	5.2	37.3	13.4	23.8	8.9
Without private flush toilet...........	79.1	94.8	62.7	86.6	76.2	91.1
Percent by bathing facilities........	100.0	100.0	100.0	100.0	100.0	100.0
With private bathtub or shower.........	23.0	5.5	39.8	13.7	29.9	10.1
Without private bathtub or shower......	77.0	94.5	60.2	86.3	70.1	89.9
Percent by electric lighting.........	100.0	100.0	100.0	100.0	100.0	100.0
With electric lights....................	82.7	26.5	94.2	48.4	67.1	19.5
Without electric lights.................	17.3	73.5	5.8	51.6	32.9	80.5
ALL OCCUPIED UNITS						
Number..................................	46,275	58,717	63,600	67,950	44,060	51,172
Percent by heating equipment.........	100.0	100.0	100.0	100.0	100.0	100.0
Steam or hot water......................	2.1	1.1	3.6	3.1	2.2	1.2
Warm air furnace........................	18.8	7.2	34.7	23.2	18.5	13.8
Heating stove, other or none...........	79.1	91.7	61.7	73.7	79.3	85.0
Percent by cooking fuel..............	100.0	100.0	100.0	100.0	100.0	100.0
Coal or coke............................	37.8	66.0	17.1	28.4	19.9	23.1
Wood....................................	6.8	21.0	12.4	41.1	25.7	64.4
Utility and bottled gas.................	28.4	3.6	44.9	3.9	31.4	0.8
Electricity.............................	16.6	1.6	20.0	1.3	9.6	0.5
Liquid fuel.............................	8.6	7.6	2.8	3.7	6.5	6.8
Other or none...........................	1.8	0.2	2.8	21.6	6.9	4.4
Percent by tenure....................	100.0	100.0	100.0	100.0	100.0	100.0
Owner...................................	74.6	62.4	49.9	46.2	57.8	40.8
Renter and rent free....................	25.4	37.6	50.1	53.8	42.2	59.2
Percent by number of persons.........	100.0	100.0	100.0	100.0	100.0	100.0
1 person................................	5.0	4.9	3.0	2.9	4.8	5.4
2 persons...............................	30.2	24.1	21.5	17.1	22.6	18.0
3 persons...............................	21.4	22.2	22.7	21.9	22.0	21.4
4 persons...............................	17.2	17.7	22.2	21.0	21.6	20.0
5 persons...............................	11.5	12.4	15.4	15.6	13.5	14.7
6 persons or more.......................	14.7	18.7	15.2	21.5	15.5	20.5
Median number of persons................	3.2	3.4	3.6	3.9	3.5	3.8
Percent by persons per room..........	100.0	100.0	100.0	100.0	100.0	100.0
1.00 or less............................	82.7	75.5	92.7	88.2	89.5	84.4
1.01 or more............................	17.3	24.5	7.3	11.8	10.5	15.6
RENTER- AND RENT-FREE-OCCUPIED UNITS						
Number..................................	11,765	22,097	31,855	36,559	18,590	30,289
Percent by persons per room..........	100.0	100.0	100.0	100.0	100.0	100.0
1.00 or less............................	75.5	65.7	91.3	85.9	87.3	82.1
1.01 or more............................	24.5	34.3	8.7	14.1	12.7	17.9

[1] The 1950 and 1940 data on condition are not entirely comparable; see glossary for explanation of differences.

Source: See page 173.

TABLE **E-8.**—Northern Wheat and Small Grains Region—Characteristics of Dwelling Units in Selected Economic Subregions: 1950 and 1940

Characteristic	Subregion 90		Subregion 110	
	1950	1940	1950	1940
ALL DWELLING UNITS				
Number...................................	40,492	46,188	24,015	32,234
Percent by year built...................	100.0	100.0	100.0	100.0
1920 or later.............................	28.5	18.5	44.9	33.0
1919 or earlier...........................	71.5	81.5	55.1	67.0
Percent by number of rooms..............	100.0	100.0	100.0	100.0
1 to 3 rooms..............................	14.2	23.2	16.0	20.8
4 rooms...................................	15.6	18.5	17.8	18.5
5 rooms...................................	18.1	16.8	21.0	19.5
6 rooms or more...........................	52.1	41.5	45.2	41.2
Median number of rooms....................	5.6	5.0	5.3	5.1
Percent by condition[1]..................	100.0	100.0	100.0	100.0
Not dilapidated...........................	89.5	57.8	87.8	64.8
Dilapidated...............................	10.5	42.2	12.2	35.2
Percent by plumbing facilities.........	100.0	100.0	100.0	100.0
With running water........................	24.5	3.4	83.9	52.6
Without running water.....................	75.5	96.6	16.1	47.4
Percent by toilet facilities...........	100.0	100.0	100.0	100.0
With private flush toilet.................	13.0	2.2	62.3	30.2
Without private flush toilet..............	87.0	97.8	37.7	69.8
Percent by bathing facilities..........	100.0	100.0	100.0	100.0
With private bathtub or shower............	16.1	2.4	66.6	34.5
Without private bathtub or shower.........	83.9	97.6	33.4	65.5
Percent by electric lighting...........	100.0	100.0	100.0	100.0
With electric lights......................	64.7	13.7	91.3	49.9
Without electric lights...................	35.3	86.3	8.7	50.1
ALL OCCUPIED UNITS				
Number...................................	34,115	41,351	18,940	28,167
Percent by heating equipment...........	100.0	100.0	100.0	100.0
Steam or hot water........................	5.0	3.9	2.6	0.8
Warm air furnace..........................	35.4	15.5	18.6	9.0
Heating stove, other or none..............	59.6	80.6	78.8	90.2
Percent by cooking fuel.................	100.0	100.0	100.0	100.0
Coal or coke..............................	36.2	77.9	10.3	6.0
Wood......................................	4.8	13.9	34.0	87.0
Utility and bottled gas...................	38.8	0.3	4.4	1.6
Electricity...............................	10.6	0.2	46.7	3.7
Liquid fuel...............................	8.3	7.3	3.7	0.9
Other or none.............................	1.3	0.4	0.9	0.8
Percent by tenure........................	100.0	100.0	100.0	100.0
Owner.....................................	73.0	50.4	69.2	63.9
Renter and rent free......................	27.0	49.6	30.8	36.1
Percent by number of persons...........	100.0	100.0	100.0	100.0
1 person..................................	5.5	6.7	7.5	9.8
2 persons.................................	17.2	13.3	25.2	23.0
3 persons.................................	20.7	17.8	21.6	20.8
4 persons.................................	19.6	18.2	21.1	18.5
5 persons.................................	14.7	14.8	12.6	12.3
6 persons or more.........................	22.3	29.2	12.0	15.6
Median number of persons..................	3.8	4.2	3.3	3.3
Percent by persons per room............	100.0	100.0	100.0	100.0
1.00 or less..............................	80.6	69.5	86.5	82.3
1.01 or more..............................	19.4	30.5	13.5	17.7
RENTER- AND RENT-FREE- OCCUPIED UNITS				
Number...................................	9,210	20,529	5,830	10,161
Percent by persons per room............	100.0	100.0	100.0	100.0
1.00 or less..............................	79.9	66.5	85.9	79.1
1.01 or more..............................	20.1	33.5	14.1	20.9

[1] The 1950 and 1940 data on condition are not entirely comparable; see glossary for explanation of differences.

Source: See page 173.

TABLE **E-9.**—SOUTHERN WHEAT AND SMALL GRAINS REGION—CHARACTERISTICS OF DWELLING UNITS IN SELECTED ECONOMIC SUBREGIONS: 1950 AND 1940

Characteristic	Subregion 94		Characteristic	Subregion 94	
	1950	1940		1950	1940
ALL DWELLING UNITS			**OCCUPIED UNITS--Cont.**		
Number........................	44,935	56,621	Percent by cooking fuel.....	100.0	100.0
			Coal or coke....................	3.3	2.9
Percent by year built.........	100.0	100.0	Wood............................	7.7	36.5
1920 or later....................	29.4	22.2	Utility and bottled gas.........	50.5	11.3
1919 or earlier..................	70.6	77.8	Electricity.....................	15.5	2.1
Percent by number of rooms....	100.0	100.0	Liquid fuel.....................	21.0	46.3
1 to 3 rooms.....................	8.4	14.0	Other or none...................	2.0	0.9
4 rooms...........................	16.3	17.2	Percent by tenure............	100.0	100.0
5 rooms...........................	22.2	19.6	Owner...........................	59.5	50.7
6 rooms or more..................	53.1	49.2	Renter and rent free............	40.5	49.3
Median number of rooms...........	5.7	5.5	Percent by number of		
Percent by condition[1]........	100.0	100.0	persons....................	100.0	100.0
Not dilapidated..................	90.1	66.6	1 person........................	5.0	5.1
Dilapidated......................	9.9	33.4	2 persons.......................	29.1	22.9
Percent by plumbing			3 persons.......................	22.7	22.4
facilities..................	100.0	100.0	4 persons.......................	19.9	19.5
With running water.............	54.1	17.1	5 persons.......................	11.7	13.0
Without running water..........	45.9	82.9	6 persons or more...............	11.6	17.1
Percent by toilet facilities..	100.0	100.0	Median number of persons........	3.2	3.5
With private flush toilet.........	32.7	11.0	Percent by persons per		
Without private flush toilet......	67.3	89.0	room......................	100.0	100.0
Percent by bathing facilities.	100.0	100.0	1.00 or less....................	90.0	82.4
With private bathtub or shower....	42.5	13.2	1.01 or more....................	10.0	17.6
Without private bathtub or shower.	57.5	86.8			
Percent by electric lighting..	100.0	100.0	**RENTER- AND RENT-FREE-**		
With electric lights..............	84.9	37.0	**OCCUPIED UNITS**		
Without electric lights...........	15.1	63.0	Number........................	16,180	26,157
ALL OCCUPIED UNITS			Percent by persons per		
			room......................	100.0	100.0
Number........................	39,951	53,098	1.00 or less....................	88.2	77.5
Percent by heating equipment..	100.0	100.0	1.01 or more....................	11.8	22.5
Steam or hot water...............	1.4	0.5			
Warm air furnace.................	19.2	8.4			
Heating stove, other or none.....	79.4	91.1			

[1] The 1950 and 1940 data on condition are not entirely comparable; see glossary for explanation of differences.

Source: See page 173.

TABLE **E-10.**—Year-Long and Seasonal Grazing Region—Characteristics of Dwelling Units in Selected Economic Subregions: 1950 and 1940

Characteristic	Subregion 98		Subregion 102		Subregion 104	
	1950	1940	1950	1940	1950	1940
ALL DWELLING UNITS						
Number....................	29,316	45,769	24,881	23,748	28,812	36,842
Percent by year built...............	100.0	100.0	100.0	100.0	100.0	100.0
1920 or later..........................	73.2	58.0	92.6	83.3	48.3	36.7
1919 or earlier........................	26.8	42.0	7.4	16.7	51.7	63.3
Percent by number of rooms...........	100.0	100.0	100.0	100.0	100.0	100.0
1 to 3 rooms...........................	38.5	55.9	44.6	49.3	26.2	38.4
4 rooms................................	24.2	19.2	27.3	26.9	20.7	20.0
5 rooms................................	18.2	12.2	15.4	13.1	19.2	15.6
6 rooms or more.......................	19.1	12.7	12.7	10.7	33.9	26.0
Median number of rooms................	4.0	3.2	3.7	3.5	4.7	4.1
Percent by condition[1]...............	100.0	100.0	100.0	100.0	100.0	100.0
Not dilapidated.......................	73.8	65.3	81.1	70.5	84.2	61.2
Dilapidated...........................	26.2	34.7	18.9	29.5	15.8	38.8
Percent by plumbing facilities.......	100.0	100.0	100.0	100.0	100.0	100.0
With running water....................	70.4	30.4	69.3	28.3	38.6	11.7
Without running water.................	29.6	69.6	30.7	71.7	61.4	88.3
Percent by toilet facilities.........	100.0	100.0	100.0	100.0	100.0	100.0
With private flush toilet.............	31.6	9.7	35.9	10.1	20.8	5.6
Without private flush toilet..........	68.4	90.3	64.1	89.9	79.2	94.4
Percent by bathing facilities........	100.0	100.0	100.0	100.0	100.0	100.0
With private bathtub or shower........	42.0	17.6	37.9	12.5	24.1	6.3
Without private bathtub or shower.....	58.0	82.4	62.1	87.5	75.9	93.7
Percent by electric lighting.........	100.0	100.0	100.0	100.0	100.0	100.0
With electric lights..................	67.0	16.0	83.4	24.5	53.3	17.9
Without electric lights...............	33.0	84.0	16.6	75.5	46.7	82.1
ALL OCCUPIED UNITS						
Number....................	24,075	36,504	17,185	19,661	24,485	31,351
Percent by heating equipment.........	100.0	100.0	100.0	100.0	100.0	100.0
Steam or hot water....................	0.8	0.2	1.1	0.1	1.5	0.7
Warm air furnace......................	1.3	0.3	2.7	0.3	14.1	6.6
Heating stove, other or none.........	97.9	99.5	96.2	99.6	84.4	92.7
Percent by cooking fuel...............	100.0	100.0	100.0	100.0	100.0	100.0
Coal or coke..........................	0.6	0.2	0.6	2.3	21.1	27.1
Wood..................................	24.6	67.0	1.6	4.4	22.1	58.3
Utility and bottled gas...............	40.9	6.7	80.9	10.8	42.6	1.6
Electricity...........................	6.8	1.2	1.7	0.3	5.4	0.4
Liquid fuel...........................	22.9	24.1	11.6	81.6	7.4	9.3
Other or none.........................	4.2	0.8	3.6	0.6	1.4	3.3
Percent by tenure.....................	100.0	100.0	100.0	100.0	100.0	100.0
Owner.................................	56.4	38.5	43.2	36.4	70.9	57.2
Renter and rent free.................	43.6	61.5	56.8	63.6	29.1	42.8
Percent by number of persons.........	100.0	100.0	100.0	100.0	100.0	100.0
1 person..............................	5.9	5.8	3.3	5.5	7.2	10.4
2 persons.............................	23.8	17.7	23.7	20.0	22.3	18.6
3 persons.............................	19.6	17.6	21.1	21.2	21.2	19.1
4 persons.............................	16.5	16.4	21.4	20.3	19.0	17.3
5 persons.............................	12.1	12.8	13.9	13.4	13.0	12.9
6 persons or more.....................	22.1	29.7	16.6	19.6	17.3	21.7
Median number of persons..............	3.5	4.0	3.6	3.7	3.5	3.6
Percent by persons per room..........	100.0	100.0	100.0	100.0	100.0	100.0
1.00 or less..........................	64.7	50.9	69.7	56.7	77.0	67.1
1.01 or more..........................	35.3	49.1	30.3	43.3	23.0	32.9
RENTER- AND RENT-FREE- OCCUPIED UNITS						
Number....................	10,490	22,450	9,765	12,502	7,130	13,412
Percent by persons per room..........	100.0	100.0	100.0	100.0	100.0	100.0
1.00 or less..........................	48.5	40.1	59.1	49.1	73.8	63.5
1.01 or more..........................	51.5	59.9	40.9	50.9	26.2	36.5

[1] The 1950 and 1940 data on condition are not entirely comparable; see glossary for explanation of differences.

Source: See page 173.

TABLE **E-11.**—UPLAND SUMMER GRAZING REGION—CHARACTERISTICS OF DWELLING UNITS IN SELECTED ECONOMIC SUBREGIONS: 1950 AND 1940

Characteristic	Subregion 112		Characteristic	Subregion 112	
	1950	1940		1950	1940
ALL DWELLING UNITS			OCCUPIED UNITS--Cont.		
Number.........................	48,637	51,517	Percent by cooking fuel.....	100.0	100.0
			Coal of coke....................	40.4	57.1
Percent by year built........	100.0	100.0	Wood............................	5.8	31.1
1920 or later....................	56.1	39.3	Utility and bottled gas.........	3.3	0.4
1919 or earlier..................	43.9	60.7	Electricity.....................	48.8	10.7
Percent by number of rooms....	100.0	100.0	Liquid fuel.....................	1.4	0.4
1 to 3 rooms.....................	21.7	34.4	Other or none...................	0.3	0.3
4 rooms..........................	27.9	25.0	Percent by tenure...........	100.0	100.0
5 rooms..........................	23.1	18.3	Owner...........................	75.6	68.5
6 rooms or more..................	27.3	22.3	Renter and rent free............	24.4	31.5
Median number of rooms...........	4.5	4.1			
Percent by condition[1]........	100.0	100.0	Percent by number of persons...................	100.0	100.0
Not dilapidated..................	91.2	69.5	1 person........................	5.6	4.5
Dilapidated......................	8.8	30.5	2 persons.......................	17.8	21.3
Percent by plumbing facilities....................	100.0	100.0	3 persons.......................	18.8	18.4
With running water...............	83.1	40.4	4 persons.......................	18.7	20.6
Without running water............	16.9	59.6	5 persons.......................	14.6	15.6
			6 persons or more...............	24.5	19.6
Percent by toilet facilities..	100.0	100.0	Median number of persons........	3.9	3.8
With private flush toilet........	56.1	24.3			
Without private flush toilet......	43.9	75.7	Percent by persons per room.....................	100.0	100.0
Percent by bathing facilities.	100.0	100.0	1.00 or less....................	73.8	61.3
With private bathtub or shower....	59.3	25.1	1.01 or more....................	26.2	38.7
Without private bathtub or shower.	40.7	74.9			
Percent by electric lighting..	100.0	100.0			
With electric lights.............	95.4	74.9	RENTER- AND RENT-FREE- OCCUPIED UNITS		
Without electric lights..........	4.6	25.1			
			Number.........................	10,745	15,160
ALL OCCUPIED UNITS					
			Percent by persons per room.....................	100.0	100.0
Number.........................	44,035	48,095	1.00 or less....................	66.8	53.8
			1.01 or more....................	33.2	46.2
Percent by heating equipment..	100.0	100.0			
Steam or hot water...............	2.7	0.9			
Warm air furnace.................	20.9	7.3			
Heating stove, other or none......	76.4	91.8			

[1] The 1950 and 1940 data on condition are not entirely comparable; see glossary for explanation of differences.

Source: See page 173.

TABLE **E-12.**—West Coast Miscellaneous Region—Characteristics of Dwelling Units
in Selected Economic Subregions: 1950 and 1940

Characteristic	Subregion 115		Subregion 116		Subregion 119	
	1950	1940	1950	1940	1950	1940
ALL DWELLING UNITS						
Number..............................	45,461	45,144	83,475	86,541	70,239	75,948
Percent by year built................	100.0	100.0	100.0	100.0	100.0	100.0
1920 or later........................	80.5	64.7	73.3	58.2	68.2	55.3
1919 or earlier......................	19.5	35.3	26.7	41.8	31.8	44.7
Percent by number of rooms...........	100.0	100.0	100.0	100.0	100.0	100.0
1 to 3 rooms.........................	26.4	29.9	27.4	34.7	22.4	23.4
4 rooms..............................	23.5	20.1	22.4	20.3	19.1	19.0
5 rooms..............................	22.3	22.0	23.1	20.4	20.9	19.5
6 rooms or more......................	27.8	28.0	27.1	24.6	37.6	38.1
Median number of rooms...............	4.5	4.5	4.5	4.3	4.9	4.9
Percent by condition[1]..............	100.0	100.0	100.0	100.0	100.0	100.0
Not dilapidated......................	90.3	85.5	84.1	78.0	87.5	80.7
Dilapidated..........................	9.7	14.5·	15.9	22.0	12.5	19.3
Percent by plumbing facilities.......	100.0	100.0	100.0	100.0	100.0	100.0
With running water...................	95.3	82.6	94.5	71.5	87.8	57.8
Without running water................	4.7	17.4	5.5	28.5	12.2	42.2
Percent by toilet facilities.........	100.0	100.0	100.0	100.0	100.0	100.0
With private flush toilet............	82.0	66.2	70.3	45.8	61.9	35.4
Without private flush toilet.........	18.0	33.8	29.7	54.2	38.1	64.6
Percent by bathing facilities.......	100.0	100.0	100.0	100.0	100.0	100.0
With private bathtub or shower.......	84.0	68.9	75.2	51.9	66.4	39.4
Without private bathtub or shower....	16.0	31.1	24.8	48.1	33.6	60.6
Percent by electric lighting........	100.0	100.0	100.0	100.0	100.0	100.0
With electric lights.................	95.0	83.5	96.8	84.7	95.4	75.2
Without electric lights..............	5.0	16.5	3.2	15.3	4.6	24.8
ALL OCCUPIED UNITS						
Number..............................	37,815	41,298	74,645	79,247	59,540	68,538
Percent by heating equipment........	100.0	100.0	100.0	100.0	100.0	100.0
Steam or hot water...................	2.1	0.7	1.2	0.3	1.3	0.7
Warm air furnace.....................	14.8	5.4	16.3	4.6	14.5	9.0
Heating stove, other or none........	83.1	93.9	82.5	95.1	84.2	90.3
Percent by cooking fuel..............	100.0	100.0	100.0	100.0	100.0	100.0
Coal or coke.........................	0.4	0.1	0.2	0.3	1.9	1.2
Wood.................................	4.1	18.3	6.7	39.6	45.5	91.1
Utility and bottled gas..............	53.0	36.4	54.7	17.9	3.7	1.1
Electricity..........................	36.3	25.6	30.3	19.8	42.9	5.5
Liquid fuel..........................	4.4	16.3	6.3	17.7	5.4	0.5
Other or none........................	1.8	3.3	1.8	4.7	0.6	0.6
Percent by tenure....................	100.0	100.0	100.0	100.0	100.0	100.0
Owner................................	64.8	56.0	63.0	53.2	83.7	75.1
Renter and rent free.................	35.2	44.0	37.0	46.8	16.3	24.9
Percent by number of persons........	100.0	100.0	100.0	100.0	100.0	100.0
1 person.............................	8.6	11.0	7.5	10.2	7.7	9.9
2 persons............................	32.9	27.4	26.4	22.4	29.9	26.1
3 persons............................	20.3	19.9	20.6	20.2	19.8	20.9
4 persons............................	17.3	16.7	19.9	17.7	18.2	17.7
5 persons............................	10.1	10.7	12.2	12.0	12.0	11.4
6 persons or more....................	10.8	14.3	13.4	17.5	12.4	14.0
Median number of persons.............	2.9	3.1	3.3	3.4	3.1	3.2
Percent by persons per room.........	100.0	100.0	100.0	100.0	100.0	100.0
1.00 or less.........................	83.6	78.4	78.9	70.9	86.1	83.3
1.01 or more.........................	16.4	21.6	21.1	29.1	13.9	16.7
RENTER- AND RENT-FREE- **OCCUPIED UNITS**						
Number..............................	13,320	18,176	27,620	37,107	9,680	17,080
Percent by persons per room.........	100.0	100.0	100.0	100.0	100.0	100.0
1.00 or less.........................	74.8	67.6	·65.1	57.6	78.2	74.9
1.01 or more.........................	25.2	32.4	34.9	42.4	21.8	25.1

[1] The 1950 and 1940 data on condition are not entirely comparable; see glossary for explanation of differences.

Source: See page 173.

G L O S S A R Y

(*Note:* Asterisked items refer to Bureau of the Census definitions used in this volume. Sometimes there is an elaboration of the definition in the regular census volumes.)

*Color of Occupants. The division of households into two groups, white and nonwhite based on color of the head of the household. The group designated as "nonwhite" consists of Negroes, Indians, Japanese, Chinese, and other nonwhite races.

*Commercial Farms, Classes of (*see* Economic Classification of Farms). Commercial farms are divided into six groups on the basis of the total value of farm products sold: Class I–$25,000 or more; Class II–$10,000 to $24,999; Class III–$5,000 to $9,999; Class IV–$2,500 to $4,999; Class V–$1,200 to $2,499; and Class VI–$250 to $1,199.

*Condition. Dwelling units were classified in 1950 as "not dilapidated" or "dilapidated." A dwelling unit was reported as dilapidated when it had serious deficiencies, was run down or neglected, or was of inadequate original construction, so that it did not provide adequate shelter or protection against the elements or endangered the safety of the occupants. A dwelling unit was reported as dilapidated if, because of either deterioration or inadequate original construction, it was below the generally accepted minimum standard for housing and should be torn down or extensively repaired or rebuilt. Specifically, a dwelling unit was reported as dilapidated if:

1. It had one or more critical deficiencies, as, for example:
   a. Holes, open cracks, rotted, loose, or missing materials over a considerable area of the foundation, outside walls, roof, or inside walls, floors, or ceilings.
   b. Substantial sagging of floors, walls, or roof.
   c. Extensive damage by storm, flood, or fire.
2. It had a combination of minor deficiencies of sufficient number and extent to make it evident that the unit did not provide adequate shelter or protection against the elements or was physically unsafe. Examples of these deficiencies are:
   a. Holes, open cracks, rotted, loose, or missing materials over a small area.
   b. Shaky or unsafe porch, steps, or railings.
   c. Broken or missing windowpanes.
   d. Rotted or loose window frames which are no longer rainproof or windproof.
   e. Damaged, unsafe, or makeshift chimney.
   f. Broken, loose, or missing inside stair treads or risers, balusters, or railings.
   g. Deep wear on doorsills, doorframes, outside or inside steps, or floors.
3. It was of inadequate original construction, of which examples are:
   a. Makeshift walls.
   b. Lack of foundation.
   c. Dirt floors.
   d. Inadequately converted cellars, garages, barns, and similar places.

Bureau of the Census data of 1940 and 1950 on the condition of a house are not comparable, because the term "dilapidation" was not used in the 1940 Census. At that time the phrase "needing major repairs" was used to provide information about the condition of a house. A dwelling unit was classified as needing major repairs when parts of the structure—such as floors, roof, plaster, walls, or foundation—required major repairs or replacement. A repair was "major" when continued neglect would have seriously impaired the soundness of the structure and made it hazardous for the occupants. (See also 1940 classification for "needing major repairs.")

Dilapidated. *See* "Condition."

*Dwelling Unit. A group of rooms or a single room occupied or intended for occupancy as separate living quarters by a family or other group of persons living together or by a person living alone. It must have separate cooking equipment or a separate entrance to be considered a dwelling unit. Excluded from the definition are rooming houses with five lodgers or more, transient accommodations, barracks for workers, and living quarters in institutions, general hospitals, and military installations.

*Economic Classification of Farms. Farms divided into two major groups: "commercial" and "other" farms. Farms with a value of sales of farm products amounting to $1,200 or more were classified as commercial. In addition, commercial farms included those with a sales value of products of $250 to $1,199, if the farm operator worked off the farm less than 100 days each year and the income of the operator and members of his family from nonfarm sources was less than the total value of total products sold. Farms with a value of sales of all other farm products of less than $250, as well as county, State, private institutional, and experimental farms, were classified as "other." "Other" farms were grouped into three classes: (a) Part-time farms—farms with a value of sales of farm products of $250 to $1,199 provided that the farm operator reported 100 or more days of work off the farm in 1949, or that the nonfarm income received by him and members of his family was greater than the value of farm products sold. (b) Residential farms—all farms except abnormal farms with a total value of sales of farm products of less than $250. Some of these represent farms on which the operator worked off the farm more than 100 days in 1949. Some represent farms on which the income from nonfarm sources was greater than the value of sales of agricultural products. Others represent subsistence and marginal farms of various kinds. Some farms are included which, under normal conditions, may have qualified as commercial farms. (c) Abnormal farms—public or private institutional farms, community enterprises, experiment station farms, grazing associations, etc.

*Economic Subregion. A combination of two or more groups of relatively homogeneous counties, sometimes cutting across State lines.

*Farm Family Income. The combined income of all members of the family, including income from wages and salaries, business income and other income. (*See* Income in 1949.)

*Farm Housing Units. In the Census of Housing, any rural dwelling unit for which the respondent affirmatively answered the question, "Is this house on a farm?"

"Good Quality" or "Poor Quality" and Similar Phrases. Used throughout the text as a device to eliminate the much longer phrases "not dilapidated, with private flush toilet and bath and hot and cold running water" and "no private flush toilet or bath, no running water or dilapidated."

*Head of Household. One person in each household who is regarded as the head by members of the household. Married women are not classified as heads if their husbands were living with them at the time of the census.

*Household. All persons who occupy a dwelling unit. Included are the related family members and also the unrelated persons, if any, such as lodgers, maids, or hired hands, who share the dwelling unit. A person living alone in a dwelling unit, or a group of unrelated persons sharing a dwelling unit as partners, is considered household.

*Income in 1949. The sum of all money received by the head of the primary family and by all related members of the primary family, less losses, from the following sources: wages or salary; net income (or loss) from the operation of a farm, ranch, business, or profession; net income (or loss) from rents, or receipts from roomers or boarders, royalties; interest, dividends and periodic income from estates and trust funds; pensions; veterans payments, Armed Forces allotments for dependents, and other governmental payments or assistance; and other income such as contributions for support from persons who are not members of the household, alimony, and periodic receipts from insurance policies or annuities.

Movers. Those persons who in April 1949 lived in a different house from the one in which they were living in April 1950.

*Needing Major Repairs. Classification used in the 1940 Census when parts of the structure such as floors, roof, plaster, walls, or foundation required major repairs or replacement. A repair was "major" when its continued neglect would have seriously impaired the soundness of the structure and created a safety hazard to the residents.

Not Dilapidated. *See* "Condition."

*Number of Rooms. All rooms which are used or suitable for use as living quarters, including kitchens, bedrooms, dining rooms, living rooms, permanently enclosed sun porches of substantial size, finished basement or attic rooms, recreation rooms, and rooms used for office purposes by person living in the dwelling unit. Not counted as rooms were bathrooms, strip or pullman kitchens, halls or foyers, alcoves, pantries, laundries, closets or storage spaces, unused basement or attic rooms not suitable for living quarters, and rooms subleased for office or business purposes by a person or persons not living in the dwelling unit.

*Occupied Dwelling Unit. A dwelling unit that had a person or group of persons living in it at the time of enumeration or if the occupants were only temporarily absent.

Open-Country Housing. Farm or nonfarm dwelling units outside of a community of 500 persons or more and designated as a "place" by the Bureau of the Census.

*Part-Time Farm. *See* "Economic classification of farms."

*Persons Per Room. The number of persons divided by the number of rooms in the dwelling unit.

*Plumbing Facilities. Dwelling units "with private toilet and bath" include those units with both a flush toilet and a bathtub or shower inside the structure for the exclusive use of the occupants of the unit. The "with running water" group includes those dwelling units having inside the structure, piped running water from a pressure or gravity system. The "no running water" group includes dwelling units for which the only source of water supply is a hand pump, a well or stream, or any source other than piped running water inside the structure.

*Primary Family. A primary family consists of the household head and all persons in the household related to him by blood, marriage, or adoption.

*Residential Farm. *See* "Economic classification of farms."

Rural Community Housing. Dwelling units in a community, not part of an urbanized area, either incorporated or unincorporated, but having from 500 to 2,500 inhabitants.

*Rural-Nonfarm Units. A variety of residences, such as isolated nonfarm homes in the open country, dwelling units in villages and in outlying portions of metropolitan areas, and units in areas around urban places of fewer than 50,000 inhabitants. The determination of whether a rural dwelling unit was nonfarm or farm was based on the respondent's answer to the question, "Is this house on a farm?"

Rural Region. Divisions of the United States made for purposes of this study based primarily on differences in the background of the people, climate, crops, soil conditions, or topography. Twelve such regions are used in this volume: Region I—Northeast Dairy Region; Region II—Great Lakes Dairy Region; Region III—East and Gulf Coast Miscellaneous Region; Region IV—General and Self-Sufficing Region; Region V—Tobacco Region; Region VI—Cotton Belt; Region VII—Corn Belt; Region VIII—Northern Wheat and Small Grains Region; Region IX—Southern Wheat and Small Grains Region; Region X—Year-Long and Seasonal Grazing Region; Region XI—Upland Summer Grazing Region; and Region XII—West Coast Miscellaneous Region.

*Sample Design. The statistics in the 1950 Census of Housing which are based on a 20-percent sample were obtained by tabulating data for all dwelling units for which the head of the household was enumerated on a sample line of the population schedule. A separate line was provided on the population schedule for each person enumerated, with every fifth line designated as a sample line.

*Tenure. Whether the dwelling unit is "occupied by owner," "occupied by renter," or "occupied rent free."

*Urban Housing. In 1950 all dwelling units in (*a*) all places of 2,500 inhabitants or more incorporated as cities, boroughs, and villages; (*b*) the densely settled urban fringe around cities of 50,000 inhabitants or more including both incorporated and unincorporated areas; and (*c*) unincorporated places of 2,500 inhabitants or more outside any urban fringe. In 1940, the urban population included all incorporated places of 2,500 inhabitants or more and in addition 140 places that were classified as urban under a special rule. Of the 2,376,000 inhabitants of these 140 places in 1950, 2,039,000 became urban according to the 1950 rule.

In 1940 housing in territory described in parts (*c*) and (*d*) were not wholly included as urban housing. This change in definition thus decreased the total number of rural-farm dwelling units to the extent that there were farms in those territories not classified as urban in 1940. It also changed the classification of rural-nonfarm units in the territory to urban units.

*Year Built. The year in which the original construction was completed, not the year in which any later remodeling, addition, reconstruction, or conversion may have taken place.

INDEX

Abrams, Charles, 117
Adams, Leonard, 115
Age of head of household, 59–61
Age of structure, *see* Year built
Agriculture, Census of, 120, 123–124
Department of, 117
Aid, government, 43, 113
housing, 113, 117
Anderson, William F., 115

Bachman, K. L., 8
Bean, L. H., 114
Benedict, M. R., 8
Beyer, Glenn H., 4, 124
Blizzard, Samuel W., 115
Bogue, Donald, 21, 132
Brunner, Edmund deS., 20

Census of Agriculture, 120, 123–124
Classification problems, economic class of farm,
8, 9, 16–20
residence, 128–130
rural, 6, 7, 131–135
Climate, 133
Commercial farms, definition of, 8
family income on, 13–20
importance of, 115–116
Concentric circles of urban influence, *see*
Urban influence
Condition, 28
definition of, 185
subregional variation in, 72, 75, 77, 79, 83,
175–186
Condition and plumbing, by economic class, 32
by electric lights, 65
by heating equipment, 65–66, 142
by income, 30, 51–52
by rooms, 51–53, 141
by tenure and rooms, 53
by type of household, 67, 143
by year built, 61–64, 140
in housing for nonwhite households, 110–112
regional comparisons of, 162–171
subregional variation in, 72–73, 75–80, 83,
86, 175–186
Construction, farm, *see* New construction
Cooking fuel, 29, 33, 34, 56–58
subregional variation in, 73, 76, 78, 81, 87,
175–186

Cooper, M. R., 116
Corn Belt (VII), changes since 1940 for selected
subregions, 77–78, 181
comparison with other regions, 46–69
detailed statistics for, 147, 151, 155, 159,
160, 163, 166, 170
farming activities, 77
Cotton Belt (VI), changes since 1940 for selected
subregions, 74–76, 180
comparison with other regions, 46–69
detailed statistics for, 146, 151, 155, 158,
160, 163, 166, 169
farming activities, 74
new construction for nonwhite families, 109
Credit, *see* Aid
Crowding, *see* Persons per room

Dilapidation, *see* Condition
Ducoff, Louis J., 7, 49, 53
Dwelling unit, definition, 186
growth in number, 4, 5

East and Gulf Coast Miscellaneous Region (III),
changes since 1940 for selected subregions,
177
comparison with other regions, 46–69
detailed statistics for, 145, 150, 153, 158,
160, 162, 165, 168
new construction for nonwhite families, 109
Economic class of farm, 8, 9
by condition and plumbing, 32
by facilities and equipment, 33–34
by rooms, 32
by tenure, 31
by year built, 42
distribution of farms, 16–20
Economic regions, *see* Regions
Economic subregions, *see* Subregions
Electric lights, 29, 65, 87, 142
regional comparisons of, 65, 162–164
subregional variations in, 73, 76, 78, 81,
87, 175–186
Ellickson, J. C., 8
Elliot, F. F., 8
Ensminger, Douglas, 7, 49, 53
Enumeration, definitions used in, 137–138
limitations of, 137–138
Equipment, *see* Electric lights and Heating
equipment

191